HIS MAJESTY SULTAN MOHAMMED V

HOME LIFE IN TURKEY.

BY

LUCY M. J. GARNETT

WITH TWENTY-ONE ILLUSTRATIONS

NEW YORK
THE MACMILLAN COMPANY
1909

TO

THE MEMORY OF

THE FATHER OF THE TURKISH CONSTITUTION

MIDHAT PASHA

STATESMAN, PATRIOT AND MARTYR

THIS VOLUME IS REVERENTLY

DEDICATED

CONTENTS

INTRODUCTION

PART I

SOCIAL LIFE

CHAPTER I

PART II

RELIGIOUS BELIEFS AND INSTITUTIONS

CHAPTER VI

PART III

DOMESTIC LIFE

LIST OF ILLUSTRATIONS

INTRODUCTION

THE ORIGIN OF THE OSMANLI TURKS

THE national Turkish traditions preserved by the Persian historians Rashid-ed-Din and Jowaini from Uigurian books, now lost, point to the region watered by the Selenga and its affluents, the Orkhon and the Tugela, as the primitive seat of the Turkish people. But already as early as the sixth century A.D. the Turks had their traditional hero in Khan Disabul, the "Master of the Seven Races, and Lord of the Seven Climates of the World," who exchanged embassies with Justinian, and whose friendship the Roman Emperor desired in order that—in the words of his Ambassador to the Golden Mountain—"a strict alliance, without envy or deceit, might for ever be maintained between the two most powerful nations of the earth."[1] Somewhere about the second decade of the thirteenth century, the little Turkish tribe destined in due course to found the Ottoman Empire was driven by invading Mongols from its original home, and, passing through Persia, entered Armenia under the leadership of Suleyman Shah, its hereditary chief. His son and successor, Ertoghrul, while wandering with his warriors over those wide Asian lands, came one day upon two armies engaged in desperate conflict. Riding at once to the assistance of what appeared to be the weaker party, their assailants—a horde of Mongols who had invaded the territories of Ala-ed-Din, Sultan of Konieh, the ancient Iconium—

[1] Gibbon, *The Decline and Fall of the Roman Empire*, vol. v. pp. 178–181.

were put to flight. In reward for this signal service, the Seljukian Prince conferred upon Ertoghrul, as a military fief, a considerable tract of land, comprising within its limits the towns of Sugut and Eski Shehir. His son Othman or Osman, surnamed "The Bonebreaker," having while still young won from the Greeks for his Suzerain several important towns, was rewarded for this service with the title of "Bey," along with the symbols pertaining to that military rank—the drum and horse-tailed standard. In 1300 the Seljukian Kingdom fell to pieces, ten separate principalities taking its place, all of which were eventually merged in that of Osman, originally the least important among them; and from this time may be dated the rise of the Ottoman Empire.

The use of the name "Turks" has never been limited in a clear and definite way by European writers. By Byzantine authors it was generally used in a collective sense to indicate certain races of Central and South-Western Asia; while at the present day Europeans restrict this term to the Osmanlis, who themselves scornfully repudiate it; their nation, as they hold, having ceased to be Turkish either in blood or in culture. As Mr. Stuart-Glennie has remarked in his essay on "The Ethnography of Turkey,"[1] "No Liberal assumption—except that perhaps as to the universal 'subjection of women'—is in such utter contradiction to historical facts as the assumption that the Osmanlis are Turks in the sense in which that term, as likewise that of Turanian, is ordinarily used—namely, to designate not only a non-Aryan, but a Coloured Race." For it is very doubtful whether even the small original following of the Central Asian chief, Suleyman Shah, were—save perhaps in their lowest ranks—what is now commonly understood by the terms Turk, Tartar, and Turanian; and it is, on the other hand, extremely probable that this small original tribe of westward wandering Osmanlis belonged to that non-Semitic and non-Aryan, "Archaian" white race which recent ethnological research has shown to have been that of the founders of the

[1] Introductory Chapter to *The Women and Folklore of Turkey*, vol. i., 1890.

Chaldean and Egyptian civilisations, and to be still, as it has from the earliest times been, widely distributed over Central Asia. And with reference to such a descent the Crescent symbol of the Osmanlis is very significant, connected, as it seems to be, with the Moon-god of the Chaldeans, masculine also in Turkish, and of whose widespread worship topographical traces may be found from Arabia to Asia Minor. It is also noteworthy that, rich as Ottoman literature is in tales, there is found in it no tradition, or trace even, connecting the Osmanlis with the Tartar race.

But whether originally a purely white race or not, the Osmanli Turks, since their appearance on the historic arena in the thirteenth century, have developed into the great nation they now constitute by admixture during more than six centuries with the best white blood both of Asia and of Europe. This admixture has been effected in various ways, not the least important having been the establishment in the reign of Orchan of the Janissary Corps (1365). This corps was originally, and until 1672 exclusively, composed of Christian boys, a certain number of whom were every year forcibly recruited from among the subject populations; and during the years of their training as soldiers not only were they carefully instructed in the tenets of Islam, but also to a certain extent, and in their more popular aspect, in the doctrines of the Bektashi Order of Dervishes in which all were enrolled as lay members, this Corps having at its formation received the blessing of its founder, Hadji Bektash, of Khorassan, poet and philosopher, fanatic and fighting monk. After a certain number of years of service in the armies of the Sultans, the Janissaries left the ranks to settle on the lands granted as a reward for their long and faithful services, married the daughters of their Moslem neighbours, and brought up their children as Osmanlis. The spoils of the cities and provinces, overrun by Turkish armies or raided by Mediterranean Corsairs, included both youths and maidens, the latter being destined to people the harems of their captors, those among the former fortunate enough to escape labour at the oar in the war-galleys

of their masters being purchased by Moslem households
for the service of the *selamlik*. Many of those who had
thus entered Moslem society through the gate of slavery
subsequently rose to high positions in the State; and
the condition of bondage not being in Moslem countries
either permanent or hereditary, their origin was speedily
lost sight of, and their descendants helped to swell the
ranks of the Osmanli nation.

In the copious ballad literature of the Modern Greeks
are to be found numerous episodes reminiscent of all these
methods of recruitment. These old popular songs, which
have been orally transmitted during centuries from one
generation to another, contain in many cases the actual
individual expression of the grief of those thus ruthlessly
torn from home and friends and faith, and of the sorrow
of their bereaved relatives. One unhappy woman of
Epirus cries—

"O cruel Sultan, cursed be thou, yea, be thou thrice accursèd,
For all the evil thou hast wrought, the ill thou still art working !
Thou send'st and biddest forth the priests, the notables, the elders,
The Tax of Children to collect, to make them Janissaries.
Fond mothers weep their sons beloved, and sisters brothers cherished.
And I'm with burning grief consumed, and all my life must sorrow—
Last year my little son they took, this year they take my brother ! "[1]

In another ballad a Greek captive, released on the
defeat of the Turks by Don John of Austria at the naval
battle of Lepanto (1574), thus briefly relates to his
deliverers the story of his captivity—

"A four days' bridegroom only I, when Turks a captive took me,
And ten long years I've passed since then on Barbary's soil in
    durance,
Ten walnut trees I planted there, within my prison dreary,
Of all of them I ate the fruit, but never found I freedom."[2]

Not always, however, as reluctant recruits do the sons
of the *rayahs* appear to have joined the ranks of the "New
Troop." In a song from North Euboea a woman boasts
that she has among other kindred of note a "Janissary
brother-in-law, who lures away the youngsters." And it

[1] *Greek Folkpoesy*, vol. i. p. 281.   [2] *Ibid.*, p. 283.

is, I believe, a matter of historical fact that, tempted by the privileges enjoyed by members of this corps, parents of Christian boys not infrequently intrigued to get their sons included among the numbers levied. And though many Christian maidens—as, for instance, Despo of Liakatà [1]— no doubt went often unwillingly enough to be the brides of their Moslem over-lords, there were exceptions then, as in modern times; and an underlying expression of satisfaction at their future prospects is occasionally allowed to appear, as in a Cretan ballad which describes the abduction by a Turkish ship's crew of a Priest's daughter, who, after begging her father to keep for himself the money he had raised as her ransom, thus naïvely adds—

"And I on costly carpets tread, on golden chair I seat me,
    And wipe the tears that dim mine eyes with gold-embroidered
        kerchief." [2]

It must not, however, be supposed that the recruitment from the neighbouring Aryan and Caucasian populations has been entirely, or even mainly, the result of the capture and enslavement of their men and women, and the forcible annual enlistment during three centuries of so many hundred thousands of the sons of the subject Christians as Janissaries. For such was the condition of security established by the Emir Orkhan in his dominions that many Asiatic subjects of the Byzantine Cæsars fled to him for the protection their own rulers could not, or would not, afford them, and abjuring their Christian Faith, were speedily merged into the Osmanli nation. And the numbers of the Osmanlis were also during its early history frequently and importantly augmented by the voluntary submission and conversion to Islam of independent Asian Princes and Chieftains who, fired with

---

[1] The daughter of a wealthy sheep-farmer belonging to the Aspropotamos district of Epirus, who with her four brothers figures frequently in folksong. While washing by the riverside she had been seen and carried off by Ali Pasha, the tyrant of Joannina, to his palace on the lake of that name, where she is said to have died of grief within fifteen days. So great, however, was the Pasha's regard for his unwilling bride, that at her death he conferred many honours and benefits on her family.

[2] *Greek Folkpoesy*, vol. i. p. 261.

admiration of the Turkish Emirs—as Orkhan and his sons were then styled—freely enlisted themselves and their followers under the banner of the Crescent. Nor only in Asia and during the earlier period of Turkish Conquests. For in the Balkan Peninsula there was at one time, owing to preparation by the widespread Protestantism of the Paulicians, such a disposition to embrace Islam that had it not been for the intervention of the Great White Tzar of the North—to whom the Christians of South-Eastern Europe looked for the preservation of their menaced national freedom—almost all the Peninsula might have been converted to the larger Protestantism of Islam. And thus in the Balkans, as in the Islands of the Ægean, the Moslem section of the population, generally referred to as "Turks," are of the purest Aryan, or, at least, *white* blood of the country.

THE TURKISH PEOPLE

PART I

SOCIAL LIFE

CHAPTER I

THE TURKS OF THE CAPITAL

O NE of the predominating instincts of the Osmanli Turks has ever been a passion for the picturesque in nature, a love of splendid sites, sparkling seas, leafy shades, cool fountains, and wide horizons; and this instinct has led them, wherever they have settled, to choose for their abodes the most charming situations, commanding views unrivalled in grandeur and beauty. At Broussa, until 1453 the Turkish Capital, the quarter of the ruling race spreads over the lower slopes of the Bithynian Olympus; at Smyrna it lies beneath the ruined walls and towers of the ancient citadel on Mount Pagus, the scene of the martyrdom of St. Polycarp and of countless sieges and sanguinary struggles with invading hosts. At Salonica, equally, the streets of the Turkish quarter extend from the new street opened out by Midhat Pasha more than thirty years ago, and named after him, to the northern walls and the castle of the " Seven Towers " at the summit of the hill on the slopes of which the city is built ; while at Constantinople not only are the seven hills of Stamboul almost entirely occupied by the homes of the Osmanlis, but they have also appropriated many a fair spot on the shores both of the Bosphorus and of the Sea of Marmora.

The streets of a Turkish quarter are often, owing to their elevated situation, steep, and also for the most part winding and narrow. The pavement, if any there be, is of cobble-stones sloping towards a gutter in the centre of the roadway, which is usually ankle-deep in dust in dry, and a rushing torrent in rainy weather. In other respects, however, the streets are, generally speaking, cleaner than those of the Christian and Jewish *mahallas*, partly owing to the natural drainage consequent on their elevated situation, partly to the greater space available in their courtyards and gardens for the bestowal of refuse, and also to the presence in their streets of the pariah dogs who act as scavengers, and, though considered unclean animals and not admitted to the houses of Moslems, are protected and treated with kindness by them. Kindness to animals, I may here remark, is a leading trait in Turkish character ; and one may often see in the streets, under a house wall, rude little temporary shelters constructed of boards and carpeted with straw for the accommodation of a canine mother and her brood of woolly pups, who speedily become the pets and protégés of the whole *mahalla*.

A *KONAK* ON THE BOSPHORUS

NOW THE "SUMMER PALACE" OF THE FRENCH EMBASSY

Life in the Capital and in the large seaport cities of the Levant presents certain aspects not discoverable in the towns of the interior, where the population, though always composed of two or more nationalities, is of a less cosmopolitan character, and where social conditions generally are less affected by European influence. But even in these great cities the difference, so far at least as the vast mass of Turkish inhabitants are concerned, is superficial and external rather than essential. For all the various nationalities, Moslem, Christian, and Jewish, of which these cosmopolitan populations are made up, live in separate quarters of the cities, and their members, after transacting business with each other during the day—honestly or otherwise according to their several codes of commercial morality—retire at sunset into worlds totally different and divided from each other by impassable barriers of language, religion, and tradition, national aspiration, and social custom ; the life and thought of a mere fraction of each section of the native races being at all influenced by those of the foreigners with whom they come into daily contact. At Smyrna and Salonica the Osmanlis form but a comparatively small section of the population ; in the Capital, however, they are exceedingly numerous, peopling almost the whole of Stamboul as well as many of the suburbs on both sides of the Bosphorus. And notwithstanding the heterogeneous character of its inhabitants generally, one can never here lose sight of the fact that the Turks are the ruling race, and that Constantinople is the capital of the Moslem world. According to an Albanian adage, "to find a representative Turk one must go to Stamboul, and to find a true Albanian to Elbassan." The term "Koniar Turk"—a Turk from Konieh, the ancient Iconium—is, however, most frequently used by Greeks and others to indicate a thoroughbred Osmanli. Pride of race is, it must be admitted, excessive in the Turks, and the habit of domination has been developed by their position as a ruling people surrounded by subject nationalities. Though—as mentioned in the introduction—to a great extent of the same blood, they as a nation display a somewhat overweening sense of their superiority to the subject races, having few interests or aspirations in common with them, seldom acquiring their languages, or attempting to understand their manners and customs, which they may be said to regard generally with a somewhat contemptuous toleration.

The social organisation of the Osmanlis themselves is, on the other hand, distinctly opposed to the principles of aristocracy and hereditary rank. A Sultan's daughters marry subjects, the connections even of the Imperial family do not form a noble or privileged class, and such Imperial descent is, in a few generations, practically lost sight of. The division of estates between all children of one father, female as well as male, and the Oriental propensity of the Government to confiscate any considerable accumulation of riches, have also constituted effectual barriers to the transmission to descendants of family position and affluence. In Asia Minor, however, there may still be found a certain number of families constituting a kind of

landed gentry whose ancestors—for the most part converted Moslems of non-Turkish origin—were at the Conquest allowed to retain their lands, holding them as
military fiefs. And previous to the introduction in 1867
of the present centralising administration the country
districts in certain provinces were ruled either by such
Turkish feudatories, or, as in Albania and Kurdistan, by
tribal chieftains, whose loyalty to the Porte was most
easily secured by allowing them entire freedom in dealing
with their own vassals. With the exception of these
provincial families, in which the title of *Bey* is hereditary,
the Ottomans have never had an aristocracy properly so
called, all the Moslem subjects of the Sultan, whether
born freemen or emancipated slaves, being virtually on
a level beneath him. There is accordingly nothing in the
social system of Turkey to prevent the poorest Osmanli
from attaining the highest dignity, that of Grand Vizier.
On the other hand, a deposed Minister may descend to an
inferior employment without losing caste, forfeiting any
of his civil rights, or becoming less eligible for office when
Fortune's wheel may again have revolved in his favour,
and to the Oriental mind there is consequently nothing
extraordinary in Joseph's having risen from the position
of a slave to that of Grand Vizier of the King of
Egypt, nor is the marriage of a handsome and adventurous "widow's son," or other hero of fairy tale, with a
king's daughter; and the Oriental possessor of wit and
audacity may indeed say with Pistol, "The world's mine
oyster!"

A still further proof of the absence from their institutions of class divisions is offered by the absence of Turkish family names. The names of men are, as a rule, Biblical or historical, and in order to differentiate one Ali or Mehmet from another, a nickname is frequently bestowed denoting some personal peculiarity, physical or moral, such as "Bajuksis (Short-legged) Ali Pasha," "Buyuk (Big) Mehmet Agha," "Kuchuk (Little) Selim Effendi," "Chapgun (Scamp) Ali Bey." The only Turkish title which carries with it any definite rank and precedence is that of *Pasha*, being conferred personally by the Sultan on the man whom he so "delighteth to honour." *Bey* and *Effendi* are merely conventional designations, as indefinite as our "Esquire" has come to be, the former being generally applied to high Government officials, colonels, and distinguished persons, including foreigners, and also to their sons. *Effendi* has the same signification as the French *Monsieur*, and is applied indiscriminately to Princes of the Royal house, to Mollahs and Sheikhs, to women, and even to native Christians. It is also used in conjunction with the other titles, a gentleman being addressed as *Bey Effendi*, or *Pasha Effendi*, and a lady as *Hanum Effendi*. *Agha* is applied to petty officers and respectable elderly Turks, and *Tchelebi* ("gentleman") to persons of the better class generally, whether Christian or Moslem. But notwithstanding this absence of hereditary rank and class distinction—perhaps because of it—every Osmanli is both by nature and tradition an aristocrat, and the same dignity of bearing and courtesy of manner may be met with in the hovel of the peasant as in the *konak* of the Pasha.

A noteworthy characteristic of Turkish town life is its extreme sobriety and consequent orderliness. Notwithstanding the mixture of races and the scarcity of policemen, street brawls or disturbances of any kind are of rare occurrence, and native Christians or foreign sailors are usually found to be responsible for them ; foot passengers make way for each other in the narrow and crowded streets and bazars with extreme good nature and mutual compliments ; the heavily laden *hamal* and the driver of cart or carriage utters continually his warning cry of " *Varda !* " and there is little of the coarseness and vulgar brutality common in Western cities. In social relations, generally, a rigid system of etiquette is observed by the Osmanlis, and respect is instinctively paid by those of a lower to those of a higher rank. A Turk when visiting another knows the precise distance from the door at which his friend should meet him, the special words which his *rutbe*—social or official standing—entitles him to be greeted with, and the exact distance from his host on the divan at which he should take his seat. A host may relax the rules of etiquette towards his guests should they be of lower official rank than himself; but a guest has not this privilege, and any breach of the rules of etiquette on either part, if apparently intentional, is considered an affront. The conditions of public safety vary, however, greatly according to locality. In Asiatic Smyrna, for instance, and also to a certain extent in Constantinople, foreign ladies could, even forty years ago, traverse the streets with safety, or travel in the Bosphorus steamers ; while in European Salonica, even under normal conditions, no lady, foreign or native, might venture abroad, save perhaps in one or two streets of the Frank quarter, without the escort of a gentleman or manservant, for fear of molestation at the hands of the Albanians and other lawless denizens of the Macedonian "hinterland ; " the long-horned draught buffaloes and files of Jew-driven pack animals with their unwieldy burdens, here con- stituting also another source of danger to pedestrians. By night public safety is, in many localities, still entrusted to the *bektchi*—a counterpart of our own obsolete watch- man—who, lantern in hand, goes his round between sunset and sunrise, giving to evildoers chivalrous warning of his approach by striking his iron-shod staff at intervals on the pavement. Many of the streets are but inadequately lighted at night, if lighted at all, and it is consequently customary for every one when out of doors after sunset to carry a lighted lantern, and any individual encountering a police patrol, or passing a guard-house without this token of his honesty of purpose, will hardly avoid getting into difficulties.

Alike in the Capital and the provincial cities or townships, the bazars form the chief centre of commercial life. The term "bazar," however, though derived from a Turkish word signifying "to bargain," is applied by the Turks only to such market-places as the *Baluk-Bazar*, or fish-market ; the term *tcharshi* being generally applied to

streets the shops in which are devoted exclusively to the
manufacture or sale of one kind of goods ; while the same
term, or that of *bezesten*, is applied to the vast walled and
roofed-in enclosures which constitute the great emporiums
in the East. The most familiar examples of these are the
Bezesten, or Grand Bazar of Stamboul, and the *Mis'r
Tcharshi*, or Cairene Bazar. This Grand Bazar forms, as
it were, a city within a city, containing arcaded streets,
tortuous and mysterious lanes and alleys, squares and
fountains, all enclosed within high protecting walls, and
covered by a vaulted roof studded with hundreds of
cupolas, through which penetrates a subdued light more
favourable, it must be admitted, to the vendor than to the
purchaser. Here, as elsewhere, each commodity has its
special habitat. In one quarter are found embroideries in
gold and silver, brocades and damasks, with gauzes of
silk, cotton, and linen from the looms of Broussa ; in
another are displayed specimens of all the rugs and
carpets woven in nomad tent, in village home, and in
town factory between Smyrna and Samarcand ; while, in
a third, footgear of every description, from a waterman's
boot to a Sultana's slipper, may be purchased ; in a fourth
the jewellers and dealers in pearls and precious stones
conceal, rather than display, in diminutive shops their
valuable stock-in-trade ; while a fifth will be found
devoted to small arms calculated to appeal to the fancy
of every Turkish subject between the Highlands of
Kurdistan and the mountains of Albania.

The khans, or caravanserais, which throughout the

East supply to native travellers the place of inns or
hostelries, have little in common with such in the
European acceptation of the term, as they furnish neither
food nor attendance to those making use of them. The
Capital contains a considerable number of khans; one
or more may be found in every large town; while others
are met with at various points on the great highways of
the interior. Not a few owe their origin to the munificence of the pious, this provision for the accommodation
of the weary wayfarer being included in the list of
"good works" required of Moslems. Among such may
be mentioned the "Lady's Khan" on the road between
Ioannina and Mezzovo, built, together with the beautiful
fountain near it, by the widow of a famous Suleyman Pasha,
and the "Khan of the Validé" in Stamboul, adjoining
the mosque of that name, founded by the able Regent
Tarkhan Sultana, mother of Mohammed IV. The architecture of this latter vast caravanserai, which is considered
a sort of model for such edifices, is quite monastic in
character. A great arched gateway gives access to a
quadrangle containing a tree-shaded fountain and surrounded by stables and storehouses for merchandise,
above which extend three superimposed cloistered
galleries on which open all the cell-like apartments.
These lodgings contain no furniture, as all Oriental
travellers carry with them their own bedding, rugs, and
utensils, and the charge made for accommodation is correspondingly small. The further wants of the guests are
easily supplied at the coffee-stall and cook-shop on the

premises, or in the numerous establishments of the kind
with which the neighbourhood abounds. In this and the
other large caravanserais at Stamboul, as also at Smyrna
and Salonica, may be found collected a motley throng
of strangers, pilgrims, and traders, together with the
donkeys and mules, horses and camels, on which they
and their varied merchandise have been transported
from the far borders of the Ottoman Empire, European,
Asiatic, and African. And, from time immemorial, these
hostelries have constituted important centres, not of trade
only, but also for the exchange of news and ideas, and
occur frequently in Oriental folk-tales.

Coffee and tobacco are, in the Western mind, indis-
solubly associated with the traditional Turk; and these
luxuries, despite the fulminations hurled against them
in past centuries by ascetic moralists, have become for
the inhabitants of Turkey generally not only the indispensable adjuncts of civility and hospitality, but almost
the necessaries of existence. Coffee and cigarettes indeed
appear to constitute an integral part of every business
transaction and every social or official interview; and so
many cups of the fragrant beverage must perforce be
partaken of in the course of a day that their consumption
must inevitably have injurious consequences but for the
special method of preparation which seems to render it
at the same time stimulant and innocuous. So continuous is the demand for freshly made "creaming"
coffee, that *kahfenes* are found on every hand—in crowded
streets, by suburban roadsides, on boat-piers and in

market-places, wherever, in a word, men resort for business or relaxation. Many are mere wooden shanties shaded by an awning or vine-covered trellis, in front of, or under which the contemplative Orientals sit contentedly on rush-bottomed stools, a cup in one hand and the mouthpiece of *narghilé* or stem of *tchibouk* in the other, for hours together. These coffee-houses, together with the public baths, in default of clubs or " institutes," have from time immemorial formed throughout the East the chief centres of union and conversation for the middle and lower classes, the men's baths being open in the evening as well as during the day. In both of these resorts those who can read impart to their unlettered neighbours the news of the day—no longer, happily, as in former years, suppressed or distorted by Press censorship—discuss political and social questions, and make acquaintance with their fellow-citizens. Turks of the lower class resort to the *kahfené* in the early morning for a cheering cup and soothing *narghilé* before betaking themselves to their daily avocations, and repair to them again at intervals during the day as opportunity may offer. Most unpretentious and by no means very inviting in appearance are these *kahfenés*, and few can boast of any arrangements for the comfort of those who frequent them, the best being furnished only with mats, rugs, and cushions, placed on a raised platform surrounding the interior. The Turks are naturally gregarious and socially inclined, and the harem system on which their homes are organised not offering facilities—especially

AT THE BATHS OF YENI KAPLIDJAH (BROUSSA)

among the lower middle and labouring classes—for social intercourse, a club of some kind has always formed a necessary element of urban life. And one of the most striking features of Constantinople under the new *régime* has been the establishment of numerous *bonâ fide* clubs to meet the requirements of every class and profession.

Personal cleanliness among Moslems certainly comes "next to godliness," being enjoined by the *Sheriat*, or Sacred Law; and to the regular and careful ablutions requisite for the maintenance of the condition · of legal purity—in which certain religious acts may alone be performed—as also no doubt to their habitual temperance, are probably due the comparative freedom of the Turks from many of the ailments which afflict their Christian and Jewish neighbours. Several *hammams*, as Turkish baths are termed, are to be found in every large town, and in the Capital they are very numerous. A few—the mineral baths at Broussa, for instance, and some of the older ones at Stamboul—present fine examples of this species of architecture, and are much resorted to by all classes. The charges made to all are extremely moderate, and for the use of the poor there are numerous minor baths attached to mosques and other pious foundations at which they may perform their ablutions gratuitously.

Nowhere perhaps in the world is itinerant commerce carried on to such an extent as in the streets of the Turkish Capital, where almost every edible and potable is hawked or exposed for sale in the public thoroughfares,

the courtyards of the very mosques not being sacred
from the intrusion of detachments of the "thousands of
people who gain a living by selling all sorts of things"—
to use the words of a Turkish chronicler of the seventeenth
century—drinks, sweets, sherbets, cakes, pistachio nuts,
and what not—where stalls with their protecting white
umbrellas encumber, uninterfered with, the precincts of
many a noble *djami*. And to this facility for carrying
on petty commerce may no doubt be attributed, in some
degree, the notable absence of the acute and squalid
poverty of Western cities ; for any man with a shilling
of capital seems able to turn a sufficiency of honest
pennies daily to provide himself and his family with the
necessaries of life. The stock-in-trade, for instance, of a
kahvedji consists but of half a dozen rush-bottomed stools
and brass *ibriks*, in which coffee is both boiled and served,
together with a few cups and glasses ; and quite a number
of coffee vendors may apparently, without any unfriendly
rivalry, eke out a living on some favourite lounging place
in a frequented spot, under spreading plane or sheltering
wall. And of this, a little incident that occurred during
my last visit to Constantinople, afforded a practical
illustration. After visiting the stately mosque of Sultan
Bayazid in Stamboul, my friends and I seated ourselves
on some stools standing outside its courtyard gate, and
called for coffee to a Turk a few yards away, whose
cotton handkerchief tucked apronwise into his girdle
denoted his calling. He, however, courteously informed
us that his domain did not extend to the steps of the

ITINERANT VENDORS—COURTYARD OF VALIDÉ MOSQUE, STAMBOUL

mosque. A second *kahvedji*, who then came up, likewise smilingly explained that only the stools on the *opposite* side of the doorway belonged to him; and after dispatching a boy in hot haste to summon his absent fellow-tradesman, he begged us not to change our places, as his neighbour would instantly return and supply our wants—affording a notable example of the prevailing courtesy of manners above referred to.

A conspicuous figure among this itinerant population is the *saka*. Pure water being highly prized by the abstemious Osmanlis, its distribution to the thirsty is accounted one of the most meritorious among the "good works" prescribed by the religion of Islam, and the *saka* is employed by charitable persons to carry water into much frequented thoroughfares for the benefit of the public, to whom he offers the welcome draught with the words, "We give thee to drink of the Kevser's spring"—*Kevser* signifying the "Water of Life." The water is usually carried by the *saka* on his back in a great leathern jack, which in hot weather is often covered with green leaves and branches; and some have an arrangement of pipes and taps by which the water can be drawn off with ease into the cups fitted into a metal receptacle strapped round the waist. Another class of *sakas* who supply water to householders in the Capital from springs in the suburbs famous for their purity, carry their jacks slung on either side of a pack-horse. All *sakas*, Christian as well as Moslem, enjoy a high degree of consideration, their persons being regarded as in a manner sacred, any offence offered to a member of this fraternity being deemed an insult to the whole quarter in which he pursues his avocation. The *sakas* form one of the *Esnafs*, or Guilds, in which members of the various trades, crafts, and callings are severally enrolled, irrespective of race and religion, for their mutual protection and support. These Guilds, though now diminished in number owing to the disappearance of many once flourishing industries, still constitute an important feature of urban industrial life, especially at Constantinople, where representatives of all the various crafts and callings practised in the Empire are to be found. Each *Esnaf* has here one or more *Lonjas*—Lodges, or Clubs—in every quarter of the city and suburbs, presided over by several officers called respectively, according to their rank, *Sheikhs*, *Naibs*, *Oustas*, and *Kiayas*, or Priors, Sub-Priors, Superintendents, and Inspectors, who are annually elected by the members from among its own master-craftsmen, these officers being formally recognised by the Government, which holds them responsible for the good behaviour of their fellow-guildsmen. Some *Esnafs* possess considerable revenues, and a few enjoy peculiar privileges granted by royal charter in bygone centuries in return for services rendered at some important crisis. Among these are the shoemakers, who, it is said, have special officers empowered to judge and punish all offenders belonging to their fraternity without the interposition of the legal authorities, this extraordinary privilege having been conferred upon them in the sixteenth

century by Suleyman "the Magnificent." Some *Esnafs*
are composed entirely of Moslems, certain callings being
exclusively in the hands of the ruling race, others
entirely of Christians. Many, however, include adherents
of both creeds; and, as members of the same *Esnaf*,
Christians and Moslems, allied by an *esprit de corps*, and
also, of course, by trade interests, pull together much
better and evince mutually a greater liberality of feeling
than is displayed generally in the social relations of
Moslems and Christians.

Though it is a matter of historical fact that certain of
these Guilds had already been long established among the
Greek, Venetian, Genoese, and other Christian nationalities
inhabiting Constantinople and the other great cities of
the Levant at the time of the Turkish Conquest, their
Moslem members assign to them an Oriental, and probably
much more ancient origin than can be historically verified.
The merchants, for instance, maintain that their *Esnaf*
was incorporated in the lifetime of the Prophet, who
himself followed the calling of a trader, and thus became
the patron of merchants. For, as with the Guilds of
Western Europe, every trade has its own patron saint,
the majority of them being the prophets and holy men
who figure alike in the Old Testament and the Koran,
each of whom, according to Moslem tradition, invented
or excelled in the craft or calling placed under his
protection. Thus Adam, besides being the patron of the
tailors' Guild, is also that of the bakers'; and among
other patron saints of *Esnafs*, Abraham, as the traditional

c

builder of the holy Kaaba at Mekka, is the protector of
masons; Cain, of the sextons, and also of all those who
shed blood in their callings; Enoch, of the scribes; Noah,
of the shipbuilders; David, of armourers and smiths
generally; Joseph, of the watch- and clock-makers; and
the Seven Sleepers of Ephesus—who are included by
the Moslems in the roll of holy men—watch, somewhat
paradoxically, together with Jonah, over the sailors,
especially those who navigate the Black Sea. The
more eminent among the "Companions of the Prophet"
also afford their protection to numerous Guilds; Selman,
one of the two to whom the Prophet promised a greeting
in Paradise, being the patron of the barbers, as it was his
privilege to shave the Servant of Allah.

Every *Esnaf* has its own special traditional laws and
usages which are no less strictly observed and enforced
than is its *kanoun*, or written constitution; and the social
customs and mode of life of the members of these various
Guilds afford in many instances curious and interesting
illustrations of manners among the labouring classes. In
a city so watergirt as Constantinople, there is naturally
a considerable section of the population whose avocations
are those of boatmen or fishermen. The fish-market of the
Turkish Capital is, perhaps, second to none in the world in
the abundance and variety of the finny tribe taken with
net or line by the fishers of the Black Sea, the Sea of
Marmora, the Golden Horn, and the Bosphorus. In the
more sheltered reaches of these waters may often be
seen rude little constructions of wood perched on high

platforms, from which the fishers watch and manipulate
their lines; and the crimson glow of their pitch-pine fires
lighted at night on the high prows of the fishing-boats,
and the drumming of the fishers' bare feet on the hollow
fore and aft decks, produce during the small hours a
weird, if not disquieting, effect on the stranger housed
for the first time in these regions. Steamboats have long
plied up and down the Bosphorus, and zigzag between
the European and Asiatic suburbs of the Capital. So
great, however, is the demand for means of communication
between the European and Asian suburbs that they have
not appreciably diminished the number of *kaïks* and other
oared craft in which one may be conveyed in more
leisurely fashion from shore to shore, and the Guild of
boatmen consequently remains not less important than
of yore. The ranks of this *Esnaf* are largely recruited
from among the Turkish, Greek, and Armenian youths,
who come in great numbers from Asia Minor to seek
their fortune in the Capital. Half a dozen or more of
these *bekiars*, or "bachelors," as they are termed, live in
common in some humble lodging, paying a fixed sum per
day or per week to an old man who acts as their steward
and cook, and also as mentor and arbiter in the disputes
that may be expected to arise occasionally in such a
mixed household. Their relations with the master *kaïkdji*,
to whom they serve a long apprenticeship, are also of
a quite filial character. Many waterside mansions have
their own private boats and boatmen; and quite a number
of the latter are attached to the service of the royal

palaces.   These are all Moslems, and constitute a
splendidly muscular set of fellows, with shaven polls, who
are apparently impervious to weather, their attire consisting only of short, full, white Turkish breeches, red girdle,
and shirt of Broussa gauze, which, worn open in front,
leaves their broad, brawny chests completely exposed.
A crew of about a dozen propel the State *kaïks*—lightly
built, flat-bottomed, double-prowed craft, some twenty
feet long and three to four feet wide—at a splendid pace
from one shore of the Bosphorus to the other, a mode
of traversing this wonderful waterway which may also
be enjoyed by Europeans who have obtained the *firman*,
or permission, requisite for visiting the Imperial palaces.
Many other callings, the exercise of which requires muscle
rather than skill—that, for instance, of the *hamal*, or porter
—are organised on similar lines to those just named ; and
a young *kaïkdji* or *hamal*, on emerging from the grade of
apprentice, is recommended by the master under whom
he has served his time to the Prior of his particular Lodge
of the Guild to which he belongs, his admittance being
attended with certain traditional ceremonies, and the
payment of the customary fees.

Another striking characteristic of Turkish urban life
is the strict specialisation of each particular branch of
industry or commerce, and the absence of the middle-man
in the generality of transactions connected with supplying
the necessaries of existence. Save in the "Frank" or
European quarters of Smyrna and the Capital, there are
as yet no "Stores," or general shops, in which goods of

various kinds are collected; and the native Osmanli
requiring a pair of shoes goes to the working shoemaker
for them, and the housewife in want of a new saucepan,
kettle, or coffee-pot, sends her husband or servant to the
street of the *bakirdjiler*, or coppersmiths where, amid the
deafening tap-tap of a hundred hammers on the resound-
ing metal, he makes his selection, and, the requisite
amount of chaffering accomplished and the " last price "
paid, carries off the purchase. For in Turkey, it may
be mentioned, it is not customary for tradesmen to send
goods home, nor—save perhaps in the case of certain
comestibles—even to wrap their wares in paper. The
Oriental accordingly, if unaccompanied by a servant,
deposits his small purchases in a handkerchief, bundle-
wrap, or basket, according to its nature, and for the
transport of weighty articles a *hâmal* will be available,
whose sturdy legs are capable of supporting anything
that can be fastened on their leathern saddles, from a
cask of oil or wine to a wardrobe.

In a country so destitute of good country roads and
level streets as Turkey, locomotion is naturally performed
to a great extent on horse-, mule-, and donkey-back. At
various points in Constantinople, Smyrna, and other towns
one may see a number of these animals, and especially the
last-named, furnished with saddlery more or less Orientally
ornate in character, waiting for hire. This method of
locomotion is also not infrequently resorted to by Turkish
women who, seated astride on the high carpet- or pack-
saddles, with their white-stockinged, yellow-shod feet

thrust into roomy shovel stirrups, look like animated bundles of bedding. In addition to being splendid horsemen, the Turks also possess great skill as drivers ; and up, or down, the worst paved and steepest of the thoroughfares of the Capital and its suburbs the native Jehu will not hesitate to drive his brakeless brougham or heavy landau and pair ; nor will he ever allow his fares to alight and walk while the willing horses are struggling, mostly on their haunches, down what appears to those behind them a declivity the foot of which can hardly be reached without mishap. " Carriage exercise," indeed, in the cities of the Levant, constitutes only too frequently the most active exercise imaginable.

The Moslem era used by the Turks dates from the Flight (*Hejra*) of Mohammed from Mekka to Medina on the night of the 15th–16th July, 622 A.D. The national calendar is lunar, the year being divided into twelve months consisting alternately of twenty-nine and thirty days, and comprising therefore only 354 days ; and no complementary days being added to adjust this calendar in accordance with astronomical events, it naturally follows that both national anniversaries and religious festivals make, in the course of every thirty-three years, the round of the seasons. The peasantry, however, in their reckoning of time, adhere for ordinary puposes to the ancient and more convenient Oriental practice of dividing the year into two seasons, Summer and Winter, the former being inaugurated by the great Nature-festival of *Khidr-Elis*, equivalent to our St. George's Day, and the latter by that of *Kassim*, held late in the Autumn. The hours of the day are still, in ancient Oriental fashion, reckoned by the Turks from sunset to sunset, which is estimated with more or less exactitude. Many of the watches now used in Turkey are made with two dials, one for Turkish and the other for European time, the former, to be correct, requiring daily regulation; and one may occasionally hear the seemingly odd question asked, "At what time is noon to-day?" In Turkey, however, few people require to catch trains or steamboats; time-tables are also as often ignored as consulted; and punctuality is not a virtue cultivated by the Oriental. On the majority of Turkish railways there is but one train a day up and down the line, and intending passengers will arrive at the station when they may happen to be ready, and, seated on their baggage, patiently wait for the next train. *Inshallah* (Allah permitting), he will ultimately arrive at his destination.

CHAPTER II

OFFICIAL AND MILITARY TURKS

THE upper classes of Osmanli society at the present day may be said to consist almost entirely of the families of Government officials and military men, as there seems to be no career open to a Turkish youth of good family but the Army or the Civil Service, and almost every member of the *jeunesse dorée* of Stamboul who has not selected the Army as his profession, looks forward to a post in one of the numerous Government offices. For the Turks, generally speaking, have not hitherto shown themselves active or intelligent as business men, and venture little into speculative commercial or financial transactions, which they appear to regard somewhat in the light of games of chance which are forbidden by their religion. To the restrictions placed especially of late years upon the free action of all Moslem subjects of the Sultan may also be attributed their abandonment to foreigners of both the import and export trade of their country, no Osmanlis being at liberty to form or join a company or to move freely from one part of the Empire to another for business purposes; and a military or official career has consequently—as apparently desired by the powers that be

24

—remained the only alternative of the present generation. The national movements among the subject races of Turkey during the past century having, on the other hand, inspired the Porte with a growing distrust of members of these nationalities as State officials, their employment in such capacities has yearly diminished, and more posts in the higher Government departments have of late been filled by Moslems of Turkish, Albanian, and Circassian descent than perhaps ever since the Conquest. The country has nominally a Civil Service entered by examination from the Government colleges, open to all Turkish subjects, and offering regular promotion. But, like many other Turkish institutions of recent date, it has remained merely nominal, and appointments have continued to be made by the time-honoured process termed *katir*, or "favour," important posts being obtainable only through influence in Yildiz Kiosk. And though a Board was constituted some years ago with the title of "Commission for the Selection of Functionaries," it was never allowed to do more than "recommend" candidates for vacant posts, and its recommendations generally received but scant attention. Posts in the Government service have continued to be treated, as of yore, as objects of commercial speculation, the favourites at Yildiz Kiosk—whose own tenure of offices was always more or less precarious—finding it to their interest not only to sell them to the highest bidder, but also to sell them as frequently as possible.

The late sudden transition from a despotic to a constitutional form of government must of necessity bring about in the near future many important changes in the organisation of the various State departments. The Sublime Porte and the *Seraskierate*, or War Office, have already ceased to be, as they for many years past have been, merely the nominal seats of Government, and ministers now themselves control their respective departments instead of being the mere mouthpieces of an arbitrary Padishah. But the Oriental modes of procedure which have been the growth of centuries and are the outcome of the Oriental attitude of mind cannot be changed by the declaration of a Constitution, and in the conduct of public affairs what has been will, in all probability, long continue to be.

The Sublime Porte in Stamboul constitutes the central seat of Government for the Empire, and here is also located the *Seraskierate*, or War Office. The great vestibule of the former, which corresponds to the "Salle des Pas Perdus" of the French Senate House and the Lobby of the House of Commons, presents a strange contrast to both, being usually crowded with a motley throng representative of all the races and classes of the Empire, among whom circulate begging Dervishes, *Kahfedjis*, itinerant vendors of various wares, and perhaps a *deli*, or madman, real or feigned, whose sallies serve to pass the long hours of waiting. Matted corridors, along which the humbler natives glide with bare or merely stockinged feet, carrying their dusty or muddy shoes, lead to the various bureaus. In the office of the head of a department there is a perpetual coming and going. The *portière*—a rug lined with leather which screens the doorway—is raised a dozen times an hour, and visitors or petitioners enter unannounced, salaam to the great man from the doorway, salaam again on approaching him, and a third time before taking a seat, if invited to do so. Oriental etiquette necessitates between equals the interchange of polite phrases before the subject-matter of the visit is entered upon, thus prolonging every interview; and it is hardly to be wondered at that under such a system an army of functionaries is found necessary to transact the business of every department. In each of the subordinate bureaus may be seen a dozen or so of clerks seated, in all kinds of attitudes, on sofas and armchairs covered with rich stuffs worn to shabbiness by the constant friction of boots and shoes. In front of each is a little stand holding the Turkish inkpot, sand-sifter, reed-pens, ashtrays, and, at frequent intervals, the inevitable coffee cup. The *kyatib*, when he happens to be occupied, holds his paper in his left hand supported on his upraised knee while inscribing on it, with his pen held vertically, the graceful Arabic characters used by the Turks, writing from right to left.

But although the Sublime Porte and its dependencies possess such large clerical staffs, admittance to a department of the public service by no means implies that a young hopeful enters at once upon regular duties with a fixed salary and expectation of certain future promotion. Things have not hitherto been managed in such prosaic

fashion in Turkey. The bureau to which a budding
Civil servant is attached constitutes for him, at the outset
at least, merely a resort in the nature of a club in the
society of whose members he may be said to graduate
socially while waiting for a salaried appointment. Here
he learns to despise the costume of his forefathers and
to become anxious about the fit of a frock coat of the
latest Paris cut, to assume the airs of a man about town,
and possibly adds to the cognomen of Ali, Achmet, or
Mehmet, which has hitherto served to identify him,
another appellation for future official use. The heads of
the various departments of State have of course special
functions, which they perform with the assistance of such
among their subordinates as they may think proper to
employ. There seems, however, hardly enough work
to go round, and a considerable number of the aspirants
to bureaucratic employment pass their time during office
hours in receiving visitors, gossiping, smoking, and coffee
drinking. At the War Office the plethora of officials is
even more remarkable ; at the Admiralty somewhat less so
—which, considering the condition hitherto of the Turkish
Navy, is hardly surprising ; the only department of State
distinguished by any degree of order and imposing gravity
being the semi-ecclesiastical one presided over by the
Sheikh-ul-Islam, the Ulema who compose its official
staff still retaining, with their ample turbans and patri-
arçhal robes, the dignified appearance and manners usually
associated with this Oriental costume.

While young men of family who have not made the

Army their vocation thus aspire to high Civil posts, those of more humble birth seek employment in the household of some official of high rank, taking places formerly filled by male slaves, such as coffee-maker, pipe-bearer, or body servant ; and from the eagerness displayed for this kind of occupation has sprung one of Turkey's greatest misfortunes, every holder of an important office being hedged around by barriers composed of successive grades of parasitic underlings through whom a suppliant could pass only with one key—*bakshish.* Orientals, it may here be remarked, do not look upon the offering and acceptance of *bakshish* as bribery. For under the disorganised and corrupt administration which has so long prevailed officials could only live by having recourse to this system, to live on their salaries being next to impossible, as, in the first place, they are generally inadequate, and, in the second, they are always in arrear. Even the most honestly disposed official has consequently been compelled, in order to support himself and family, to supplement his meagre and irregularly paid salary by this ancient and approved method. It may here be remarked parentheti- cally that the absence of punctuality in paying salaries, or wages, is characteristic not of the Turks only, but of Orientals generally. Domestic servants, for instance, are engaged at a yearly wage and are fed and clothed by their employers. Their wages are not, however, paid to them at any stated period, but are as a rule allowed to accumulate in the master's hands and are only drawn on leaving. As savings banks are not yet common in Turkey, this practice, when the employer is honest, has no doubt its advantages. In the case of military officers and Government employees, however, who have themselves and their families to support, this irregularity in the payment of salaries often entails great hardships, and I have personally known heads of households holding the rank of Pasha, and consequently entitled to high pay, at a loss how to meet their butcher's and baker's bills.

The methods of the Turkish Paymaster-General's Office are also peculiar. Both salaries and other claims on the State are paid by means of *havalés*—or orders on some provincial treasury. After much petitioning, an official may receive such an order for the sum due to him, or perhaps only a part of it. This order does not, however, bear the name of any special treasury, so the recipient takes it to a *saraf*, or professional discounter, from whom he may perhaps receive a third or half its value. For not only this functionary, but also the provincial governor on whose treasury it is made payable, and the financial authorities of the province through whose hands the *havalé* must pass before final payment in full by the Treasury, will all make their own profit out of the remaining half, or third, of the sum of which the unfortunate officer is thus mulcted. Stories are rife in the country, and especially in the Capital, of enormous bribes being received and vast sums appropriated by dishonest officials ; but somehow few seem to be much the richer for these transactions. Exaggeration is a foible peculiarly Oriental, and even a *bakshish* running into four figures

does not amount to much when perhaps two-thirds of it
have to be distributed among subordinates and others
who are parties to the transaction.

Since the destruction in 1826 of the Janissaries by
Sultan Mahmoud II., "The Reformer"—a measure forced
upon him by the dangerously hostile attitude of this
formidable but reactionary corps—the organisation of the
Turkish Army has undergone radical changes, the re-
formed system on which the Army of the present day
is based having been initiated sixteen years later. The
Empire was then, as now, divided into seven military
districts, three in Europe and four in Asia, each of which
furnishes an Army Corps for the defence of the Father-
land, recruitment being effected by conscription. Under
this system all Moslem men are, nominally at least, liable
to be called upon to serve their country in the field, non-
Moslem subjects of the Sultan paying a tax in lieu of
military service. Wealthy Moslems may, however, by
paying a fine of £50 and providing a substitute, evade
this patriotic duty, and young men whose labour constitutes the sole support of their parents may also claim
complete exemption. Very curiously there are certain
localities of the Empire—the Capital, Scutari in Albania,
and the Yemen—residence in which confers freedom from
the conscription. Members also of the learned professions,
theological, legal, and medical, together with students preparing to enter them, are everywhere excluded from the
number available for military service; and many young
men who have no vocation for the study of the *Sheriat*,

or Sacred Law, endeavour to pass at least the preliminary examination in Arabic and other subjects which entitles them to this privilege, even if they subsequently adopt another career.   Half a century ago, notwithstanding these numerous exemptions, the burden of this blood-tax fell lightly enough on the population generally, seeing that the Moslem subjects in the Empire could be computed at a figure approaching 20 millions.   With the shrinkage of the Empire, however, since 1876, the recruits are now drawn chiefly from among the seven million or so of Moslems inhabiting European Turkey, Asia Minor, and Syria, and military service is yearly becoming a heavier burden to the agricultural population who are now chiefly called upon to fill the ranks.   The vast number of men thus enabled to claim exemption constitutes a serious blot on an otherwise admirable system, and calls loudly for reform.   Since the establishment of the Constitution, non-Moslems are, in some localities, being called upon to bear their part in the defence of the Empire of which they are subjects.   Whether this scheme will prove to work satisfactorily, remains of course to be seen.   Possibly, however, the recruits drawn from the Christian and Jewish races will be organised into separate corps, officered by their own co-religionists.

In Asia Minor this obligatory military service constitutes a more grievous burden than elsewhere.   For as the Moslem population in Europe (exclusive of the exempted cities) numbers less than a million and a half of souls, a considerable proportion of the recruits annually

ARTILLERY OF THE 1ST BRIGADE.

required for the three nominally European Army Corps have to be sought beyond the confines of their own strategic circles; and accordingly, out of the forty-eight recruiting districts into which the Empire is now divided, no fewer than forty are situated in Asia, these districts being called upon to supply 53 regiments of cavalry, 315 regiments of infantry of various classes, and 276 batteries of artillery, horse, field, heavy, and mountain.

For the purposes of conscription a register of births in each recruiting district is kept at the battalion head-quarters, annual returns of births being made by the municipal officials of provincial towns and the headmen of villages. As each youth arrives at the age for service, his number is drawn according to rule, and if he cannot claim exemption under any of the foregoing pretexts, he is either sent to the military depôt for training, or, should there be at the moment no vacancies for service with the colours, he is at once passed, without training, into the second-class reserve. Cavalry, Artillery, and Engineers are recruited indiscriminately from all the various districts, each centre furnishing a certain proportion to each arm. On completing his nine years of service in the *Nizam*, as the regular Army is termed, a soldier returns to his home as a *Redif*, or first-class Reservist, being attached to the battalion of his district, and still liable to be called out for active service in such cases of emergency as have recently arisen in Macedonia and on the Persian frontier. Of these regimental districts of *Redifs* there are no fewer than 384, each under the command of a major with a

D

small permanent staff; and as arms, accoutrements, and equipment are stored at the battalion headquarters, and the *Redif* brigades are always complete as to their cadres, a body of highly trained and seasoned men can, on an order for mobilisation being received from the War Office, be despatched without delay from each district.

As to the *Mustafis*, or Reservists of the second class, ten divisions of this body are attached to each of the five Army Corps, having their headquarters at Constantinople, Adrianople, Salonica, Erzinghian, and Damascus. They, however, are only liable to be called upon for active service in the event of grave national danger, and as they possess no military qualifications beyond regimental organisation, their lack of training renders them unavailable as a fighting contingent. But as hewers of wood and drawers of water, and in similar subordinate capacities, they no doubt form a valuable asset to the regular army during a campaign. The officers of the Reserve consist largely of men who have risen from the ranks through the intermediate grades. They are said to make excellent company commanders, owing to their possessing in a marked degree the affection and confidence of their subordinates, but lack of education renders the majority unfit for superior commands. Examinations for promotion have recently been introduced into the Turkish Army, but the numbers who can profit by such facilities for advancement are limited. Books on military subjects are not easily obtainable in the remoter provincial towns, and officers whose regiments are quartered far from the

Capital, however ambitious of promotion, have few opportunities of keeping abreast of the times in military
matters. At such great centres as Constantinople, Smyrna,
and Salonica, however, the Military clubs, which number
among their patrons and benefactors the Sultan and
other members of the Imperial family, offer all these
facilities; for neither the Military nor the hitherto less
numerous Naval clubs are in any sense political, their
primary object being, in common with the generality of
such institutions in Turkey, study, self-improvement, and
social intercourse.

The rations to which officers are entitled are valued
at £1 Turkish (about 18s.) per unit, this being the sum
which a lieutenant can draw in lieu. Senior officers
receive in an increasing rate up to the maximum of
twenty-four rations, the allowance of a Field Marshal.
Officers receive the same pay in all arms, and are entitled
in addition to receive rations and forage for their horses
as well as a liberal outfit in the matter of kit and
uniform, graduated according to rank, each officer according to his grade having the right to a certain number
of soldier servants for whom he also draws rations and
forage. The rate of officers' pay is low, according to
our notions. But, on the other hand, they receive their
uniforms from the Government as well as their rations;
they are not, as a rule, addicted to expensive habits,
being accustomed to a simple life; and even for those
who are married and have to provide houses for their
families, living in Turkey is cheap, especially in the

provinces. Few complaints are therefore heard on the
score of pay. The real hardship has consisted in the fact
that regimental, as well as civil, pay has for many years
past been always in arrear. Nor have the higher fared
in this respect better than the lower grades of officers
and civilians. The rations supplied to the men are of
good quality and ample in quantity, a Turkish soldier
being said to fare far better in barracks than ever in
his village home, for he is entitled to an *oka*[1] of bread
and half an *oka* of meat, with certain quantities of rice,
vegetables, and cooking butter per diem. The barracks
in which the regimental officers and men are housed are,
on the whole, sufficiently spacious and airy, and notwithstanding the frequent defects in the sanitary arrangements the troops are, generally speaking, strong and
healthy. Barrack life is no doubt in many respects
trying for the sons of the soil who form the majority
of the recruits. But taken as a whole, the physique of
the Turkish Army is indeed magnificent, and in marching and staying powers the rank-and-file are admitted
by competent authorities to be second to those of no
other country. Accustomed to frugal fare and a total
abstainer from strong drink, the Turkish soldier, when
on active service, like his remote nomadic forbears of
Central Asia, is ever ready at the bugle call to strike
or pitch his tent, saddle or unsaddle his charger, and
hang his camp kettle wherever he may happen to bivouac.
Content with the simplest fare, he takes his frugal meal

[1] An *oka* is equivalent to about 2 lbs. 12 ozs.

seated on the ground, bears with infinite patience the toils of march and the pains of privations, and obeys with unquestioning alacrity the orders of his superiors. Though often in rags and shoeless—as I have myself seen them on their arrival at the coast towns for tranship- ment after a long campaign on the frontiers of the Empire—with months of pay in arrear, their behaviour is blameless, and their discipline perfect. And with the sound of the sunrise and sunset gun from citadel or warship there ever rises enthusiastically from a thousand throats the loyal cry, *Padishahim chok yashar !*—" Long live our Padishah ! " The requirements of the soldiery being so easily satisfied, and those of their officers being proportionately modest, the commissariat of the Turkish Army during a campaign is simple to arrange, and to this fact is chiefly due its extreme mobility in the field. The Transport service has certainly often proved lament- ably defective ; but efforts are now being made to bring it up to modern requirements. Owing to the absence of good roads, it is, however, impossible for commissariat waggons to be used, and pack animals are consequently the usual mode of conveyance for all the necessaries of an army.

In the opinion of English and other European military men who have had opportunities for observing the difference, an immense improvement has taken place in the Turkish Army since the Russo-Turkish war of thirty years ago, some indeed going so far as to assert that the chief factor making for peace in South Eastern

Europe has been rather the Turkish Army than that somewhat fictitious entity known as the "European Concert." At the time of the Crimean War, Turkey could only with difficulty send 100,000 trained soldiers to the front. Now she has at her disposal nearly ten times that number, and at the present moment has some 200,000 engaged in active operations in Macedonia and on the Eastern frontiers of the Empire. The Transport service has also been completely reorganised since 1897. It now possesses thirty-four well-found vessels, and the harbours at Haidar Pasha—the Asiatic port of the Capital—at Salonica, and at Beyrout have been greatly improved. Owing to the state of unrest which has for so many years past prevailed in Macedonia, and to the disturbed state of Yemen and the Persian frontier, a large proportion of troops of all arms have seen active service, and a considerable proportion of the Reserves were at the front in the Turco-Greek war.

With regard to the medical requirements of the Army, each Army Corps headquarters has its own hospital, as have also most of the divisional centres, the majority having hospital accommodation for from 300 to 500 patients. The Military hospitals in the Capital, and also at Adrianople, are large and well equipped, the former containing no fewer than 4000 beds and the latter 1200; and the Hamidieh Hospital above Pera—so named after its founder and patron the Sultan, who maintains it at his own personal expense—is considered one of the most complete and up-to-date institutions of its kind in Europe. Each Infantry regiment has also on its rolls twelve medical officers, three for each battalion, under a surgeon-major, who is attached to the regimental staff; while Cavalry regiments have four medical officers, batteries of Artillery one, and Engineer battalions three, veterinary officers being also attached to all mounted corps. A considerable proportion of military medical officers are either foreigners or non-Moslem Turkish subjects, who are equally eligible with Osmanlis for the highest posts.

CHAPTER III

DENIZENS OF THE PALACES

ESKI SERAI—the Old Palace—the ancestral home of the Ottoman Sultans during four hundred years, so charmingly situated on the triangular point of land washed by the waters of the Golden Horn, the Bosphorus, and the Sea of Marmora, was unfortunately in great part destroyed by fire about fifty years ago. It had, however, previously been more or less abandoned as a place of residence since the time of Mahmoud II., who, together with his successors, preferred the modern palaces they had caused to be erected on the immediate shores of the Bosphorus to this somewhat gloomy abode with its high enclosing walls, its dungeons, and its gilded bowers, tainted with the fratricidal crimes of their ancestors. At the time of its destruction Eski Serai was occupied by the numerous harem of the defunct Sultan Abdul Medjid, some members of which, according to common report, finding existence here insupportable after their accustomed freedom under that mild and indulgent Padishah, on two occasions (1863 and 1865) purposely set fire to it, in order to obtain a more congenial place of residence.

The ancient throne-room, together with other interesting

State apartments, was, however, fortunately saved, and the walls of the Imperial demesne still enclose in addition a number of the elegant detached buildings termed "kiosks," many of which still serve their original purposes.   Among these is the Sultan's treasure-house, in which are kept a variety of valuable and interesting objects, including bowls of uncut gems, ancient Imperial costumes and jewelled arms, and—perhaps most interesting of all—the golden throne and footstool set with pearls and rubies, taken by Sultan Selim I. from the Persians in 1514.   There is also the "Kiosk of Bagdad," so called from the model in that city from which it was copied, which is esteemed the finest existing specimen of Turkish decorative art, the artistic blending of colour being strikingly successful.   Both the inner and the outer walls are covered with beautifully patterned blue and white tiles, the doors and shutters are of walnut-wood inlaid with ivory and mother-of-pearl, and the carpets, draperies, and divan stuffs are most elaborate and costly.   The friezes in this kind of wall decoration, which is found in other buildings forming part of the Serai as also in some of the mosques of Stamboul, consist of

> " Soft Persian sentences in lilac letters,
> From poets, or the moralists, their betters,"

the Arabic characters composing them being peculiarly adapted to arrangement in conventional patterns most artistic in their general effect.

In the course of the past century "the European with the Asian shore" have been "sprinkled with palaces" by the later wearers of the sword of Osman, and especially by the extravagant, luxury-loving Sultans Abdul Medjid and his son Abdul Aziz. And besides palaces proper there are *Yaklis* and *Kiosks*, elegant villas, ancient and modern, occupying elevated and picturesque spots over-looking the winding and swiftly rushing Bosphorus, and embowered amid flowers and foliage. The three splendid waterside palaces of Dolma Baktché, Tcheragan, and Begler-Bey have not, however, been favourite abodes of the reigning Sultan, who has for many years past resided exclusively at the less pretentious Yildiz Kiosk—the " Kiosk of the Star "—situated on the summit of the hill behind Dolma Baktché. Around this once modest villa have, however, now grown up a vast assemblage of buildings, the whole being surrounded on every side by extensive wooded grounds forming a sort of park enclosed within high walls. These are flanked at intervals by ugly yellow barracks, in which are quartered the troops of the Imperial bodyguard, Arabian, Albanian, and Kurdish, who watch over each other while watching over the safety of the mighty Padishah. Beyond these walls again the hills and valleys are occupied by an outer circle of block-houses and sentry-boxes, extending down to the shore of the Bosphorus, where stretches the long frontage of the palace in which the deposed ex-Sultan, poor mad Murad Effendi, lived for thirty years the solitary existence of a strictly guarded captive.

Like the abodes of private individuals, and in common with the other Imperial palaces, Yildiz Kiosk is divided

into *haremlik* and *selamlik*, the buildings which crown
the hill constituting the latter, in which the Court
functionaries and their attendants have their quarters;
while the edifice containing the Sultan's private apartments forms the *mabeyn*, as the connecting neutral
ground between these two divisions of a residence is
termed. The ladies of the harem are accommodated in a
mansion connected with the *mabeyn* by a long corridor,
and agreeably situated in the Imperial demesne, being
surrounded by delightful flower gardens, artificial lakes,
and woods intersected with winding paths leading to
various pleasure kiosks. In the Imperial park are also
situated the Sultan's private theatre and various detached
pavilions and villas. One of the latter, styled the palace
Merassim, has been specially erected and furnished for
the reception of foreign visitors of high rank, in order
that the Commander of the Faithful might be able to
fulfil all the duties of hospitality and courtesy to his
occasional Royal guests without going beyond the walls
of his private domain.

Ancient custom and established precedent, however,
require the Padishah on certain occasions to do violence
to his desire for seclusion and to show himself to his
loyal subjects, one of these occasions being the weekly
function termed the *Selamlik*, from *selam*, "salutation."
For many centuries past it has been customary for
Turkish Sultans to proceed in state to one of the
principal mosques of the Capital for the performance
of the midday prayers on Friday, the Moslem Day of

Rest, and no consideration of any kind has been allowed
to prevent the present sovereign fulfilling this religious
obligation, his failure to show himself on this day being
calculated to create rumours of his illness or death, and
subsequent political complications.   And however indis-
posed the Padishah may be, at the important hour he
is invariably reported by his courtiers to be in the best
of health, and nerves himself for his weekly public
appearance. But even in this particular, Sultan Abdul
Hamid has deviated from the habits of his ancestors,
and, instead of making a weekly progress on horseback
through the streets of his Capital, amid the acclamations
of loyal subjects, has performed the Friday *namas* in
the private Hamidieh Mosque, built by himself in the
palace precincts. This ceremony of the *Selamlik* presents
a most animated and striking spectacle which is regularly
witnessed by ambassadors and other foreigners of distinction from the windows of a pavilion erected at the gate
leading into the palace grounds. On the other side is a
railed-in enclosure, surrounding the mosque, which is new
and white, and of a pseudo-Oriental and somewhat rococo
style of architecture. During the forenoon on Fridays the
roads surrounding the mosque are gradually lined with
troops belonging to the first and second Army divisions.
First come the battalions of the Albanian or Arab
Zouaves with their quaintly twisted red turbans, and
take up their positions near the palace gates ; the Marines
arrive next, and are followed by battalions of Anatolian
Infantry, who form in lines several deep on either side of

CALIFORNIA

THE SULTAN'S VICTORIA

the roadway, while Cavalry regiments take up their
positions behind them, flanked again by gendarmes in
couples. The Turkish populace, composed largely of
women and children, occupies every available inch of the
roadway on the lower side of the mosque, eager for a
glimpse of their Padishah as he passes down the sloping
drive between the palace gates and those of the mosque ;
but it is now impossible to approach and present petitions
personally, as in previous reigns had always been the
privilege of subjects during a Sultan's weekly Friday
progress to and from the mosque. Strains of military
music fill the air ; officers in smart well-fitting uniforms
ride to and fro on beautiful Arabs ; well - appointed
carriages pass conveying high civil functionaries to the
mosque or members of the various foreign Embassies
and Legations to the pavilion. Presently broughams
arrive from the palace bearing uniform-clad princes and
white-veiled princesses ; and lastly, driven very slowly
in a smart landau, appears the Padishah himself. A
bugle sounds, and simultaneously from a thousand throats
the cry of *Padishahim chok yashar !*—"Long live our
Padishah !"—thrice repeated, greets the Commander of
the Faithful. Salaaming continually in acknowledgment of the cheers and salutes, Abdul Hamid passes
down the road and through the gates to the curved and
carpeted stairway leading to his private entrance and
divan khané, or reception room, a passing glimpse only
being meanwhile caught of him—a figure of medium
height in simple fez and undress uniform, a pale and

somewhat sad, yet keen and dignified face, with longish hooked nose and well-trimmed grey beard and moustache. On alighting, the Sultan is received and surrounded by a little crowd of obsequiously bowing dignitaries, civil and military, and having mounted the short flight of steps, he, before entering, courteously turns to acknowledge with the military salute the homage of his troops and subjects, who again cry in response, "Long live our Padishah ! "

Half an hour or so elapses, during which the waiting multitude—or at least that section of it sufficiently well placed—has leisure to contemplate the wide view of the Bosphorus and Stamboul extending below to the south ; to admire the half-dozen superb saddle-horses which have been led behind the Imperial carriage ; and to watch the regimental *sakas*, or water-carriers, distribute the contents of their leathern jacks among the soldiery. Presently the battalions are called to attention, form again into line, and march past the northern side of the mosque before the Sultan, who is stationed at a window of the *divan khané*. A stir follows at the door, the Padishah emerges, and now, seated in a victoria drawn by a pair of spirited greys, the reins of which he himself holds, again passes, closely surrounded by staff officers on horseback and running footmen in the Imperial red and gold livery, and disappears through the gates of Yildiz Kiosk.

Besides the Friday *Selamlik* there are also five other annual occasions on which the Sultan is required to show himself in public. These are the ceremonies connected

respectively with the opening of the Greater and the
Lesser Bairam; the veneration in mid-Ramazan of that
sacred relic, the Prophet's Mantle, which is kept in the
Old Serai together with his standard, his staff, and sword
and bow; the *Mevlud*, or Birthday of the Prophet; and
the departure of the Caravan of Pilgrims to Mekka, all of
which are elsewhere described.

The Commander of the Faithful is no *Roi fainéant*.
Like the humblest of his subjects, he rises with the sun
all the year round, often commencing his morning's work
at five o'clock after partaking with his first cigarette of a
cup of coffee prepared in his study by the chief coffee-
maker. For the Sultan is a great smoker and coffee-
drinker, and is never, it is said, without a cigarette—made
in his presence by his *tchiboukdji*—between his fingers;
and when he takes walking or riding exercise about the
palace grounds he is followed everywhere by his *kahvédji-
bashi*, or chief coffee-maker, who carries the paraphernalia
requisite for preparing at a moment's notice a cup of his
favourite beverage. Abdul Hamid, like most of his
ancestors, has also his little superstitions; and as it was
once prophesied to him by a Gypsy that he would reign as
long as he continued to drink the water from the springs
of Kiathané in the valley of the "Sweet Waters of
Europe," his daily supplies are regularly brought thence
in sealed jars, and no other water passes his lips. The
Sultan is most abstemious in his habits. At about six
o'clock he partakes of a light breakfast of eggs and milk;
at ten o'clock he indulges in a rather more substantial

déjeuner, and, like the rest of his subjects, dines at sunset. The Imperial dinner, usually eaten in solitary state and served with great ceremonial, consists of a number of courses all of a very simple character, and in obedience to the advice of his physician, as also of St. Paul, he occasionally takes, "for his stomach's sake," a little brandy, champagne, or punch; but, of course, as a rigid Moslem, no "wine." During the lifetime of the Validé Sultan, as had been customary in previous reigns, the dishes for the Imperial table were invariably prepared in the kitchen of the Empress Mother's establishment and sent in sealed napkins to the *mabeyn*. The mother of his Majesty Abdul Hamid having, however, long since been summoned away by the "Cupbearer of the Sphere" to "the goodly plains in the Garden of Eden," prepared "for all resigned and believing women," the Padishah guards against the possibility of poison by having for the service of his own table a private kitchen fortified against access from without by barred windows and a massive door. When the Sultan intimates to his attendants that he wishes to dine, a table is placed before him laid for one, and the bread, water, and dishes, all severally enveloped in napkins sealed by the *Kilerdji*, or chief steward, are carried in solemn procession from the kitchen by a number of lackeys, any persons whom the Sultan's dinner may encounter on its passage to the Presence habitually doing homage to it by bowing low with their hands clasped on their stomachs. The seals are broken in the Sultan's presence, and the dishes placed in succession on the table by the *Kilerdji*, who may possibly—should his Imperial master be suddenly seized with an apprehension of poison—be commanded to partake of the viands himself; and to the same motive is also attributed his habit of feeding several cats from his table. After partaking of one or two of the dishes placed before him, the Sultan, as a mark of royal favour, names those of his courtiers and ministers to whom he wishes the rest to be conveyed. And in the midst of the great military display awaiting the Sultan's appearance at the gates of Yildiz Kiosk on Fridays, it is rather curious to see palace attendants sallying forth bearing dishes enveloped in white napkins tied at the four corners, destined for the Court dignitaries their Imperial master thus delights to honour.

The intervals between these simple Royal repasts are occupied chiefly with the transaction of State business. Every Sultan of Turkey has been, theoretically at least, an autocratic ruler, but the degree of power exerted by each of the descendants of Osman has varied according to the vigour of his character and the social and political conditions of his time. The present reign has, however, witnessed the most remarkable union of all the conditions requisite for real autocracy—a prince who " scorns delights, and spends laborious days "—an extension of the telegraph system throughout the Empire, and, until the proclamation of the Constitution last year, an absence of all elements capable of thwarting or resisting the sovereign will. Many as have no doubt been the tyrannical acts of Abdul Hamid, the degree of progress attained by Turkey as an

E

Empire during the past thirty years is mainly due to the unflagging industry of her ruler, who may be literally said to work night and day. The supreme head of the military forces of the country, all who have been brought into personal contact with him pay tribute to his knowledge of military affairs, the minutest detail of which does not escape his keen interest. And critical as the state of Turkey undoubtedly now is, it is certainly far less so than when, in 1876, he was suddenly and unexpectedly called upon to ascend the throne. War with a great Power was then impending, the Treasury was well-nigh empty, and the State saddled with a debt of over two hundred millions, a national debt now reduced by the Sultan's exertions to less than eighty millions, notwithstanding the payment to Russia of nearly ten millions of war indemnity.

Strenuous worker though he habitually is, the Sultan has, however, his occasional hours of relaxation, his favourite diversions being drawing, painting, wood-carving, and chemical experiments. An expert marksman, he keeps his hand in by regular target practice and firing at glass balls and other moving objects. Report says that fear of assassination incited the Padishah to attain this proficiency in the use of firearms, and that he always carries a pistol on his person. In his partiality for dramatic and operatic representations Abdul Hamid resembles his father Abdul Medjid; and to the little theatre in the palace grounds are permanently attached a company of light comedians and an operatic troupe, whose rehearsals the Padishah often supervises in person. The foreign troupes which

periodically make the tour of the Levant are also often
"commanded" to give performances here to which high
officials or Royal guests are sometimes invited.   The
Sultan, however, as well as the ladies of his family and
their attendants seated in the Royal boxes, are concealed
from view by gilded lattices and vouchsafe no audible sign
of approval or the reverse, though courteous messages,
usually accompanied by presents or decorations, may be
sent to the leading artistes after the performance.   The
floor of the auditorium is occupied only by foreign visitors
and palace functionaries, an arrangement which must have
a somewhat chilling effect on actors accustomed to a
crowded house.   The Sultan has also, like all Orientals,
a weakness for mechanical toys and shows of all sorts, and
cinematographs, phonographs, pianolas, musical boxes, and
other products of Western civilisation, as well as the native
Oriental shows described in a subsequent chapter, are in
great favour at the Kiosk.   A genuine Turk also in his
kindness of and interest in animals, the Sultan has
tenanted his park with numbers of wild creatures which
he delights to feed with his own hands.   And in addition
to the multitude of birds of many species which enliven
the hills and vales, large numbers of pigeons and parrots—
including a collection presented to the Sultan by the
Mikado—build and breed in the Imperial demesne; while
well-appointed kennels to which a veterinary hospital is
also attached—a great innovation—are tenanted by
favourite dogs of various breeds.   The Royal stables contain nearly a hundred and fifty horses, including some

valuable thoroughbred saddle-horses reserved for his Majesty's own use, his favourite being a white Arab, "Azyl" by name. Half a dozen of these beautiful creatures are on Fridays led behind their master's carriage by grooms dressed in the handsome Imperial livery. Attached to the stables is a riding school for the use of the young princes, whose equestrian exercises are occasionally supervised by their Imperial father from a glazed gallery overlooking the ring.

As has been remarked in a previous chapter, Oriental sentiment is opposed to the formation of an aristocratic class occupying an intermediate position between the Sovereign and the people; even the connexions of the Imperial family forming no such noble or privileged class. With the exception of the Sultan's sons, the male members of the Imperial family, including the Heir apparent—who, according to the Turkish law of succession, is the senior among his relatives—have hitherto led dull useless lives of compulsory seclusion in separate palaces; and but a limited number of persons belonging to collateral branches of the dynasty which has reigned for five centuries at Constantinople appear to exist in the country. Under the new *régime*, however, these princes of the Imperial house are able to enter the Services and play their part in social life. One may, for instance, now read in the Constantinople papers that Lieutenant Prince Burhaneddin Effendi has presented a piano and the sum of £300 to the naval club of which he is the honorary president, or that

S. A. I. Youssouf Izzedin Effendi has graciously accorded his patronage to the concert to be given under the auspices of the Armenian Benevolent Society. It is also no longer an act of *lèse majesté*, as formerly, to enumerate the sons and daughters of the Sultan, whose olive branches are sufficiently numerous, and Turkish almanacks may now venture to publish such information to the world without being promptly suppressed. The daughters of Sultans, who also bear the title of "Sultan"—there being in Turkish no feminine form of complimentary titles— assume, in virtue of their Royal birth, precedence of their husbands, and have in many cases treated with scorn the conventional restraints imposed by Oriental custom on their sex. The sons of these princesses have, however, hitherto in common with other scions of the family of the Padishah, been ineligible for the higher civil and military offices, the whole system of the Imperial harem appearing to have been, like the Turkish social system, framed with the view of preventing the formation of a hereditary aristocratic class in the nation.

The household of Sultan Abdul Hamid, large as it may appear, is organised on a quite modest scale compared with that of his brother and predecessor Abdul Aziz, at whose deposition in 1876, no fewer than three thousand persons were dismissed from the palace of Dolma Baktché; and it was computed that less than one-third of these were women, the rest being function-aries, menials, and hangers-on of every degree. The Imperial harem, however, still contains many hundreds of women, who form a society apart from the rest of the population, live their own life, and have their own code of traditions, manners, customs, and etiquette. They may also be said to have their own peculiar dialect, for the speech of the *Serailis*—as the denizens of this strange abode are termed—differs in pronunciation and expression from that of the outer world; and their extraction can always be at once detected by this peculiarity. But large as is the number of women thus brought together under one roof, so complete is the organisation of the whole, and so absolute the discipline, that there is no confusion or disorder, each member of the household having her assigned position and functions. The *Serai* possesses a sort of constitution of its own, having its own customary laws—unwritten, it is true, but none the less rigidly enforced—its high dignitaries, and its intermediary and lower ranks. The titular head of this feminine Court is the *Validé Sultan*, the mother of the reigning Sultan, next to whom ranks the mother of the eldest son—the *Khastki Sultan*, and after her the second, third, and fourth Kadin Effendis, should there be so many. To each of these ladies is assigned a *daïra*, or establishment, which comprises an allowance in money, a suite of apartments, and a train of female slaves and eunuchs. The chief female officials of the Queen Mother's Court are twelve in number, each of these Ladies of the Household, or *kalfas*, as they are called, having under her an assistant and six or more pupils, who are all designated according to their several departments. The *daïras* of the other ladies are formed on the same model, but the number of attendants composing them varies according to the rank of the Kadin Effendi.

On the accession of a new Sultan, the various ladies of the deceased, or deposed, Sultan's harem are, together with their personal attendants, removed to one of the smaller palaces in order to make room for the household of the young Padishah, whose mother is immediately elevated to the rank of Validé Sultan, and at once invested with almost Imperial dignity. The new Sultan now requires all the persons composing his household, from his wives down to the lowest menials, to take an oath of obedience to his Mother, who is henceforth only addressed or referred to as "The Crown of Veiled Heads," a title with which every petition to her must begin. No one may venture to appear before her unless an audience has previously been asked for and granted, or sit uninvited in her presence, and all stand before her in the Oriental posture of respect—arms crossed on the breast and heads bent, and accompany every reply with a lowly reverence and the words "Our Lady." Nor may any one of the inmates of the Serai, whatever her rank, leave her own apartments without her permission, or address any request to the Sultan, save through her. Such supreme authority naturally entails much responsibility and duties sufficiently arduous. Of these a Validé is, however, in great part relieved by her *Hasnadar Ousta*, or "First Lady of the Treasury," and also by the chief eunuch, known as the *Kisler Bey* or *Kisler Agha*—" Bey," or "Agha of the Women," through whom all intercourse with the outer world is carried on. This functionary, under the old *régime*, ranked next to the Grand Vizier, and, in the Serai the *Hasnadar* ranks next to the Empress Mother herself. She is generally, on being appointed to this important post, a woman of middle age, who has been brought up in the *daïra* of the Validé, and whose seniority, coupled with her devotion to the interests of her mistress, has entitled her to this important post. Her office gives her absolute authority in every matter with which the Validé does not choose to concern herself personally; and should the latter die before her Imperial son, the *Hasnadar Ousta* succeeds during the whole of his lifetime to her position and prerogatives, and ever since the death of the late Validé Sultan, the harem of Yildiz Kiosk has thus been ruled over by her "First Lady of the Treasury."

Slaves for the service of the palace are, as a rule, purchased as children in order that they may be suitably trained for the positions they will be required to occupy. Abyssinians and Negresses, as also white girls who give no promise of future beauty, are placed under the care of *kalfas*, or "matrons," who bring them up as cooks, housemaids, bath-women, laundry maids, etc. The finer specimens of humanity, who may be called upon to f'l high positions, are taught elegance of deportment, dancing, singing and music, by the various Ladies of the Household, and initiated into all the graceful formalities of Oriental etiquette and deportment. A certain number who may be destined for such posts as those of Secretary, or " Lady Chaplain "—whose duties comprise reading the Koran aloud and imparting religious instruction—are also taught to read fluently and write with elegance. There is thus always on hand a supply of these *aläiks*, or pupil-slaves, ready to fill any vacancies that may occur in the various establishments which constitute the Imperial harem. Separated for ever from her own kindred, the slave child becomes the adopted daughter of the *kalfa* who has purchased her for the service of her department, and who is at the same time her mistress and instructor. Each *kalfa* takes a pride in the appearance and the efficiency of her pupils, watches over their interests with the utmost vigilance, and, should marriage with an out-sider be the *Kismet* of any one of them—as not infre-quently happens—does all in her power to secure for her adopted child as good a match as possible. Slaves both, the *kalfa* and the *aläik* look to each other for mutual support, and the affection that arises between them is a touching proof of the need of the human heart for sympathy and love ; and even when removed by marriage to another sphere, a girl of slave origin maintains the same intimate relations with her adopted mother, who will on her side make use of her position in the Serai to forward the interests of her former pupil.

The *kalfas* are generally those slaves who, having neither attracted the notice of the Sultan, nor been given in marriage to a subject, have attained their position by right of seniority. Some may still look forward to

matrimony, but the majority, contented with the life which
has become habitual to them, and devoted to their respective mistresses, look for their only promotion within the
walls of the Serai. It is these old *serailis* who are the
faithful guardians of all the palace traditions and usages,
which they cherish with jealous conservatism and, in their
turn, transmit to their successors in office. The denizens
of the Serai, however, even when not given in marriage
to outsiders, are by no means, as is generally supposed,
imprisoned for life within the palace precincts. Many
of their amusements, indeed, lie outside its walls, for
Sultanas and their ladies-in-waiting, like the generality
of uncultured women in all countries, find their chief
distractions in their toilettes, in visits, and drives and
excursions. Pilgrimages to the shrines of Moslem Saints,
and attendance at the services in Dervish Tekkehs, vary
their mundane pursuits, and are made the opportunity
of atoning for some of their sins by pious gifts and alms-
deeds. Each lady has usually her favourite Sheikh and
her favourite shrine, to whom and to which she periodically makes offerings, either in money or in the shape
of rich shawls and draperies for the tombs of the departed
Saints. In their excursions beyond the palace precincts,
the Ladies of the Imperial harem are, however, invariably
attended by negro eunuchs resplendent in frock coats,
light trousers, kid gloves, and diamond jewellery. For
these gentry, though valued chiefly for their size and
ugliness, are preposterously vain, and their owners gladly
gratify the amiable weaknesses of such generally attached

and trustworthy servants. Mounted on prancing Arabs, they ride on either side of the smart closed broughams, through the windows of which a passing glimpse may be caught of a filmy white *yashmak*, athwart which dark eyes peer curiously at the denizens of the strange outside world whom they may encounter on the way to one of the fashionable resorts of Turkish holiday-makers.

The above described elaborate organisation of the Imperial household was by no means of Turkish origin, but was evidently copied in great measure, together with other social institutions, from that of the Court of Byzantium to which the Turkish Sultans served themselves heirs, the practice of making Sultanas of slave women having apparently been introduced about that period. For the earlier rulers of Turkey, who contented themselves with the unassuming title of *Emir*, or " Prince," were in the habit of contracting legal marriages with free women. Orkhan, for instance, wedded the daughter of John VI. of Byzantium; Bayazid I., before his accession, espoused the daughter of the Asian Prince Jacob of Kermian, who brought him for dowry Kutayia and other important territories situated in the former Seljukian Kingdom; while six years later his father Murad I., and two of his brothers wedded on the same day three Byzantine princesses, their espousals being celebrated with great pomp and splendour on the plain of Yeni-Shehir in Asia Minor, in the presence of the Army there encamped. And later Ottoman legists, while seeking to guard against female influence at the

Imperial Court by limiting the wives of Sultans to slave women, would appear to have overlooked the fact that a Sultan is after all but a man, and consequently liable to be influenced by any woman, whatever her origin, clever enough to gain ascendancy over him. It is related that one of the "four rules of conduct" given by the famous Vizier Mohammed Kiupruli, when on his death-bed, to the young Sultan Mohammed IV. was "never to listen to the counsels of women." Yet the great Kiupruli himself owed his long maintenance in office to the able Validé Sultan Tarkhan, and his son and successor in the Vizierate owed the freedom of action which he enjoyed under the same prince to the patronage of Mohammed's favourite wife. The *rôle* played by the women of the Serai in Turkish history has, indeed, been by no means unimportant. To give a few instances only—the Sultana Safiyé, a lady of Venetian extraction, exercised for some twenty years of the lifetime of her incapable consort, Sultan Murad III., a predominant sway in the government, and ruled generally in the Court and Councils of her son Mohammed III. The mother of Mustapha I. exercised supreme authority in his name. And when his successor Murad IV. mounted the throne at the age of twelve, the Validé Mahpeiker, a slave of Greek extraction, became regent. She appears to have been a woman of remarkable talent and energy, and both were taxed to the uttermost to combat the dangers and disasters that clouded the dawn of her son's sovereignty. A Venetian Ambassador who met this princess when she was about forty-five years of age, described her as "virtuous, wise, prudent, and liberal, loving pious works."

The present Sultan is, however, by no means, as so many of his predecessors have been, and as he is by some foreign writers reported to be, under the influence of the women of his harem, those most hostile to his rule admitting the irreproachability of his private life. He has now but one wife living, is somewhat advanced in years, and has moreover for many years past been too completely engrossed with affairs of State to concern himself with the affairs of the *haremlik*, the conduct of which is left in the hands of the functionaries above mentioned.

The harems of the Imperial Serais have, however, always constituted a perfect hot-bed of intrigue, which indeed forms the main occupation of the generality of their inhabitants. The law of primogeniture not being recognised in the succession to the throne, each prince born in the Serai has the chance of becoming Sultan in his turn; and every mother of a son being in consequence an aspirant for supreme power in the harem, she, together with all the members of her *daïra*, makes the event of his succession the supreme object of her life, working day and night for its accomplishment. As the Sultan is styled the "Lion of Lions," each prince is called by his mother and her attendants "My Lion," and is worshipped by the whole of her miniature Court. There are consequently in the Imperial palaces as many coteries as there are Kadin Effendis and *daïras*, each of which forms a centre having ramifications extending beyond the walls of the

Serai. For the brothers and other male relatives of a
reigning Sultan—or rather the respective mothers of these
princes—being always in quest of partisans, the Validé
Sultan or her representative is on her side vigilantly
occupied in safeguarding the interests of her Imperial son.
The possible successors to Sultan Abdul Hamid are
somewhat numerous, as they include besides his own six
sons—the eldest of whom he himself desires should be
the next to gird the sword of Osman—his half-brother
Reshid Effendi, the legitimate heir, whose claim is supported by the reactionary party, and other scions of the
Imperial House. Each of these possible future claimants
to the throne has his following as well among the inmates
of the palace both male and female as in the Army and
thoughout the Empire generally. The Padishah is sixty-
seven years of age, and in the natural course of events the
Osmanli nation will ere long be called upon to make choice
of a new ruler. A strong man is wanted at this crisis of
Turkish history ; and, if report says true, such a successor
may be found among the princes of the Royal house
other than those above mentioned, whose candidature
would be strongly supported by leading members of the
progressive party.

H.I.H. PRINCE SELIM EFFENDI, ELDEST SON OF THE SULTAN

A CHANDLER'S SHOP AT AIDIN (ASIA MINOR)

CHAPTER IV

PROVINCIAL AND COUNTRY FOLK

ALTHOUGH Smyrna, Salonica, and also to a certain extent Adrianople, since its connexion by rail with Central Europe, present many features in common with the Capital, the manners and customs and even the languages of the non-Turkish element of the towns of the interior, where Turkish influences chiefly predominate, are considerably affected by those of the ruling race. Many provincial towns of European Turkey present, indeed, features far more characteristically Oriental than are to be found on the Eastern shores of the Ægean Sea. The same system of administration obtains, of course, in the remoter provinces as in the cities, the higher judicial Courts being supplemented by the local *Medjliss*, or Town Council, comprised of the representatives of the various communities, Christian, Jewish, and Moslem, which usually make up the population of a township, and the *Konak*, or Government House, forms the centre of municipal life. A provincial *konak* is, generally speaking, a many-windowed, barrack-like edifice, coloured red or yellow without, whitewashed within, and approached by a spacious

courtyard on either side of the great roofed gateway of
which sit, on rush-bottomed stools, a couple of stalwart
Zaptiehs, as the Turkish armed police are termed.
The internal arrangements are those of most Oriental
houses—a wide central hall, or corridor, on which all
the rooms open, the upper floor, or floors, being precisely
similar in plan. Over the doorways are inscribed the names
of the various departments—" Secretary," " Treasurer,"
" Keeper of Archives," etc. ; and among the motley throng
loitering in the courtyard and entrance hall during office
hours may always be found a heterogeneous collection
of litigants, witnesses, and petitioners, servants, soldiers,
and loafers, varying in race according to province, and
clad in garments denoting every degree of Eastern
civilisation, from sheepskin cap and jacket to fez and
frock coat.   The new Constitution, young as it is yet,
has already worked important changes in the administration of justice ; but things move slowly in the East,
and time-honoured abuses are not abolished in a day.
The majority of the frequenters of a provincial *konak*
may still be divided into two classes—those who seek
to gain some unfair advantage over their fellows, and
those who would avert, or seek redress for, some act of
injustice or spoliation.   Here will be a group of Turkish
peasants, ragged probably, but dignified, discussing the
justice of a sentence just announced, adverse to their
village and in favour of the *beylikdji,* or tax-farmer,
whose demands they have appealed against.   And outside
the door of another office may stand a party of flock-masters

having a triangular dispute with the forest inspectors
and the inhabitants of a village, both parties claiming
rights over some neighbouring pasturages which the
shepherds have been in the habit of renting from the
former. Formerly, almost every village in Turkey had
its own common and forest in which the peasant proprietors had the right to cut wood, burn charcoal, and
rent the pasturage annually to the nomad herdsmen
and shepherds—a great resource for the peasantry, though
most destructive to the forests. All this was, however,
changed when what is known as the Vilayet system
was organised, and the forests and the pasturages were
placed under Government supervision. But though the
laws regulating the new arrangement were excellent on
paper, the acts of injustice and the abuses connected with
their administration have proved most prejudicial to the
rural population.

Upstairs in a large scantily furnished room the
Governor holds his court, seated—if an "old-fashioned"
Turk—cross-legged in an angle of the divan which
furnishes three sides of the apartment. Accommodated on
either side of him—their rank being easily ascertained
by their proximity to the great man and the degree of
ease in the posture they assume—are a number of individuals, some in turbans and flowing robes, others in
semi-European garb, members of the *Medjliss*, or Municipal
Council, magnates, officials, and others. The Jewish
doctor, for instance, sits at a distance on the extreme
edge of the divan, with his hands on his stomach, speaks

F

only when spoken to, and with a deferential salaam; the Greek dragoman occupies an uncomfortable corner of his rush-seated chair near the door, from which he rises and salaams obsequiously every time the *Vali Pasha* addresses him; and these subordinates are served by the bare-footed attendants with coffee only, though cigarettes or *tchibouks* will also be handed to the *Kadi*, or Judge, and to the other magnates seated on the great man's right and left.   In the small towns and villages of Turkey, the immediate supreme authority is, however, vested in the *Kodjabashi*—Headman, or Mayor—who settles petty disputes and is held responsible for the good behaviour of his township.   It is also. his business, as, save in large towns inns are non-existent, to provide lodging for travellers, and to arrange for the accommodation of troops and *saptiehs*—armed police—passing through on their way from one town to another. The office of *Kodjabashi* naturally entails considerable responsibility upon its holder, and under the social and political conditions which have so long obtained in Turkey is frequently one of no little difficulty. It has, however, no doubt its compensations, and places its possessor in a position superior to that of his fellows.

An ill-paved and often mud-pooled market-place usually occupies the centre of Turkish villages and small towns, and here the peasants collect from the neighbouring country with their sheep and cattle, and their carts and beasts of burden laden with produce of all kinds for sale or barter. Bulgarian weavers come, too, with rolls of cloth, and Gypsies with pots and pans, sieves, coarse baskets, and other articles for domestic use. Surrounding the square are the *bakals*, or chandlers' shop, the butchers' stall, and, of course, the shanty which does duty as a *café*, at which the market-folk refresh themselves in frugal fashion and hear the news of the country side, perhaps also some faint echo of political events from the nearest city. Close by, in a Turkish village, stands the little white-washed mosque with its cypress-shadowed cemetery. At one end of the green is the threshing-floor, generally of beaten earth, but sometimes paved with flags, used by all the villagers in turn, and on feast days by the youth for their wrestling matches; and at the other end is the village well, to which the maidens come towards sunset carrying on their shoulders the large red earthen water-jars, unchanged in shape since the days of Homer.

A considerable proportion of the agricultural land of Asia Minor is held and cultivated by peasant proprietors; and in other parts of Turkey are also to be found a considerable number of so-called " Head villages," or " Free villages," the lands adjoining which are owned and tilled by small farmers. In Macedonia and Thrace, however, landed property is less equally divided, great areas being united in large estates called *tchiftliks*, owned either by native Beys, or by absentee landlords who reside in the towns and cities, leaving the management of their estates to an agent called the *Soubashi*. The large estates belonging to absentee landlords are cultivated to a great

extent on what is called in France the *Métayer* system—
that is, the landlord provides the seed corn in the first
instance, while the peasant, who also finds his own yoke
of oxen or buffaloes, performs all the labour.   When the
harvest has been reaped, the seed for the next season
set aside, and the tithe deducted, the remainder of the
produce is shared with the proprietor.   If equitably
carried out, this arrangement proves, as in other countries,
by no means an unfavourable one for the *yeradji*, as the
peasants working under this system are called.   In
Turkey, however, "might" is but too often "right," and
the tiller of the soil frequently gets a quite inadequate
return for his labour.   One serious grievance of the farmer
is that when the grain has been cut he may not remove
it from the field until the tithe collector has been pleased
to come and inspect the crop, no matter what weather
may threaten, or what depredations be committed by the
immense flocks of birds that are robbing the peasant of
his profit.   The computation of shares is also too often
very unfairly made.   A certain number of sheaves, forty
perhaps, of the finest and heaviest, are threshed separately,
and the seed for the next year, the tithes, and the landlord's share are deducted according to this standard,
which often leaves the *yeradji* an unfairly small portion
of the produce.   The *soubashi* is also entitled to receive
six measures each of barley and wheat for every head
of cattle possessed by the peasant; and among other
burdens which press hardly upon him are the Government taxes, the conscription, the frequent quartering in

his cottage—especially if near a high-road—of *saptiehs* and soldiers, and the obligation of performing statute labour whenever called upon, often with disastrous results to farm labour and damage to carts and implements. The small agriculturist in Turkey is, indeed, perhaps the most highly taxed individual in the world.   His taxes may also be demanded at any time during the year, and perhaps more than once.   The Imperial taxes are also for the most part farmed, and the expenses of their collection, to say nothing of the tax-farmer's profit, is added to the burden of the peasant.   As to their assessment, the system pursued is a masterpiece of simplicity. The question is not how much such and such a village ought to pay, according to the number of adult males it may contain, but how much it *can* pay, rich villages being called upon to make up the deficit of those in less prosperous circumstances.   This point settled by the powers that be, the village council responsible for the payment of the lump sum meet to apportion to each householder of the community his share of the common burden. Seated cross-legged on a mat or on rush-bottomed stools under a leafy plane tree, or in the shadow of the mosque, the village fathers and their scribes, in coarse baggy breeches of brown homespun, brightly coloured shirts and ample waist-shawls, discuss the financial position of their neighbours and allot to each what they consider his rightful portion of the tax.   The council is, however, collectively responsible for the taxes due from each householder, and bound to make up all deficits.

Native farming is still for the most part conducted according to most primitive methods and with the aid of implements the most archaic. The ground is broken to-day, as it was two thousand years ago, by the clumsy one-handled wooden Pelasgian plough drawn by a yoke or team of buffaloes, and in some places the grain is merely scattered over the stubble and ploughed in, threshing and winnowing being performed in equally primitive fashion. Agriculture is consequently, notwithstanding the great fertility of soil and the favourable climatic conditions, which allow of the cultivation of the products of both the old and the new world, and a coast-line of 1100 miles in extent, in a most backward state. The explanation of this is hardly to be found in any peculiarity of the Ottoman character which, though warlike and pastoral, is also essentially agricultural, but rather in a variety of causes, the chief of which consists in the forms of land tenure, other contributing causes being the lack of scientific knowledge, of capital, and, owing to the conscription, of labour. Deficiency in means of communication is also another cause, for there are no great waterways as in Russia; railways as yet are only in their infancy, and leave untouched great tracts of land over which "the ship of the desert" still swings his slow way to the ports of the Ægean, laden with great bales of produce from the interior, raw cotton and wool, vallonia, jute, hemp, hides, and cereals. Large tracts of land in Asia Minor remain uncultivated, or have fallen out of cultivation, the quantity of corn grown being, it is computed, but a tenth of what the country might yield, if properly worked. Nor is any regular system of rotation of crops observed by the peasants, though on large estates the ordinary rule for rich lands is two crops of wheat to one of oats, then fallow one or more years, after which wheat, followed by sesame, is again sown. In Macedonia, where arable land abounds, it is allowed to lie fallow more frequently. The only dressing the fields owned by natives receive is the treading of the sheep in spring and autumn ; but the soil is naturally so fertile, and the crops ripen so early, especially in the southern provinces, that a bad harvest is of rare occurrence. Occasionally, however, occurs a long drought, when the crops in the great open plains perish for want of moisture, and the cattle die by hundreds unless driven off in time and sold—much under their value—to those living in more fortunate localities. At such times it is customary for both Moslems and Christians to invoke the aid of the celestial powers by special ceremonies, as in former days the pagan rain-god was propitiated in the same localities in times of drought. With the Turks all the children attending the *mektebs*, or parish schools, march in procession, headed by their *hodjas*, through the streets of the towns to the open plain, where, after spreading their carpets, they offer up prayers interspersed with many prostrations. After continuing this religious exercise for nearly an hour, the children fall into rank again, wailing, as they trail slowly back to the town, a monotonous and weirdly melancholy chant.

the vulgar by semicircular tilts or awnings which sway
balloon-like with the motion of the steed as he staggers
along under the weight of his double burden. Travelling
is indeed, in Turkey, no very pleasant matter, the roads
are generally in a deplorable state, knee-deep in dust in
summer, and in winter full of treacherous mud-filled holes ;
and in mountainous districts the torrent beds often constitute the only highway. Bridges over the great rivers
are few and far between, and frequently out of repair ;
and fording, though easy enough in the dry season, offers
considerable dangers when the streams are swollen after
rain.

The way in which an absentee proprietor spends his
time when on an occasional visit to his estate naturally
depends upon his pecuniary means and personal tastes.
A sportsman will occasionally have a hunting or coursing
party, or go out with his sons, guests, and servants for
a day's expedition in quest of more distant game—deer
and boar on the hills, or snipe and quail in the marshlands.
His duties as landlord are confined to regulating accounts
with his agent, hearing and deciding cases between that
functionary and the tenants, giving instructions for future
farming operations, and last, but not least, to realising the
profits. As to improving the soil, introducing modern
and labour-saving machinery, building model cottages and
otherwise ameliorating the moral and material condition
of his tenants—these are things which have not so far
been considered necessary by a Turkish landed proprietor.
In the mean time, the Bey's womenkind contrive to amuse

TURKISH PEASANTS

themselves in their own fashion during their annual *villeggiatura*. Turkish women are passionately fond of the open air, and when in the country spend a great part of every day in roaming about freely in the most *negligé* of costumes, picnicking, singing and amusing themselves according to their wont. Included in the "house party" are generally a number of relatives or hangers-on, who lend willing aid in preparing the stores of winter provisions to be carried back to town by the family. These comprise tomato sauce and pickles of various kinds; a kind of molasses made from grape juice, used in the confection of the commoner kinds of preserves for household consumption; macaroni pastes for soups and other dishes; fruit syrups for making sherbets; and the great variety of elegant and carefully prepared sweets which are served to harem visitors on great occasions. For the *kiler*, as a Turkish storeroom for provisions is called, is a very important department of every Oriental household. Here, besides the above-mentioned confections, oil and honey are stored in great jars of red earthenware, which recall those in which the "Forty Thieves" were hidden, together with sacks of rice, flour, nuts, and dried fruit of all kinds for winter consumption.

Whatever may be the opinion of European travellers and residents in Turkey as to the character of its towns-people, all who have ever come into personal contact with the Turkish peasantry have been unanimous in praise of their simple honesty and sobriety, their passive contentment and dignified resignation to the will of Allah and their Padishah, and their passionate attachment to the land which has been bought by the blood of their forefathers. Physically, a Turkish peasant is well built, healthy, and, owing no doubt to his habitual abstemiousness, possesses remarkable powers of endurance. With him days and seasons succeed each other in a dull round of laborious and frugal monotony ; for, unlike his Christian neighbours, he has no weekly dance, no frequently recurring village feast, and but little music to vary the uniformity of his life. His cup of coffee, taken before the labours of the day begin and at their close, and his poor *tchibouk* at intervals, constitute for him all the luxuries of life. His cottage, often a mere mud hovel, though clean, is comfortless enough, cold in winter and hot in summer, and contains little in the way of furniture beyond a scanty supply of bedding and a few rugs, stools, and cooking utensils. Turkish villages, indeed, throughout the Empire wear a much more impoverished and much less animated aspect than do those of their Christian neighbours. For a Turkish peasant's wife and daughters take, as a rule, a less active part in field and farm work than do the Christian peasant women, and are never seen, like them, spinning, knitting, and sewing at their cottage doors. As mentioned in a previous chapter, the abolition of the feudal system, and also of the Janissary corps, at the beginning of last century, and the placing of the army on a European footing, created a demand for soldiers from the peasant class unknown in previous centuries ; while, owing to the method pursued in levying conscripts, the agricultural communities labour under the permanent disadvantage of being deprived of the co-operation of a considerable proportion of their younger and more energetic members.   And when, in time of war, the majority of the able-bodied are, as reservists, also called to the colours, the situation becomes one of real hardship.   The old men, the raw boys, and the women—unused to labour and consequently incapable of coping with it—struggle on for a time as best they can, often finding themselves at length compelled to abandon their holdings and take refuge in some neighbouring town or larger village.   Thus deserted, their little homesteads—too often built merely of mud and wattle, thatched with reeds—fall into ruin, and their untilled fields either pass into the hands of Christian or Jewish mortgagees, or are added to the vast waste-lands of the Empire.   The larger villages will also, there is grave reason to fear, in time share the fate of the hamlets unless the new administration speedily introduces such radical changes as will permanently ameliorate the condition of the peasantry, who constitute morally and physically the backbone of the Turkish nation.

CHAPTER V

HOLIDAY LIFE

THERE is perhaps hardly a town in Turkey which does not possess in its immediate neighbourhood one or more picturesque spots to which its inhabitants resort on Friday, the Moslem Day of Rest, and on other festive days, and round about the Capital may be found many such. Among the most frequented in the vicinity of Constantinople are, on the European side, the "Sweet Waters of Europe," the Forest of Belgrade near Buyukdéré, and the Vale of Lindens; and on the opposite shore, the "Sweet Waters of Asia," the "Sultan's Valley," and Merdevenkeui. The "Sweet Waters of Europe" is the foreign designation of the charming valley to the west of the Capital, watered by the river Barbyses, which here meanders among green meadows and shady trees before losing itself in the waters of the Golden Horn. Rustic wooden bridges span the stream at intervals; in the neighbourhood elegant villas are dotted about; while among the meadows may be found a number of verandah-shaded *kahfinés*, whose customers, seated in the pleasant shade by the cool flowing water, watch the performances of the various jugglers, mountebanks, showmen, and strolling

78

players, who never fail to present themselves. Among them will probably be *Kara Gues*—a kind of Chinese shadow-play—and also plays by Marionettes—both of which, it must be admitted, usually leave much to be desired in the matter of decency. Egyptian musicians with rebeck and flute fill the air with their strange melodies, often harsh and discordant, occasionally tuneful, but always melancholy. Gypsies wander from one group of holiday makers to another with bears or monkeys, whose performances they accompany with excruciating sounds from drum, tambourine, bag-pipe, and reed-pipe, while their women execute unwearyingly their wild nautch-like pantomimic dances. Dancing, it may here be remarked, though a favourite recreation of all the Christian nationalities, as also of the Albanians, Kurds, and other races professing the creed of Islam, is not indulged in personally by the sedate Osmanlis, who consider such exercises beneath their dignity, and prefer to see slave girls and Gypsy women dance for their amusement. Swinging boats and rotary horses, barrel organs, and cinematographs have also been introduced into Turkey, and may be found as far east as Mosul. The hours passed at the *kahfinés* in these popular holiday resorts are also frequently beguiled with various sedentary games such as draughts, dominoes, and backgammon. Cards are seldom resorted to, games of hazard being forbidden to Moslems. Nor can gambling be said to be at all a popular vice in the country, the stakes played for among the Christian populace seldom rising above the price of a glass of *raki* or cube of *rahat lokoum*. When lack of piastres, or *groosh*, as the natives term this modest coin, or lack of sufficient leisure makes any of these resorts inaccessible, the Turk betakes himself contentedly to the nearest cemetery where, seated on a fallen turbaned tombstone under the shade of the tall cypresses, he may enjoy with his fellows the amenities of conversation flavoured with "the inevitable, the eternal, the universal cigarette."

In addition to the holidays observed by the nation generally, every Trade Guild observes a special annual festival in honour of its patron saint, the expenses of which are defrayed either by subscription among the guildsmen themselves, or from the corporation funds. This festival usually takes the form of a picnic at one of the above-mentioned resorts, and to the substantial and even sumptuous repast provided on such occasions are usually invited friends of members of the Guild, irrespective of creed; and any stranger who may happen to pass the spot chosen for the festivities is also hospitably entertained by the revellers. The amusements indulged in after the conclusion of the midday repast include besides the usual variety of juggling and acrobatic performances, wrestling matches between the guildsmen, and, for the Christians and Albanians, their national dances, during the execution of which their Turkish fellow-craftsmen, seated on rush-bottomed stools in front of a rustic coffee-house, one hand occupied with the beads of their rosary, and the other with a short-stemmed *tchibouk*, cigarette, or bubbling *narghileh*, according to their calling, enjoy their *kaif* in more passive fashion. Disputes are of rare occurrence at these *al fresco* gatherings, and the greatest harmony prevails. "Strict, stern, stony decorum" is, indeed, according to a recent traveller in Turkey, "the keynote to all Turkish *fêtes*." And certainly a total absence of anything approaching to vulgarity or rowdyism is noticeable in Oriental merry-makings generally, whatever the class of those who participate in them.

Here and there among these holiday crowds may be seen the picturesque figure of a Turkish musician and story-teller in the immemorial costume of his profession, which, together with its repertory of song and stories, is handed down from generation to generation of the same family. These will include mythical stories extolling the magical exploits of King David and King Solomon; religious and semi-religious legends connected with the Prophet and the saints of Islam; charming animal tales, and fables with a moral application; besides satirical stories relating to the impostures of pseudo-saintly dervishes, the rapacity of *Mollahs*, and the corruption of *Kadis*, together with comic and humorous anecdotes innumerable. Many of these tales also, like those of the "Thousand and One Nights," deal with *Peris* and *Djins*—the race of beings created before Adam, and to which his second wife, Lilith, is held to have belonged—with wicked magicians, enchanted princesses, and valiant and ready-witted heroes. No allusion is, however, to be found in them to the original home of the Turkish race in Central Asia. Such a total absence of any legends connected

G

with the former habitat of the Turks is, however, only
what one might expect to find on consideration of the
history of the Osmanli nation. For—as pointed out in
the Introduction—the original small band which invaded
Asia Minor in the thirteenth century has for the last
six hundred years been increased, first, by the adherence
and conversion of whole populations, and, secondly, by
intermarriage in every succeeding generation with the
best blood both of South-Eastern Europe and Asia Minor.
The women belonging to all the surrounding peoples—
Kurdish, Georgian, Circassian, Byzantine-Greek, Armenian,
Slav, and even Venetian and Genoese—naturally brought
with them into the harems of the Osmanlis their own
folk-lore which, gradually falling under the influence of
Moslem ideas, has attained its present distinctive character.
A proportion of tales of the humorous class have for
their hero Nasr-ed-Din Hodja, a semi-mythical Turkish
parson, who became a sort of Court-jester to the terrible
Timour the Tartar during his invasion and occupation of
Asia Minor. Many of these stories are, however, presumably of much greater antiquity than the end of the
fourteenth and the beginning of the fifteenth century, the
date assigned to this famous Oriental wit. In character
they are most varied; some are proverbial or didactic;
the weaknesses and shortcomings of the female sex form
the subject of others; while in yet another class the
honesty and integrity of the Hodja himself are more than
questionable. Domestic and social manners and customs
are admirably depicted in many; and underlying the

majority is a vein of the fine irony peculiar to Orientals,
though very frequently the point lies entirely in a subtle
play upon words impossible to reproduce in another
language. Much of this popular literature has still only
an oral existence, though during the last century a considerable portion has been collected in book form; and
it is said that the volumes in which are related the
exploits of the famous Hodja have, next to the Koran,
more readers than any other class of literature. Almost
every witty or comic anecdote is, indeed, fathered upon
this parson-buffoon, who has become a sort of type
personifying the humorous side of the national character.
The two following, which I have often heard related, but
which have not hitherto, I believe, appeared in English,
may serve as specimens.

The Hodja's Wager

One day, as the Hodja was sitting with his gossips,
he was twitted with being a man fond of ease and comfort
and lacking powers of endurance. Resenting the insinua-
tion, Nasr-ed-Din wagered a supper that he would remain
for a whole night on the terrace of his house without fire
or light. The wager was accepted, and the Hodja performed his vigil, and claimed the forfeit,

"Oh, but," objected his friends, "thou wert not altogether
without fire or light, for there was a fire on the mountain
all the time."

The Hodja submitted, and after a few days invited

his friends to supper at his house. Towards sunset the
company assembled at the mosque parsonage, and after
performing the *Namas* with their host, seated themselves
on the divan till the meal should be ready. Half an hour
passed, an hour, but still the *sofra*, or dinner-tray, was
not brought in. Hunger finally got the better of good
manners, and one of the guests ventured to suggest that
the usual supper-hour was past.

"Have patience, my souls, I beg, the pilaf will very
shortly be ready," was the reply of the smiling host, who,
according to his wont, had meanwhile been entertaining
his guests with anecdotes and sallies of wit. But after
another hour of polite endurance, one hardier, or hungrier,
than the rest, exclaimed—

"Hodja, I am beginning to think that you are playing
us a trick, and that there is no pilaf at all cooking
for us!"

"By Allah! thou misjudgest me! Come into the
kitchen then, my soul, and see for thyself if the pilaf
is not cooking," exclaimed the host. Leading the way,
he pointed triumphantly to the copper pilaf-cauldron
which was suspended from a rafter, while on the floor
below it stood the brazier of charcoal embers.

"But, Hodja! Art mad? How can the pilaf cook at
that distance from the fire?"

"Quite as easily as I could warm myself the other
night by the fire on the mountain opposite," dryly quoth
Nasr-ed-Din Hodja.

THE HODJA AND THE OLD-CLOTHES MAN

One day Nasr-ed-Din Hodja, finding that his every-day pelisse had grown the worse for wear, sold it to a Jew, but forgot to take out of the lining a gold piece which he had sewn there for safety. During the night, however, he remembered the oversight, and next morning went to demand back his coat from the dealer.

"A bargain is a bargain," replied the *eskedji*; "what I have bought I have bought."

So the Hodja bided his time. After a while he had another pelisse to dispose of, but before taking it to the Jew, he carefully stitched a five-para piece—a coin worth about a farthing—into the lining. While examining the garment, the purchaser felt the coin, and thinking it was another gold piece, he paid a fair price for the pelisse. On the following morning the Hodja was strolling past his shop when the Jew called to him—

"Hodja Effendi, I paid thee too much for that pelisse; take it back and pay me the money I gave thee."

"A bargain is a bargain," replied the Hodja; "what I have sold I have sold."

But the Jew was angry and insisted, and finally demanded that the question should be settled before the *Kadi*.

"By all means," replied Nasr-ed-Din. "But as you
see, I am without a pelisse, and it were unseemly to
go before the judge save in my best."

"I will lend thee a handsome one, so thou come
with me at once to the *Kadi*."

So the pair went off together to the Court, and the
Jew laid his case before the *Kadi*. When he had done
so, the Hodja gave the judge his version of the matter,
and then exclaimed—

"See you, my Lord, the wickedness and dishonesty
of this man. By Allah! it has no bounds. He will next
tell your worship that the pelisse on my back belongs
to him!"

"So it does, by Allah!" exclaimed the other. Upon
which the Kadi bade the attendants turn him out for
an impudent cheat and impostor; and Nasr-ed-Din
Hodja went home chuckling to tell his wife the story of
the *eskedji's* discomfiture.

The numerous and various stories about King—or,
as he is more generally termed, "Saint"—Solomon, to
be found in Oriental folk-literature, are considered by
scholars to be reminiscences, not of the vaunted Son of
David, but rather of the Chaldean "King of the Gods,"
the wise Ea, one of whose names, Sallimanu, was adopted
by the Hebrew prince, whose proper name was Jedidiah.[1]
In the story of "Why the Swallow's Tail is Forked," we

[1] Compare Sayce, *Religion of the Ancient Babylonians*, pp. 57,
58; and 2 Sam. xii. 24, 25.

find illustrated one set of the wonderful powers attributed to this monarch.

A long, a very long time ago, Solomon, the Son of David, reigned over all things. This powerful King understood the languages of all mortals, the voices of the forest beasts and the cries of the smaller animals, the hiss of the serpents, the warblings of birds, the hum of insects, the speech of the lofty trees and the whisper of the woodland flowerets, the roar of the mighty ocean, and the murmur of river stream and summer breeze.

To each creature Solomon had assigned his fitting food. To some he had given the flesh of weaker animals; to others the herbs of the field, or the fruits of the trees. But to the Serpent the Son of David had said—

"Thou shalt be nourished with the blood of Man."

And the Serpent, therefore, hiding in the bushes and long grasses, lay in wait for Man and seized upon him in order to drain his blood. But Mankind protested so loudly against this evil that the sound at length reached the ears of the great King, and he asked of Man, "Why dost thou complain?"

"O King, the Serpent lives on our blood; our race will soon disappear!"

"Go in peace, I will bear in mind thy prayer."

The great Solomon reflected long. At last he summoned all living creatures to assemble in the middle of a great plain. The Lion, the Tiger and the Elephant, the Wolf, the Horse and the Camel, the Eagle, the Vulture and the Ostrich, and thousands and thousands of the birds and animals came together at the bidding of the King. Solomon sat on his throne, and thus addressed them—

"I have called you together that I may hear your complaints. Speak!"

Man first approached the throne, made his obeisance, and said—

"O King, I ask that the Serpent may be assigned as his food the blood of some other animal."

"And why?"

"Because I am the first of created Beings."

At this the assembly began to protest, with roars, growls and howls, yelps, barks, and screams.

"Be silent," commanded Solomon. "Let the Mosquito, the smallest of animals, find out whose blood is the most delicate in all creation. Whosesoever it may be, even to that of Man, I mean to give it to the Serpent. A year from to-day ye will meet me in this place to hear the decision of the Mosquito."

The animals dispersed, and during the year the little insect visited them all in turn and tasted their blood. As he was on his way back to the assembly of King Solomon, he overtook the Swallow, whom he saluted.

"Peace be also upon thee," replied the Swallow. "Thou art welcome, friend Mosquito. Whither fliest so swiftly?"

"I go to the Great Assembly."

"In truth. Well, whose blood hast thou found most delicate?"

" That of Man."

" That of——? "

The Mosquito, who thought the Swallow had not heard, opened his mouth to repeat the words ; but this was but a ruse on the part of the Swallow, who fell upon him and tore out his tongue. Furious, the Mosquito pursued his way, always closely followed by the Swallow, and finally arrived in the presence of King Solomon.

" Well," said the Son of David, " hast thou indeed tasted the blood of every animal ? "

The insect made a sign in the affirmative.

" Which then is the most delicate ? "

Great was the embarrassment of the Mosquito, who, now that he was tongueless, could no longer speak.

" *Ksss ! Kssssss ! Kssssssss !* " repeated the insect in a frenzy.

Solomon was greatly puzzled, until the Swallow presented himself before the throne.

" O King ! " he said, " O King, the Mosquito has been stricken dumb. But on the road hither, he confided to me the result of his year's experiences."

" Speak, then ! "

" O King, the *Frog* is the animal whose blood is the most exquisite—that is what the Mosquito would say."

" *Ksss ! Ksssssss ! Kssssssss !* " gurgled again the insect, beside himself with impotent rage.

" It is well," observed Solomon. " From this day forth the Serpent will feed on the blood of the Frog. Man may now live in peace." And he dismissed the assembly.

But the Serpent was by no means satisfied with this judgment; and as the Swallow dived past him—still chuckling over the successful part she had played on behalf of Man, who shelters her nest under the eaves of his dwelling—the reptile darted upon her. But the bird, aware in time of his intention, gave him a smart blow with her wings, and the Serpent succeeded only in seizing her by the middle of the tail. And since that time the Swallow's tail has been forked, and the Serpent has lived on the blood of the Frog.

The moral of the following story of "Saint Solomon and the Sparrow" will, no doubt, be appreciated by others than Orientals.

There was once in the blessed service of Saint Solomon —*on whom be peace !*—a little cock-sparrow, whose lively tricks and gambols were even pleasing to this Sultan. One day Saint Solomon saw not the Sparrow by him, and he commanded the *Simurgh* (a mythical bird frequently referred to by Oriental Poets) to go fetch the Sparrow wherever he might be. Now for many days previously the Sparrow had not visited his mate, and she had upbraided him, saying, " For this long time thou hast left me, and hast been with Solomon. Dost thou then love him more than me, or dost thou fear him ? Tell me ! "

"By Allah !" replied the Sparrow, "I would not exchange thee for the world !—I am come but once on earth and shall not come again. I go to Solomon for diversion—I have no fear of him."

While he was thus talking with many such vauntings and boastings, the *Simurgh* arrived in haste, and hearing him, said harshly, "Up, up! Let us be off, for Saint Solomon is asking for thee."

Then the Sparrow, being with his mate, plucked up courage and replied, "Off with thee, I will not go!"

Said the *Simurgh*, "But I will indeed take thee with me."

"Off with thee!" cried again the Sparrow, "or I will seize and rend thee in twain!"

Quoth the *Simurgh*, "I will not go without thee."

Yet the Sparrow heeded him not; and the *Simurgh* waited awhile, but in vain. So he said again, "O my life, give me an answer!"

"I tell thee to begone," replied the Sparrow. "If thou speak to me again my heart will bid me do somewhat to thee! But no!—I would not slay thee. Yet begone, or I shall do thee some hurt, and then will I go to Solomon's Palace, and smite it with my foot, and overturn it from its foundations, and pull it down on his head. So away, fool, return the road thou camest. Thou chatterest here and sayest not, 'This is the Sparrow's harem; he is ill,'" and he gave the *Simurgh* a kick. The noble bird felt it not; but he flew thence and reported to Saint Solomon the audacious words of the Sparrow.

"Where was the Sparrow when he spoke thus?" asked Solomon.

"With his mate," replied the *Simurgh.*

"Then," quoth Saint Solomon—*on whom be peace !*—"there was no harm in his thus boasting and bragging in his own house and before his wife. Though every stone of this my palace was raised by the toil of those many *Djins,* yet wonder not at his saying, when beside his wife, that he could shatter it with one foot—*for a man should be a hero to his own household.*"

So this was pleasing to Saint Solomon—*on whom be peace !*—and when the Sparrow again returned, he made him one of his boon companions.[1]

The fatalistic notion of Kismet alluded to in the following chapter finds its illustration in such stories as that of

The Woodcutter and Fortune

In the Island of Mitylene there once lived a woodcutter with his wife and two children. All the stock-in-trade the poor man possessed was his axe, billhook, and pair of mules. Every morning at break of day, this woodman arose and went into the woods to fell trees. Having laden his mules with faggots and logs, he set off to sell them in the neighbouring town. Thus he had lived for a score of years; Fortune had for him no favours ; and to-morrow found him no richer than yesterday. Weary at last of such a life, and seeing no hope

---

[1] Adapted from *The Tales of the Forty Visiers.*

of any betterment of his lot, the woodcutter at last lost heart altogether. "What," said he to himself, ".is the use of all this toiling and moiling? If I were to lie in bed from morning till night, perhaps Fortune might take pity on me, and come to me whilst I slept—it shall be so; I will go no more to the forest."

So on the following day the good man remained in bed. His wife, finding that he did not get up as usual, left her work and came to wake him.

"Come, husband," she cried, "it is time to rise—the cock crowed long ago."

"What sayest thou? for what is it time?"

"It is time for thee to go forth to cut wood."

"Yea, truly—to earn what will keep us but for the day, such is our wretched lot!"

"But what canst thou do, my poor husband? We must needs submit to our fate, and Fortune has never yet come our way."

"Well, wife, I for one am weary of the caprices of Fortune. Should she wish to find me, she will seek me here in my poor hut. But I go not to the wood to-day."

"Come, come, my poor husband, are you mad? Do you think Fortune will come to you if you do not run after her? Come now, get up, take your axe and bill-hook to the forest, or we shall all die of hunger—you know we have food only for the day."

"I care not. I will neither get up nor go to the forest, and nothing shall move me. Leave me in peace, wife."

In vain the poor woman wept and entreated ; her good-man would lie abed and wait for Fortune to come to him.

By-and-by a man came from a neighbouring village, knocked at the door, and greeted him.

"Peace be with you, Yussuf. Luckily for me you are not yet gone forth. I have a load to remove, and I want you to bring your mules and help me with the job."

"I am sorry to refuse you, neighbour, but to-day I have sworn to lie in bed, and for no one will I break my oath."

"Then let me take the mules and I will pay you hire for them ;" and to this the woodman agreed.

Now the villager had found in his field a buried treasure which he wished to remove at once to his house. He took the mules to the place, loaded them, and was leading them homewards when he saw coming along the road a party of *zaptiehs* (armed police). Well knowing that treasure-trove is the property of the Sultan, and that to appropriate it is punishable with death, the peasant ran off, abandoning the mules, who, left to their own devices, forthwith made their way back to their stable with their loads. The good wife, seeing the beasts enter the courtyard staggering under the weight of the sacks, ran to inform her husband.

"*Effendi, Effendi,* get up, get up at once, the mules have come back alone laden with sacks so heavy that they are ready to drop."

"O wife, have I not told thee that I rise not to-day ? Cease, I prithee, from troubling me."

So the goodwife, left to herself, went back to the yard, and set about cutting the cords which bound the sacks to the pack-saddles. Down they fell with a bang and burst open, when a stream of coins—gold sequins, silver *beshliks* and *medjidiehs*, and copper *piastres*—rang merrily over the stones. For the sacks were brimming with them, and to right and left the courtyard was strewn with a carpet more precious by far than the carpets of Smyrna or the Indies.

"*Inshallah*, a treasure!" she cried, and ran again to her husband's bedside.

"*Effendi, Effendi*, you were right not to go to the forest to-day, but to wait at home for Fortune. But get up now, for she has come! Our mules have returned laden with treasure. All the gold of the world is in our courtyard. We are richer than the richest!"

At this the woodman jumped up from his couch and hurried to the courtyard, where he stood for a moment dazzled by the glitter of the sequins and gold pieces.

"You see, my dear wife," he finally exclaimed, "how right I was to stay in bed and wait for Fortune! So capricious is she that if you run after her you will never catch her; but give up the chase, and she will come to you!"

Tales of a religious character also find ready listeners. Many of these are connected with the miraculous appearances and disappearances of that saintly and mysterious being known as Khidhr or Khidhr-Elias, about whom more will be said in the next chapter. One of these stories relates that a pious Turk, who earnestly desired to see Khidhr, and had with that object frequented for thirty-nine days the mosque of Ayia Sofía, a favourite resort of the Saint, met on the morning of the fortieth day in the courtyard a stranger, who said to him—

"The mosque is not yet open, why comest thou to disturb the sleep of its keepers?"

"I come to seek Khidhr," was the reply.

"Dost thou know him?"

"I know him not."

"Then follow me, and I will show him to thee."

Khidhr—for it was indeed he whom the True Believer had met—went on before him, and the pious man observed that his feet left an imprint even on stones.

"Dost thou know what Khidhr can do?" asked the Stranger.

"No," replied the pious man.

"Khidhr can thrust his finger into stone even as I do."

His finger entered the stone as he spoke, and the stone "perspired"[1] abundantly. "When thou seest a man who does wonders such as these, say to thyself, 'This is Khidhr!' and hold him fast."

"I will not fail," he replied, and his companion disappeared.

---

[1] Stones into which Khidhr-Elias has thrust his finger are believed to cure those afflicted with profuse perspiration. The patient inserts his finger in the cavity, strokes with it his forehead and eyes, and, it is asserted, "goes away cured."

The pious man entered the mosque and related his adventure to the guardians.

"'Twas Khidhr himself!" they cried. "If thou see him again, fail not to hold him fast, and let him go only when he has fulfilled thy desire."

The man performed his devotions in the mosque for another forty days, and on the morning of the fortieth he met a stranger who accosted him as the other had done.

"I would see Khidhr," he again replied.

"What seekest thou from him?" asked the Stranger.

Then the pious man concluded that this was indeed Khidhr, and he seized and held him fast.

"I am not Khidhr," said the Stranger.

"Yea, thou art he!"

"I am not. Suffer me to go on my way, and I will show thee Khidhr."

"Yea, thou art indeed Khidhr," insisted the pious man. "Fulfil my desire, or I will proclaim aloud who thou art, and others will then likewise seize and hold thee."

"I tell thee again I am not he whom thou seekest. Thou wilt see Khidhr on Friday in the mosque at the hour of the noontide *Namas*. HE who shall place himself on thy right hand at the moment the public prayers begin will be Khidhr—hold him fast." So saying, the Stranger disappeared.

Friday came, and the True Believer repaired to the mosque of Ayia Sofïa for the morning prayer.

Just as the service was beginning, a man, dressed as an Usher of the Sublime Porte, placed himself on his right.

H

As they came out of the mosque the pious man seized the
Usher, saying—

"Thou art Khidhr! I will not let thee go!"

The Usher stoutly denied that he was other than his
dress betokened him, and did his best to get away from
the pious man. A long struggle ensued. The two men
wrestled, fell, and rose again, until they came to the
cemetery outside the Adrianople Gate of the city. The
window of a *turbé* [1] stood open, and the Usher climbed
through it, closely followed by the pious man who still
held on to his clothing, and, after various turns, they came
into a splendid subterranean hall. Round it were ranged
forty sheepskin mats, thirty-eight of which were occupied
by venerable-looking men. The Usher was the chief
of the Forty, one of whom had just died, and the pious
man was allowed to take his place.

"Thou mayst seat thee on any mat thou wilt save that
which is reserved to me," said the Usher, who was the
Sheikh of the Forty, as he and his companions prepared
to go out on the morrow.

The pious man obeyed, and remained in the under-
ground dwelling for eight days, during which he was left
alone from morning until sunset. But on the eighth day
the True Believer, moved by curiosity, seated himself on
the sheepskin of the Chief. Suddenly he saw as in one
glance the whole world with everything in and upon it,
even to the innermost thoughts of men, and was filled

[1] See Chapter X. Many famous Dervishes are buried in this
cemetery.

with wonder and delight.[1] As the hour for the return of
the Thirty-nine approached he took another seat, where
they found him.

"What hast thou done?" they demanded in voices of
thunder.

"I have done nought."

"Yea, thou didst sit in the forbidden seat!"

"Nay, I did not."

But scarcely had he said the words than the hall
became dark, and he found himself again in the cemetery
outside the Adrianople Gate.

Of the various manly sports in which the Osmanlis of
former centuries, from Sultans downwards, may be said to
have excelled—among which were tennis and quoits,
leaping, wrestling, and throwing the *djereed*—the two last
only appear to be practised at the present day. Wrestling
has indeed remained a popular pastime with all nationalities and creeds, Turks and Kurds, Greeks and Armenians
Bulgarians and Gypsies freely entering the lists—often the
village threshing floor—against each other, and continuing
for hours the contest which is watched by a large crowd
of spectators, undemonstrative for the most part, but none
the less deeply interested and critical. The game of
djereed is more exciting, and, I believe, now peculiar to
Asia Minor, the land *par excellence* of legendary champions
and deeds of "derring-do" celebrated in ballad and story;
at all events I have never seen or heard of it in European

[1] This is a very common occurrence in Eastern folk-tale.

Turkey. It is played on horseback, and affords opportunities for the display of all those equestrian tricks on which Osmanli horsemen pride themselves. The number of players, perhaps twenty on each side, armed with *djereeds* —long, heavy, spear-like sticks, or rather poles—take up positions about fifty yards from each other on some open space, preferably at the foot of a rising ground, from which the game can be watched without danger to the spectators. The game is opened by one of the horsemen, who dashes forward and hurls his *djereed* at an opponent, who in his turn endeavours to intercept him before he can return to his place. It is then the turn of the other side. Sometimes a player mounted on an exceptionally swift horse will, instead of returning to his place in the lists after making his throw, create a diversion by riding off to a distance, when several of the other side pursue him and endeavour to overtake him. A player who has got rid of all his *djereeds* is at liberty to appropriate any found lying on the ground, which he contrives to do without dismounting, dexterously bending down and snatching up a weapon as his steed gallops past it. The rules of the game are strictly observed, and no unfairness or unnecessary roughness is permitted. The poles, which should not be aimed at the head of an opponent, may be dodged by any of the expedients at the command of expert horsemen, some appearing to leave their saddles when ducking to avoid a flying *djereed*. As inevitable in a game of this description, there are frequent mishaps and collisions, and horses and men may occasionally be seen struggling together on the ground in dangerous confusion. In Asia Minor young men forming part of the procession when a bride is being conveyed to her new home, carry *djereeds* and vie with each other in feats of horsemanship and agility as they alternately hurl forward and catch the weapon.

Not only, however, has the old Turkish love of racing and hunting been revived in a remarkable manner during the last few months, but a perfect craze for athletics as practised in England has also manifested itself in the Capital, where various clubs have already sprung into existence devoted to the furtherance of sport and athletic games. This movement is in great part a result of the reaction against the—to Englishmen—almost unimaginable restrictions placed by the late Government on both individual and social liberty, and especially as regarded public assemblies—even pictorial representations of crowds having for years past been prohibited by the Press Censor! Not a week now passes without a football match in which Turks, Greeks, and Armenians jostle each other in good-fellowship, and almost every evening the Turkish Eustace Miles—Captain Selim Serri Bey—lectures to the enthusiastic youth of the Capital at one or other of the athletic clubs which have been established by him in Pera and Stamboul. Foreign cricket clubs have long existed in the country, and it is confidently anticipated that this game will, in its due season, become as popular as the winter game has lately been. It is also more than probable that Turkish horses and jockeys will ere long be seen on French and English racecourses. Splendid horsemen the Osmanlis have ever been, and cavalry officers now vie with each other in long rides and forced marches, covering, for instance, even such long distances as lie between Adrianople and the Capital—no slight feat considering the state of country roads in Turkey during the winter season. The hunting club lately founded in Constantinople, to which foreigners are also eligible as members, owes its origin to the initiative and enthusiastic support of a Turkish military man, General Izzet Fuad Pasha, renowned for his knowledge of horses and everything pertaining to them.

THE "GREAT MOSQUE" AT BROUSSA

PART II

RELIGIOUS BELIEFS AND INSTITUTIONS

CHAPTER VI

MOSQUES AND THEIR GUARDIANS

THE most ancient and at the same time some of the most beautiful of the Moslem places of worship were originally Christian Churches which were converted to their present use at the Conquest. One of these, a *rotondo* at Salonica, is indeed of earlier date, having been a pagan temple dedicated to the Kabeirian deities once worshipped in these regions before its dedication, early in the Christian era, to St. George. The crosses of these Byzantine churches were everywhere replaced by the Crescent, the symbol of the conquering Osmanlis; and their frescoes and mosaics representing saints, angels, and other members of the Christian spiritual hierarchy, were concealed from view by a thick coat of whitewash. Few other modifications were, however, found necessary to meet the requirements of the simple form of Mohammedan worship beyond the substitution of the *mihrab*—as the shallow semicircular recess indicating the direction of

Mekka is termed—for the Sanctuary of the Eastern Church guarded by the "Golden Gates." The direction of Mekka being south-easterly, this orientation produces a somewhat discordant effect on Europeans, as the prayer mats and carpets are all arranged askew, and the worshippers on them stand in lines oblique to the axis of the building. The principal external additions to the Byzantine form of architecture are the minarets, which may be one, two, four, or even six in number, as at the great Mosque of Sultan Achmed I., who is said to have worked with his own hands at its erection. Previously to this date, the holy Kaaba at Mekka had been the only mosque with six minarets, and to silence the outcry made by the guardians of this Moslem Holy of Holies, Sultan Achmed offered to build a seventh minaret for the Kaaba.

The Byzantine churches were indeed practically adopted as the architectural model for the numerous mosques subsequently erected by the Conquerors in all parts of the Empire, as many as 230, large and small, now existing in the Capital alone. The great Cathedral Church originally founded by Constantine in the fourth century and rebuilt and dedicated by Justinian in the sixth century to the " Holy Wisdom," is now, under its Turkish designation of *Ayia Sofia Djamisi*, the chief Mosque of Stamboul ; and subsequently erected mosques are designed on a similar general plan. In front is a noble forecourt planted with trees ; at the rear of the edifice is a spacious garden ; and the whole is surrounded by a great walled-in space inclosing the various institutions connected with the mosque —the *Mekteb*, or primary school, the *Medresseh*, or theological college, the *Imaret*, or kitchen for the poor, the Library, Bath, and Hospital, and the *Khan*, or Guest-house, in which strangers and travellers are accommodated. A description of the beautiful mosque known as the Suleymanieh may here serve to illustrate the arrangements of mosques generally. This " Imperial " *djami* was built in the sixteenth century with materials taken from the Church of St. Euphemia at Chalcedon. The stately rectangular forecourt by which the Suleymanieh is approached is surrounded by cloisters roofed with a number of cupolas resting on pillars of porphyry, granite, and marble, under which, on three of its sides, are benches also of marble, for the occupation of the meditative Osmanli public, while in the centre a dome supported on slender pillars protects the ablutionary fountain around which the pigeons and other birds perpetually coo, twitter, and preen themselves. At each corner a tall, slender minaret, surrounded by balconies, lifts its pointed leaden roof to the sky, those at the outer corners being not only of different design but shorter than the others, an arrangement which produces a good effect.

The Mosque itself is nearly square. Its internal construction rests on four great piers ; the screen of windows on each side under the great lateral arches of the dome being supported on four monolithic shafts of great beauty; and the interior decorations generally are marked by a wealth of artistic detail. Walls and pillars are veneered with rare coloured marbles, and the stained glass windows, two of which are spoils of the Persian wars, and the rest the work of a native artist-craftsman, glow with rich and varied colour. The *mihrab* is of pure white sculptured marble bordered with exquisite blue-and-white tiles. The marble *mimber*, or pulpit, with its straight, steep staircase, is decorated with delicately sculptured tracery, as is also the screen of the *maksura*, the tribune appropriated to the use of the Sultan. Great pillar-shaped candelabra stand on either side of the *mihrab ;* others of different form, and hung with countless tiny oil lamps, are suspended from the ceiling, while here and there are affixed to the walls great circular discs emblazoned in Arabic characters with the names of Mohammed, Ali the First Khalif, and his immediate successors. There are no seats, but the floors are covered with clean matting Entering from the bustle and glare of the crowded streets into the cool dim quiet of these beautiful buildings at the hour of noontide prayer, the contrast is most striking and impressive ; and it is at such moments that something of the deep mystery of Oriental life may perhaps occasionally, if transiently, be understood by the foreigner. In the cool gloom—or what appears gloom after the sunpervaded air without—Moslems of all races, ages, and conditions, from the jetty Nubian to the fair blue-eyed Anatolian Turk, are ranged in rows facing the *mihrab*, and alternately stand erect, kneel, and prostrate themselves while accomplishing the simple form of worship described in the following chapter.

The spacious gardens at the rear of the mosques

INTERIOR OF THE SULEYMANIEH MOSQUE

peaceful, picturesque, cypress-shaded spots, usually contain the tomb of the founder and his family, and are
sometimes fairly filled with tombstones of all descriptions,
which fall away from the perpendicular at every angle
amid a riot of roses and flowering shrubs.   In that
attached to the Suleymanieh rise the two noble *turbehs*,
or mausoleums, erected by this Sultan, under the larger of
which he himself lies with two of his successors and
various members of his family, while the second covers
the remains of his beloved Khurrem—"the Joyous One"
who, having entered the Serai as a Russian slave, was
elevated to the exceptional rank of legal wife of the mighty
Suleyman.   In this garden lies also Ali Pasha, the famous
reforming Grand Vizier of Sultan Abdul Aziz, together
with other men of note and power in their brief day.
Turbehs like these of Suleyman and his Consort are
richly decorated, and in them may be found choice specimens of the beautifully inscribed tiles elsewhere mentioned.
Over the actual graves stand wooden catafalques termed
simply *sunduk*—"boxes," varying in size with the worldly
rank and importance of the deceased, and draped with
palls of velvet or with costly Eastern shawls, all of
which were conveyed to Medina and laid upon the
Prophet's tomb there before being applied to their
present purpose.   These *turbehs* rank in religious
estimation as mosques, *fatihas*—chapters from the Koran
used as prayers for the dead—being daily read in them
by the Sheikh in charge, a folding book-rest of beautiful
workmanship for holding the illuminated copy of the

Sacred Book being part of the appointments of the edifice.

The endowments of the larger mosques were formerly very considerable ; but owing to various causes the revenues of many have of late years been considerably diminished. The Suleymanieh is, however, said still to possess property the revenues from which amount to nearly £3000 a year, devoted chiefly to the support of the various educational and charitable dependencies above enumerated. The revenues of the mosques generally, out of which are also of course paid the salaries of their guardians, consists in the rents derived from the class of landed property termed *vakouf*—that is, "dedicated to Allah "—which include all real property the proceeds of which are applied to the support of such religious and charitable institutions, as also to the maintenance of aqueducts and street fountains. No official report is available of the extent of these *vakouf* lands, but it is estimated at as much as two-thirds of the whole area of the country. For at the Conquest numerous grants of large tracts of land were made as endowments not only of mosques and their dependencies, but also of the monastic establishments of the Dervishes who accompanied the victorious armies into the battlefield. To these original endowments private munificence has also constantly and richly added ; for the piety, as well as the vanity, of Moslems has ever incited to the erection and endowment of religious and beneficent institutions, both as a religious duty well pleasing ; to Allah, and also as the surest method of obtaining the praise of their

A STREET FOUNTAIN (*SEBIL*) IN STAMBOUL

contemporaries and of posterity. Such acts of munificence were formerly very frequent on the part of private individuals, though in more recent times they have been practised chiefly by members of the Imperial family and by grandees of the Empire. Church lands have also been very largely increased from a third source. As such estates, together with the tenants living on them, enjoy special privileges, a Moslem freeholder—or, for that matter, a Christian— worried by tax-gatherers or creditors, would sell his land to the "Dean and Chapter" of a mosque for a merely nominal sum, while at the same time retaining the right of hereditary lease and becoming tenant at a fixed rent, a transaction by which both he and the mosque were the gainers, and only the Government and its corrupt officials the losers. For the trustees of the mosque receive a large interest for their trifling investment of capital, and are also entitled to the reversion, in default of direct heirs; while the tenant on land which has thus become *vakouf* pays no taxes, and is secure from extortion by Government officials, as also from persecution on the part of private creditors. This system is, however, now menaced with reform.

The distribution of water being, as elsewhere mentioned, accounted by Mohammedans one of the most important among the "good works" which form such an integral part of their religion, drinking fountains are everywhere found attached to mosques. A *sebil*, as such fountains are termed, is usually situated in the forecourt of the mosque, and consists of a cistern surrounded on the inner side by a wall of sculptured marble, and on the

street side by a screen or grating of gilded bronze, often
of beautiful design, resting on a low wall of masonry, and
having at its base small semicircular openings through
which the brass drinking cups filled by the attendants are
passed to the thirsty public standing without. The roof
is in the form of a low dome, and the wide extending
eaves, boarded beneath, give to these little edifices, which
are also usually shaded by waving trees, a most pleasing
and picturesque appearance. Water is indeed, to the
Oriental, the symbol of life, and the words of the Koran,
" By water all things live," may be found inscribed on
the majority of the principal fountains of Stamboul.

The important body of Moslem legists termed collectively *Ulema*, of which the Sheikh-ul-Islam is the head,
comprises in its ranks the guardians of the mosques and
those charged with the conduct of public worship in them,
as well as the higher administrations of the *Sheriat*, or
Sacred Law, on which, notwithstanding the establishment
early in the last century of a system of Common Law, the
judicial system of Turkey is still based. It must, however,
be borne in mind that the *Ulema* do not constitute a
sacerdotal caste, or even an ecclesiastical body in the
Christian acceptation of those terms. There is, indeed,
no country in Europe in which the clerical element
exercises so little and the legal so great authority; and
yet spiritual and temporal functions are strangely and
inextricably interwoven in the conduct of internal affairs
in Turkey. The Sheikh-ul-Islam, though the highest
ecclesiastical dignitary, without whose sanction no Imperial

decree can be issued, is at the same time but an official whose appointment and dismissal are equally in the hands of the Sultan, his importance being due rather to his legal standing as judge of the highest Court of Appeal than to his religious office.   For though on occasions of ceremony he appears at the head of the *Ulema*, he in no sense possesses the religious authority of a Christian archbishop, and various holders of this high office have been regarded with popular contempt as mere subservient tools of a tyrannical Padishah. The *Mollahs*, or Doctors of Law, preach sermons in the mosques on special occasions, and the *Imāms* in their religious capacity lead the prayers in the mosques and conduct funerals ; but it is as legal functionaries that they attest marriage and other contracts and accompany police officers when making domiciliary visits—for unless preceded by the *Imām* of the parish no police officer may cross the threshold of a Moslem dwelling. The *Khatibs* and *Hodjas* also assist in leading the prayers at the midday Friday service, the chief religious event of the week ; the *Muezzim* chants five times daily from the lofty balcony of the minaret the *Ezan*, or call to prayer ; and the *Kaïms* perform the lower offices in the sacred edifice.

All the members of this numerous *Ulema* class, from the highest to the lowest, have passed some years as *Softas*, or undergraduates, in the Theological Colleges. As a body these *Softas* exercise considerable public influence, and have almost invariably taken a prominent part in revolutions and other political events. Generally

speaking, they have hitherto been regarded as the most
fanatical section of the population, hostile to every innovation or attempt at reform; and the authorities have on
occasion not scrupled to make use of their agency for the
purpose of awakening that spirit of savage bigotry which,
save when so stirred, slumbers peacefully enough in the
heart of the Turkish peasant and artisan. In modern
times an energetic Sultan has, on the other hand, more
than once found it expedient to disperse some of these
communities and close their colleges, and the present
Sultan, in the late pursuance of his policy of suppression,
on more than one occasion adopted measures calculated
to prevent any collective action against his government
on the part of this redoubtable corporation. In carrying
out the revolution of last summer, the " Young Turks "
appear, however, to have obtained the ready and energetic
support and co-operation of a large section of this supposed reactionary element, which, although it had upheld
Midhad Pasha in proposing his short-lived Constitution of
1876, subsequently petitioned the Grand Vizier against the
clauses extending citizenship to the Christian elements of
the population.

As just observed, the actual ministers of public worship,
such as the *Imâms*, who pronounce the public prayers, the
Hodjas, Muezzims, and others, constitute but a subordinate
section of the Ulema. The *Imâms*, who form the nearest
approach to a beneficed clergy, pass an examination,
and are appointed to their office by the Sheikh-ul-Islam.
Imperial mosques such as Ayia Sofía, the Suleymanieh,

the Achmedieh, etc., have several *Imāms*, to the chief of whom are subordinate all the others, as also the guardians of the mosques of inferior rank. An *Imām* is required to marry, and may bequeath his office to his son who, if unlettered, appoints a deputy to perform his duties. This lower class of the *Ulema*, who, like the *Softas*, are distinguished by a white turban bound round the fez, and by wearing the old Turkish dress, are drawn from the lower middle class of Turkish society, and exercise little or no influence, intellectual or other, in their parishes.   An *Imām* or *Hodja* lives rent free in a house attached to the mosque, and receives a small annual stipend, which he is able to supplement by the fees received for teaching in the *Mekteb*, or elementary school, and for issuing licences, officiating at circumcisions, weddings and funerals, and for washing the dead.   The *Imām* of a village mosque occupies a position somewhat superior to that of the Christian or secular priests who provide for the religious needs of the Greek, Armenian, and Bulgarian peasantry, he having generally received a fair education, according to Turkish ideas, in the Medresseh of a provincial town, and his mosque generally possessing an adequate endowment bequeathed by some pious departed Moslem.   Generally, however, a village *Imām* or *Hodja* has to combine in his own person all the above enumerated offices, religious and legal, which in a town mosque are performed by half a dozen functionaries belonging to different grades.

I

CHAPTER VII

BELIEFS AND SUPERSTITIONS

"IN what consists Islamism?" Mohammed was asked by the Angel Gabriel, in the guise of a Bedouin.

"In professing," replied the Prophet, "that there is but one God and that I am His Prophet; in observing strictly the hours of prayer; in giving alms; in fasting during the month of Ramazan; and in making the pilgrimage to Mekka."

"It is so, in truth," responded Gabriel, making himself known.

These main tenets of Mohammedanism are figuratively termed the "Five Pillars of Practice," and comprise all that is of supreme importance in the religion of Islam. The Moslem confession of faith is thus expressed, "I believe in Allah and His Angels and His Prophets, in the predestination of good and evil by Allah, and in the resurrection after death. I bear witness that there is no God but Allah, and I testify that Mohammed is His servant and His Prophet."

The term *Moslem* signifies "resigned"—resigned to the mysterious decrees of an irresponsible Ruler who, though He has revealed a certain moral Law for the guidance of His creatures, is Himself above all law and morality. This view of the Almighty as "the only potentate, Lord of Lords, and King of Kings," recurs all through the Koran, and is curiously illustrated by the formula of devotion, termed the *namaz*, instituted by Mohammed. In Islam there is, properly speaking, no ritual, no sacrifice of horned beasts as in Judaism, nor of the Mass, as in Christianism; there is also a marked absence of sacerdotalism, for the *Ulema* form no spiritual hierarchy, and the *Imām*, who is also a legal functionary, lays claim to no priestly rank, but merely for convenience sake leads the collective devotions of the congregation in the mosque. The mosque itself is indeed merely a convenience, for so long as the worshipper's face is turned towards Mekka the *namaz* may be equally well recited elsewhere—in the privacy of the harem, in the public thoroughfares, or in the Council chamber.

This obligatory form of devotion, which is performed five times daily, consists merely of two or more repetitions of a ceremony called the *rikat*, or "prostration," which is little more than the recitation in various prescribed attitudes of certain formulæ, such as "God is most Great!" "We give praise unto Allah!" A few minutes before the hour of each of these prayers a servant of the mosque, called the *Muezzim*, generally chosen for his vocal abilities ascends the spiral staircase of the minaret and, emerging on its lofty circular balcony, chants in Arabic the *ezan*, or call to prayer—"*Allahu Akbar!*" (repeated four times). "God is most Great! Come to prayer! Prayer is better than sleep! (for the sunrise *esan* only). There is no God save Allah! He giveth life and dieth not! My sins are great, greater is Allah's mercy! I extol His perfections! *Allahu Akbar*—God is most Great!" This act of worship is invariably preceded by ablution, as prayer must be made in a state of "legal purity," and for this facilities are offered by the fountains with which the courtyard of every mosque is supplied. This ablution is called the *abtest*, and consists in washing the hands and forearms, the face and feet in running water. When water is not procurable, the *abtest* may be made with sand, gravel, or dust. Prayer-carpets are used when possible in order to guard against any impurity on the spot where prayer is offered. The observance of the Moslem Day of Rest— Friday—is unattended by any special Sabbatarian rites beyond the public midday service in the mosques. The provision markets are in full swing, and itinerant vendors of refreshments are everywhere seeking custom. Here a *kahvedji* has installed his charcoal brazier under the shadow of a sculptured and gilded fountain, and is busy preparing and distributing to his customers cups of fragrant coffee. Close by a *simitjdi* has halted, and· removes from his head to the tripod stand carried in his hand the circular tray piled with ring-shaped fancy bread fresh from the oven ; and over the way, seated on rush-bottomed stools, a row of burly Turks of the labouring class are passively smoking their wooden *tchibouks* or *narghilis*, while awaiting their turn at the hands of the open-air barber. As the hour of noon approaches, the

Muezzim's cry floats melodiously down to the True Believers who are already making their way to the mosque. Crossing the *harem*, as the enclosing spacious courtyard is termed, they perform the customary ablution at the bird-haunted fountain in its midst, and discarding their shoes in the marble-paved and pillared vestibule, pass into the sanctuary. Here, side by side, irrespective of rank, in rows facing the *kibleh*—the niche in the south-eastern wall indicating the direction of Mekka—sit the variously garbed worshippers, some still wearing the ample turban and flowing robe of their forefathers; others in tightly buttoned uniform or official frock coat and scanty fez; sons of toil in coarse baggy breeches and short jacket; and dervishes of every grade and order, from the decorous *Mevlevi* in his sugar-loaf hat and mantle of fine cloth, to the shaggy-haired and ragged *Kalenderi* or *Bektashi* with staff and begging-bowl. No female form is visible, as any women who may be present are concealed behind the carved and gilded screen of the gallery, which is approached by a separate entrance.. The Moslem's public worship is peculiar in the absence of all elaborate ceremonial or sacramental rite in which priest and people take different parts. The *Imām* stands alone facing the *kibleh* with his back to the congregation, who, led by him, perform simultaneously the prescribed gestures with the precision of soldiers at drill. First he places his thumbs behind his ears with the fingers extended while he ejaculates, "God is most Great," then with his hands folded on his stomach and with downcast

eyes he recites a collect and the *fatiha*, the Moslem
equivalent of the "Lord's Prayer": "Praise be to Allah,
Lord of the Universe, the Merciful, the Compassionate
Lord of the Day of Judgment; Thee only do we worship;
to Thee do we cry for help; guide us in the right way—
in the way of those whom Thou hast laden with Thy
blessings, and not in the way of those who have en-
countered Thy wrath, or have gone astray." Other
passages from the Koran may follow, after which the
Imām inclines himself, placing his hands on his knees,
with the words "God is most Great! I praise Allah!"
three times repeated. Rising, he exclaims, "God hears
those who praise Him! O Lord, Thou art praised!"
and then falling on his knees, "God is most Great;"
he next prostrates himself with his forehead touching
the ground, repeating thrice, "I extol Thee, O God."
This formula of recitation and posture constitutes
what is termed a *rikat*, the ordinary midday prayers
consisting of ten, and on Friday of twelve *rikats*. At
the conclusion of the *namaz*, the worshippers stand
erect, with outstretched arms and extended palms, as if
to receive the promised blessing from on high. Most
impressive is the simple faith, reverence, and absorbed
devotion with which this service of worship is performed
by the mixed congregation, composed chiefly of the
working classes, in Turkey the most devout section of
the population. There is no sermon on week-days, but
after the Friday *namaz* the *Mollah* ascends the pulpit, and
delivers a discourse. Save, however, when the *Mollah* has

some special message to deliver, this is hardly a sermon
in our sense of the word, being largely addressed to the
Deity, and including prayers for the protection and
triumph of Islam, followed by mention of the early Khalifs
and companions of the Prophet, each name being greeted
by the congregation with the words, "May he find
acceptance with Allah!" To say of a man that he
performs his *namaz* five times daily is the highest praise
that can be awarded, and Moslems who are themselves
careless in this matter, respect the punctiliousness of the
devout who, in the fulfilment of their religious duties,
disdain concealment, reck not of ridicule or comment; and
believe too utterly themselves to care if others disbelieve.

The fatalistic notion of *kismet* inculcated by the
doctrine of predestination above mentioned importantly
influences Turkish thought and action—or inaction—as
it assumes that all events affecting mankind are absolutely
pre-ordained by Allah, who has written them down in
"the preserved Tablets," delivered to the Angels on the
"Night of Destiny."[1] Many people beside Turks are
fatalists, but they consult a doctor when they are ill,
and take other ordinary precautions against disaster. In
the opinion of old-fashioned Moslems, however, all such
precautions are vain; if it is their *kismet* that calamity
shall overtake them, overtake them it will, and what, then,
is the good of troubling oneself with efforts to avert it?
That fortune helps those who help themselves is a doctrine
incomprehensible to Orientals. Whatever energy a man

[1] See p. 146.

may display, *kismet* will override his endeavours, or
crown his supineness with equally unmerited and unex-
pected prosperity ; and many are the folk-tales, some not
without humour, illustrating and confirming popular
belief in this great factor in human affairs, one of which
will be found in the preceding chapter. The effects of
such a mental attitude are naturally far-reaching. For
not only are lives constantly sacrificed and wealth and
happiness missed by this fatal principle of passivity,
but the whole character of the nation is enfeebled.
Neglect of all sanitary precautions—not to say hostility
towards them—is one important result of *kismet*. Owing
to its geographical position, Turkey is especially liable to
epidemics, which, among so passive a population, naturally
create terrible havoc. Quarantine regulations are certainly
now officially observed at Constantinople and the other
large seaports. But in the towns of the interior the
Moslem population manifest the greatest dislike to such
sanitary regulations, which they regard as profane inter-
ference with the will of Allah, and do their best to avoid
carrying out.

The religious laws by which men are ruled in Moslem
countries aimed at the establishment of a certain degree
of equality among a people by lessening the sufferings
of the poor. Thus while Christians merely pray for " Peace
on earth and good-will among men," Mohammed, being
eminently a practical reformer, made it incumbent on
his followers not merely to give of their superfluity to the
poor, but to share with them a considerable proportion of

their worldly goods. *Salaam aleikum*, "Peace be to thee," is the Moslem's greeting to his fellow, and in no more practical way than by such self-denying alleviation of the miseries of the less fortunate can men be made brothers, and be literally "at peace" with each other. That the merely secular laws by which the West has been governed have fallen lamentably short of such happy results is abundantly proved by the growth in all European countries of Socialism and Nihilism. Almsgiving, which includes also hospitality, being thus one of the "Pillars of Practice" of the religion of Islam, though more especially exercised during religious festivals and on the occasion of family ceremonies, is practised by Moslems whenever opportunity occurs. An Arabic proverb says, "Whoso visits a living person and eats nothing at his house, might as well visit the tomb of a dead man." And the following may serve as a specimen of the many charming parables and stories in which this virtue of hospitality is inculcated :—

In the days of the Prophet there lived at Mekka a man who had a wife and two children, and this poor family for a whole week had had nothing to eat, when one day they received some victuals—not enough, however, to satisfy a single hungry person ; and at the same time a stranger arrived and demanded hospitality. Then the goodman said to his wife, "Praised be Allah who gives us His blessing by sending this guest ! What is there to put before him ? "

" There is barely enough for one," replied the woman.

" Then have the goodness to put the children to bed, for our guest must eat what food we have. As soon as it is dark do thou light the lamp and bring in the supper at the same time. Then must thou upset the lamp and say, 'The lamp went out in falling; I will relight it,' and I will say, ' No, let us sit down ; we can sup without a light.' Then in the darkness we can put our hands into the dish, and our guest will think that we are eating, and will not perceive that he alone eats."

And so they did. The stranger passed the night, and when morning dawned he rose and departed. The goodman, after performing his ablution, betook himself to the noble mosque, where he beheld the Prophet—*on whom be peace !*—seated with his back against the pulpit; and as the pious man approached him Mohammed exclaimed, " Happy art thou, for Gabriel has promised to thee and thy wife blessings innumerable."

As formerly in the Christian monasteries of the West, so now in the Dervish *Tekkehs* of the East, the traveller is sure of finding food and shelter ; *Imarets*, or almshouses, founded by private charity, are of ancient institution in the Empire ; and general almsgiving is so largely practised that, notwithstanding the absence of anything in the shape of poor-law relief, there exists—save in times of scarcity, as unfortunately at present—no such squalid destitution as disgraces the large cities of Europe and the United States. Blind Bartimæus and Lazarus still sit by the wayside begging, and the True Believer fulfils the precepts of his religion by supplying the wants of these afflicted ones, and of the fatherless and the widow.

It is important to note that Mohammed, in announcing his mission as the Prophet of God, connected himself with the past as the last of the Prophets. The Moslem hierarchy of inspired Seers begins with Adam, and includes the patriarchs Noah and Abraham, as well as the greater Jewish Prophets and Jesus, each successive one being esteemed greater than his predecessor. But in addition to this historical hierarchy of Prophets, there exists, in Moslem belief, another of an entirely mythical character— a succession of saintly men unto whom the Will of Allah is revealed, and through whose instrumentality the destinies of mankind are governed. Supreme among these Saints of the Moslem Calendar is Khidhr, the mythical personage already referred to, who from time immemorial, and in various forms, has filled a prominent place in the religions of the world. This Protean Saint, or Demi-God, appears also to be identical with the Prophet Elijah, or Elias, as well as with the Christian hero St. George, who, in his turn, has been identified with Horus. Khidhr is held to have had his original abode in the terrestrial Paradise which contained a Tree of Life and a Fountain of Life, and, having eaten of the fruit of the one, and drunk of the water of the other, he became immortal.[1] As the

[1] This "Water," "Fountain," "Stream," or "River of Life," believed to exist in a Land of Darkness in the extreme East, is an Oriental myth alluded to in Rev. xxii. 1, and often made use of by

wisest of created beings, he was consulted by Moses, who, accompanied by Joshua, journeyed to a place where two rivers meet, or, according to other writers, to an "Isle of the Isles of the Sea," where they found the sage from whom Moses received the "Secret of Secrets." Khidhr is also credited in Moslem belief with having led the Israelites out of Egypt and guided them through the Red Sea and the Desert, taking the place of the "pillars of cloud and of fire" in the Biblical account of this incident. Moslems also hold that Khidhr-Elias, as he is often termed, though really one single individual, has a dual personality. He is regarded as the special protector of travellers, being invoked under the former name by those journeying on the sea, and under the latter by those journeying on land. Both parts of this dual personage are believed to be perpetually wandering over the world, Khidhr on the sea, and Elias on the land, and to meet once a year at Moona, near Mekka, on the day of "the Station of the Pilgrims." He is thus connected with St. Nicholas, who performs the same good offices for the Greeks, and is the special patron of sailors.[1] St. Nicholas is also further confounded with Ἥλιος, with Ali, the nephew of the Prophet, and with Phineas, the immortal hero of Talmudic legend, who is held to have performed twelve

Turkish and Persian poets. It frequently occurs also in the folk-tales of the Christian as well as the Moslem races of South-Eastern Europe.

[1] A Greek couplet says of this Saint—

> "He to our aid comes on the sea,
> And on the land works wondrously."

miracles, and, according to this authority, is destined, like Elias, to play an important part at the end of the world. This belief would appear to be illustrated in the question addressed to Jesus by His disciples, " Why say the Scribes that Elias must first come ? " and in His answer that " Elias is come already, and they knew him not ; "[1] as also in the popular Eastern belief in the periodic incarnation of this mythical personage.   Numerous instances are recorded in Moslem literature and legend of the sudden appearances and disappearances of Khidhr-Elias.   By many he is held to be always visibly present somewhere on the earth, and, like his prototype the Tishbite, is often " carried by the Spirit of the Lord " from place to place. Could he be recognised, a knowledge of the secret of immortality might be demanded of him ; but it is only a saintly man who can distinguish Khidhr from another. A Moslem desirous of an interview with this mysterious being must, according to popular belief, perform his *namas* during forty consecutive days under the central dome of St. Sophia at Constantinople, and on the fortieth day he is certain to be rewarded with a sight of Khidhr.   Evliya Effendi, the seventeenth-century Turkish traveller and author, asserts in his *Travels* that " Thousands of pious men have here enjoyed the happiness of conversing with that great Prophet."   A specimen of the strange and fantastic legends current in Stamboul of the adventures of those who have undertaken this quest, has already been given in the preceding chapter.

[1] St. Matt. xvii. 10, 12.

Various European writers, from Montesquieu downwards, have assumed and asserted—though on what authority it would be difficult to ascertain—that the religion of Islam denies to woman the possession of a soul and, consequently, admission to Paradise.[1] Although such an assertion could not honestly be made by any one acquainted either with Islamic religious books or religious thought, this assumed Moslem debasement of women has been eagerly seized upon by the "Subjection of Women" theorists; and it may not, therefore, be superfluous to point out briefly how utterly at variance with facts is such an assumption. In the first place, the Koran is most explicit on this point, and numerous texts, of which the following may serve as examples, promise the joys of Paradise to all "true Moslems" irrespective of sex.

"God has promised to believers, men and women, gardens beneath which rivers flow, to dwell therein for ever, and goodly places in the Garden of Eden."[2]

"The Gardens of Eden, into which they shall enter

---

[1] Many instances might be adduced of this prevailing vulgar misconception. I will, however, only give here the latest that has come to my notice. In her recent article on "Woman's Place in the World" (*North American Review*), the Duchess of Marlborough informs her readers that "the Mohammedan religion degraded women even lower [? than primitive man], consigning her, as far as psychic qualities are concerned, to the level of the beasts, forbidding her for ever the hope of future salvation."

[2] *Koran*, chap. ix. v. 73.

with the righteous amongst their fathers and their wives and their seed."[1]

"Verily men resigned and women resigned, and believing men and believing women, and devout men and devout women, and truthful men and truthful women, and patient men and patient women, and humble men and humble women, and almsgiving men and almsgiving women, and fasting men and fasting women, . . . and men who remember God much and women who remember Him—God has prepared for them forgiveness and a mighty reward."[2]

"Enter into paradise, ye and your wives, happy."[3]

The *Hadith*, or "Traditional Sayings" of Mohammed, also record that the Prophet of Islam imparted to his followers his divinely acquired knowledge that certain of their deceased friends had been rewarded for their faith by admission to Paradise. Among them, he said, was his departed wife and first convert, Khadija, whom he had been "commanded to gladden with the good tidings of a chamber of hollow pearl in which is no clamour and no fatigue"[4]—surely a delightful vision of the "rest that remaineth for the people of God." And in the following little elegy on a Sultana who died in the bloom of youth, the poet Fazil admirably depicts the Oriental belief in both physical and spiritual consciousness after death :—

[1] *Koran*, chap. xiii. v. 23.   [2] *Ibid.*, chap. xxxiii. v. 35.
[3] *Ibid.*, chap. xiii. v. 70. Other similar passages may also be found in chaps. ix. v. 66 ; xxx. v. 56 ; xviii. v. 5 ; vii. v. 12, etc.
[4] Redhouse, *The Mesnevi*, p. 11, quoting from Wustenfeld's *Ibnu-Hishan*, vol. i. p. 156.

"Ah ! thou'st laid her low, yet flushed with life, Cupbearer of the
  Sphere ! [1]
Scarce the cup of joy was tasted when the bowl of Fate brimmed
  o'er.
Cradle her, O Earth ! full gently ; smile on her, O Trusted One ! [2]
For a wide world's King this Fair Pearl as his heart's own darling
  wore." [3]

If further evidences were necessary to prove that the
slavish subjection of women which is generally assumed
to be inseparable from Mohammedanism, was neither
preached nor practised by the Prophet, it may be found
also in the honour and regard paid by him to his wives,
and especially to Khadija and A'isha. The latter had
been married to him at the age of nine, and was the
favourite wife of Mohammed, who had taken the greatest
pains with her education. She was esteemed the most
polished and learned of Arab women, and after enjoying
for eleven years the confidence and affection of her illustrious husband, was, on his death, honoured by the True
Believers with the title of "Prophetess" and "Mother of
the Faithful." A'isha lived in virtuous and honourable
widowhood for forty-eight years, during which, having
been the most intimate confidante of the Prophet, she
was consulted in all difficulties that arose after his death
in points of religion and law. A large proportion of the
"Traditional Sayings" were indeed, according to the
Moslem doctors, compiled from her replies, which were
based on the opinion she had heard him express. After

[1] The poetical name given by Moslems to Death.
[2] The Angel Gabriel.
[3] Gibb, *Ottoman Poems*, Appendix.

uttering the names of A'isha and other saintly women, Moslems invariably add, " May they find acceptance with Allah ! "   Although regular attendance at public worship on the Day of Rest is not required of Moslem, any more than it is of Christian or Jewish women in the East, all the usual ordinances of their religion—performance of the five daily *namaz* with their accompanying ablutions, fasting, pilgrimage, and "good works" generally—are as obligatory for Moslem women as they are for Moslem men. Children of both sexes are taught their prayers at the age of seven ; and the honourable title of *Hafiz* is conferred on any Moslem who may have committed to memory the whole of the Koran, a by no means unusual feat, it would seem, if we are to credit the seventeenth-century traveller and author Evliya Effendi, who records that the city of Angora at the time of his visit to it contained no fewer than two thousand boys and girls who were *Hafiz*.[1]

The Osmanlis have many graceful folk-beliefs connected with animals, most of which possess also some religious significance.   According to one of these, the stork goes every autumn on a pilgrimage to the holy Kaaba at Mekka, and hence it is called *Baba Hadji*— "Father Pilgrim." This bird, they say, builds his nest only on the mosques and other edifices of the True Believers, avoiding the Christian churches and quarters. When the Father Pilgrim returns in spring to his nest on their house-top or cypress tree, the women and children look anxiously to see what he carries in his beak—if a bit

[1] *Narrative of Travels*, Book II. p. 231.

K

of glass, it is a good sign, the year will be free from plague
and famine, and every one will be happy and prosperous;
if a bit of rag, it will be a year of sickness; if an ear of
corn, the harvest will be abundant. If the stork arrives
with his beak pointed skywards, it signifies that he is dis-
satisfied with men, and will not deign to look at them;
if, on the contrary, his beak is pointed earthwards, and
towards the dwellings of men, they say that he murmurs,
" *Salaam aleikoum!* "—" Peace be with you!" And the pious
Moslems exclaim in reply, " *Aleikoumi es Salaam! Khosh
gueldiniz, Hadji Baba*"—" On thee be peace, welcome Father
Pilgrim!" Another popular belief connected with animals
is that in the promised admission to Paradise of the following twelve animals which are found mentioned in Moslem
Holy Writ or Traditional lore as connected with the
histories of Prophets and other famous personages. Among
these are the whale which swallowed Jonah; the asses on
which the Prophet and the Queen of Sheba respectively
rode; Solomon's ant and Belki's cuckoo; Ishmail's ram
and Abraham's calf; Moses' ox and the dog of the " Seven
Sleepers of Ephesus."

Superstition plays an important part in the lives of the
Turkish people, every ailment or misfortune being ascribed
to the baneful effects of an " Evil Eye " or to the influence
of witchcraft, and even the educated classes have difficulty
in completely throwing off the beliefs inculcated with
their nurses' milk. As an illustration of this it may be
recalled that among the members of the " Camarilla " dismissed from the Palace at the recent revolution was the

Sultan's Astrologer, a Dervish Sheikh, whose prognostications, inspired no doubt by his *confrères*, were often effectual in influencing the actions of his Padishah.   Not the least superstitious are naturally the women, for whom every trivial event of the day possesses a significance prophetic of good or foreboding evil.   It would be a stupendous task to collect all the folk beliefs and superstitions of the Osmanlis, so intimately connected are they with every detail of domestic life and with every varying circumstance, and a European is, indeed, as a rule, made aware of their existence only by inadvertently transgressing them.   There are no laws in Turkey which interfere with the time-honoured calling of the Witch, and in every part of the Empire she and her magical powers are held in high esteem, not only by the Turks, but also by their Christian and Jewish neighbours.   To the Witch-wife repair love-sick maidens and jealous wives, childless women and mothers with ailing children, seekers of lost or stolen property, and for each of her clients the wise woman has a specific.   Fortune-telling is also largely practised by the Witch, and is performed by means of cards, or a tray of dried beans, coins, beads, and other small objects which are manipulated according to some traditional formula.   I once formed one of a party of Europeans at a Witch's fortune-telling at Salonica.   Her cottage was approached through a tidily swept little courtyard, and the room in which the séances were held was comfortably enough furnished in native fashion with rugs and divan.   The old woman squatted on her heels on the

floor, the implements of her trade before her on a *sofra*—
the low circular tray-stand used by the Turks in lieu of
table.   One by one we also, at her invitation, sat on the
rug at her side until three or four of our number had been
told their future, and had added a piece of silver to those
on her tray.   The "Spay-wife," however, was keen enough
to perceive that she had no credulous Orientals to deal
with, and presently she summarily dismissed us.   When
the courtyard gate was re-opened we found gathered outside in the street a motley group of Jews, Greeks, and
Moslems, awaiting their turn to consult the Witch, whose
fame was evidently great in this Macedonian capital.

A considerable branch of the Witch's trade consists
in providing love-spells and potions, and occasionally, it
may be added, spells of a less innocent character.   Persons
believing themselves to be suffering from the effects of magic
—for a hint is generally conveyed to the subject of a spell
—must naturally have recourse to the Witch to remove
it.   Her skill is also resorted to when ordinary measures
apparently fail to exorcise that most dreaded of all
mysterious powers—the "Evil Eye."   For, notwithstanding
all precautions, persons are often found to be suffering
from the effects of the enviously malignant gaze of some
evilly disposed neighbour.   As elsewhere mentioned,[1] fumi-
gations are in some cases made for the purpose of dispelling
this baneful influence.   It would, however, be difficult to
enumerate all the magical practices which are had recourse
to with this object, as they are as numerous as are the

[1] See p. 231.

preservatives against the dreaded *fena gues*. Among the latter I may, however, mention the bunches of charms consisting of gold coins, horn-shaped bits of coral, and blue glass, turquoise ornaments, engraved bloodstones and cornelians, cloves of garlic sewn in silk, and other small objects which are tied to the caps or hung round the necks of children, and also ornament the headstalls of horses, mules, and donkeys ; and the horseshoes, boars' tusks, and hares' heads hung on the walls of houses and other buildings. Blue glass bracelets are also frequently worn for the same purpose ; and when they get broken, as, considering the material of which they are made, is certain sooner or later to happen, the accident is attributed to the *fena gues* having luckily fallen upon them instead of upon their wearers. Some individuals are quite notorious for their power of "casting the Evil Eye," any person or object of which they may speak with commendation being certain to come to grief in some way or other, and on this account they even enjoy a certain amount of consideration, as their neighbours are very fearful of in any way offending them. Red-haired persons are more particularly suspected of this proclivity, and blue or gray eyes, being somewhat rare in the East, are considered specially baneful. The latter defect in my personal appearance, indeed, caused me on more than one occasion to be accused of exercising this spell.

The supernatural beings with whom the Osmanlis terrify themselves and their children have by no means the variety of those of their neighbours belonging to other

nationalities, and fall, for the most part, under the de-
nomination either of *Djins* or *Peris*. Under this term are,
however, popularly classed Supernals generally, including
the *Tellestims* which haunt ancient buildings and guard
buried treasures, besides other uncanny beings whose
propensities resemble those of the goblins and pixies of
Western Europe. Some houses are believed to be haunted
by *Djins* of the last-named description who are called *Ev-
Sahibi*—"Lords of the House." If these are good *Djins*,
they bring all kinds of prosperity to their hosts; and no
matter how idle or extravagant the goodwife may be,
everything goes well with the household. The *Ev-Sahibi*
are popularly said to be clothed in bridal garments edged
with tiny bells, the tinkling of which announces their
passage through the house, and they sometimes allow
themselves to be perceived by those whom they specially
honour with their favour. The malevolent *Ev-Sahibi*, on
the other hand, are most mischievous in disposition, and
destroy the property of the family, besides annoying its
members with intolerable nocturnal noises. In common
with other magical beings, these *Djins* have the power of
assuming any shape they please, from that of a shadowy
being of colossal proportions, or a beautiful youth or
maiden, down to that of a cat or dog, or even a pitcher or
broom. Both the good *Djins*, or Peris, who serve Allah,
and the evil *Djins*, the followers of Eblis, the Spirit of
Darkness, are believed to have been created before man,
Adam having, according to Oriental legend, married as
his second wife a woman belonging to this race, whose

name was Lilith. The evilly disposed *Djins* were cast out from heaven with Eblis, whose rebellion against the Most High consisted in his refusal to pay homage to the newly created Adam, when so commanded by his Creator. *Djins* are popularly held to be of both sexes, and appear also to propagate their kind. One of their propensities is to carry off by night the clothes of humans—especially the gala dresses of women—to wear at their nocturnal revels. And if such a garment appears to its owner to be rapidly losing its freshness, she concludes that the *Djins* have taken a fancy to it, and regrets not having had it " blessed " by some holy man before wearing it—which precaution would have rendered it safe from the depredations of these uncanny folk.

The magical practices of the Osmanlis, though derived in great part from legendary lore, are also borrowed to a considerable extent from so-called " Occult Science." Not only all classes of Turks—save perhaps the most " advanced " section—but also the lower classes among their neighbours of other races, Christian and Jewish as well as Moslem, credit the professional wizards and witches, and especially the dervishes, who are the chief exponents of this "science," with the possession of an extraordinary degree of magical power. As sickness as well as every other calamity is usually attributed to the influence of a magical spell, when any one falls ill the women of the family—for it need hardly be said that the firmest believers in this mode of spiritual cure are of the female sex—send for some saintly Sheikh in order that he may remove the spell, or avert its maleficent influence. This holy man, whose breath, sanctified by the constant repetition of the name of the Deity, has acquired a supernatural healing power, proceeds to make a series of breathings on the head and the afflicted parts of the sufferer, accompanied by the imposition of his hands. These concluded, he produces a tiny scroll of paper inscribed with some words from the Koran, and orders it either to be swallowed by the patient or soaked in water and the liquid to be drunk, or perhaps to be worn on the person for a given number of days. The efficacy of these little scrolls can only be relied upon—according to the Sheikhs who prescribe them—if administered with their own hands. But whatever the success, or lack of success, of these strange remedies, nothing shakes the faith in them of the meek-minded. If they fail, it is from a want of faith on the part of the recipient. The holy man in any case receives a fee for his services either in coin or kind ; and if a speedy recovery follow his visit this will be proportionately liberal. The words used as exorcisms and counterspells are, for the most part, taken from the two chapters of the Koran relating to witchcraft and malevolence— [1]

"Say, I fly for refuge unto the Lord of the Daybreak, that he may deliver me from the mischief of these things

---

[1] Chaps. cxiii. and cxiv. Compare *Cymbeline*, act ii. scene 2—

> "To your protection I commend me, Gods!
> From fairies, and the tempters of the night
> Guard me, beseech ye ! "

which he hath created, and from the mischief of the night
when it cometh on, and from the mischief of women
blowing on knots, and from the mischief of the envious,"
etc.

Moslem commentators relate that the reason for the
revelation of the above chapter of the Koran and the
one following it was that a Jew named Lobeid had, with
the assistance of his daughters, bewitched Mohammed
himself by tying with evil intent eleven knots in a
cord which they hid in a well. The Prophet falling ill in
consequence, this chapter and the following were revealed,
the Angel Gabriel acquainting him with the use he was to
make of them, and telling him where the cord was hidden.
The cord being found and brought to Mohammed by Ali
his nephew, he repeated these chapters over it; at every
verse a knot was loosed, and on finishing the recitation,
he found himself set free from the charm. Knots are also
tied with good intent, as I have myself witnessed. It
was by the tomb of St. Demetrius in the fine basilica
of that name at Salonica, converted into a mosque at
the conquest by the Turks of that city. St. Demetrius
belongs to the class of saints termed by the Greeks
myroblutai, whose relics exude a sweet savour;[1] and the

---

[1] An odoriferous unguent (μύρον) is supposed to exude from the
bones of certain saints who from this circumstance are called μυροβλύται.
Of these St. Nicholas is one; another is one of the companions of
St. Clara, buried in the little convent of St. Damiano near Assisi; a
third is St. Catherine. Referring to the relics of the last named in
Mount Sinai, Sir John Mandeville wrote: " The Prelate of the Monkes
schewethe the Relykes to the Pilgrymes; and with an instrument of

Dervish guardian of his tomb, taking from under the slab
a piece of cord, proceeded to tie knots in it for the benefit
of a young matron of our party, a knot for each relative of
the first degree of herself and her husband. This he
directed her to wear, girdlewise, round her waist whenever
assailed by any of the ills to which female flesh is especially heir, when the results would be—in a word—magical !

Calculations intended as charms or talismans are made,
among other methods, by cabalistic calculations based on
, the numerical value of the letters comprising the name of
the person interested. In a divination for the purpose of
fortune-telling, these numerical values are multiplied and
divided, and their cubes and squares added and subtracted
according to some conventional formula, to obtain a result,
odd or even, odd being considered lucky, and even the
reverse. Some of the charms purchased from these
diviners are believed to possess, like the magical objects
of folk-tales, the power of compelling visits from beneficent *Djins*, who cure the suffering in body, ease the
troubled in mind, and grant the wishes of the invokers.
The sacred and mysterious character attributed by
Orientals to the letters of the alphabet has given rise to
the notion that Allah has appointed to each its special
attendant *Djin*, who may be invoked singly or in company
with his fellows. In order to secure the presence —

Sylver he frotethe the Bones : and thanne ther gothe out a lytylle
Oyle, as thoughe it were in a manner swatynge, that is nouther like to
Oyle ne to Bawme ; but it is fulle swete of smelle " (quoted by
Mr. Athelstan Riley in *Mount Athos*, p. 127 n.).

invisible, of course—of these "Slaves of the Letter," the calculations must be drawn up at special phases of the moon and positions of the stars, on certain days and at stated hours. Texts from the Koran, or invocations of the Prophet or the Khalif Ali, engraved on stones brought from the Holy Cities of Islam or from the vicinity of the tombs of the sainted dead, are also worn on the person as charms. In former centuries it was customary to inscribe over the gates of conquered cities, and on such public edifices as fountains and mosques, "talismans" in verse, composed by the eminent dervishes always to be found with the armies of the conquering Sultans; and some of these may still be seen on ancient edifices at Constantinople and at various towns of Asia Minor. When the assistance of the "Slaves of the Letter" is invoked for the purpose of inspiring an indifferent person with the tender passion, the *Djins* summoned devise in council a series of influences which will compel the person in question to obey their behests. The only means of resisting their influence lies in procuring a counter-charm composed of letters that will ensure the attendance of another set of *Djins* who will either overcome the first, or compel them to agree to a compromise, and thus release the victim from the power of the spell.

In Asiatic Turkey, during the long winter nights between the 27th November and the 5th January (Old Style), when elemental spirits are generally supposed to be especially alert, uncanny beings called *Fishoti* are believed to haunt the abodes of men; and throughout this period

infants and children of tender age must be specially
guarded against the malevolence of these nocturnal
visitants. If a window should after sunset happen to be
left the least bit open, or a door ajar, the *Fishoti* will enter
and call the inmates by their names. Woe to him who
should be so imprudent as to answer, for the *Djin* would
then tear out his tongue and carry it off, shrieking meanwhile with demoniacal laughter. After the 5th January,
however, the *Fishoti* ceases from troubling, being, it is
supposed, frightened away to his desert haunts by the
bonfires lighted by the Christians on that date in honour
of St. John. As the word *Fishóti* has no meaning in any
of the languages of the present inhabitants of these regions,
it is supposed to be, together with the superstition attached
to it, a survival from some other race formerly inhabiting
Eastern Asia Minor.

Perhaps, however, the most gruesome among Oriental
superstitions is belief in the existence of Vampires. This
notion, which is common to all the races of South-Eastern
Europe, has been traced by scholars to an Asiatic origin,
as, in the great Chaldean Epic of the third millennium
B.C., Istar in Hades gives utterance to the threat, " I will
cause the dead to rise and devour the living." For the
Vampire is no nebulous "ghost," but the actual resuscitated body of a man—the *Vurkolak* is generally, if not
invariably, of the masculine sex—supposed to be possessed
of the power of emerging from his grave in the dead of
night, when he roams abroad, revelling in blood. The
causes of vampirism are various, and among them are the

following : The fact either of having perpetrated, or of
having been the victim of, the crime of murder ; having
grievously wronged some person who has died resenting
the wrong ; or having been made the subject of a curse,
lay or ecclesiastical.   Vampirism is also held to be
hereditary in certain families, the unfortunate members
of which are naturally regarded with aversion, and shunned
by their neighbours.   Their services may, however, be
requisitioned when there is a vampire to be " laid," as
they have the reputation of possessing special powers in
that direction.   It is popularly believed that a vampire,
like a ghost, must return to his grave before cockcrow, and
if possible he will be tracked to it by such of his neighbours
as are found bold enough for the exploit, accompanied,
probably, both by Moslem Hodja and Christian Priest ;
and the various exorcisms to which recourse is had will
probably be effectual in putting an end to the nocturnal
wanderings of the ghoul.   Many vampire panics are no
doubt attributable to rumours set on foot by persons who
profit by such superstitions, and the following is, I think,
a case in point.   Some years ago the whole population
of Adrianople was thrown into a state of commotion by
the reported nightly appearance of a spectre in an elevated
part of the town known as Kyik, inhabited both by Turks
and Greeks.   This spectre was represented as a *Vurkolak*
by persons who affirmed that they had seen it lurking
in the shadows—a long, lank object with a cadaverous
visage, clad in a winding-sheet.   Priest and Hodja strove
in vain during a fortnight to exorcise the wanderer by

their prayers and incantations ; and finally a rumour was circulated that the only person possessed of the power of freeing the city from this haunting spectre was a Turkish *djindji*, or magician, famous for his influence over apparitions, who lived in a distant town, and who would consequently require a substantial fee for his services. Seven hundred piastres—about £6 sterling—were, however, speedily raised by the panic-stricken townsfolk. The *djindji* came, and the *Vurkolak* was put to flight.[1] Should all exorcisms prove futile, as sometimes happens, the people of the neighbourhood proceed by daylight to the grave of the reputed vampire, and either drive a stake through the heart of the undissolving corpse, or disinter and consume it with fire.[2]

[1] See Lady Blunt's *The People of Turkey*. (Murray, 1878.)

[2] Pashley's *Travels in Crete* contains (p. 226) a graphic account of this last method of disposing of a vampire.

CHAPTER VIII

FASTS, FEASTS, AND PILGRIMAGE

THE annual fasts observed by Moslems are seven in number, the most important being the month-long fast of Ramazan. This period of abstinence is held to be of divine institution, and its observance is therefore compulsory for all True Believers over the age of fourteen, travellers and the sick being alone exempt. Ramazan is celebrated in the ninth month of the Moham-medan year, during the whole of which food, drink, and tobacco are rigidly abstained from between sunrise and sunset. The year consisting, as previously mentioned, of twelve lunar months only, the fast makes in the course of time the round of the seasons. To the wealthy this annual period of penitence offers no great hardship, as they merely turn night into day, and official duties are reduced to a minimum in the departments of State. But to the labouring section of the population, who are the most punctilious in the performance of religious observances, Ramazan, especially when it falls in summer, constitutes a period of real penance and mortification of the flesh. For Moslems generally this fast constitutes a sort of revival time, during which Western innovations,

wherever adopted, are for the time being abandoned, and
the simpler native customs reverted to. Services are held
every evening in the mosques, hospitality is largely
exercised, and the poor are loaded with benefits in
response to the exhortation of the *Muessim*, who concludes
the usual call to prayer with the words, "Give food, all ye
Faithful, unto the orphan and the indigent, the wayfarer
and the bondsman, for His sake, saying, We feed you for
Allah's sake, and we desire no word of thanks from you,
nor any recompense." Much time is also devoted during
this season to religious observances and devotional acts,
many devout persons of both sexes habitually secluding
themselves for a part of each day, either at home or in the
mosques, and—especially during the last ten days of the
fast—abstaining from all worldly conversation. An hour
or so before dawn the "awakeners"—a Hodja carrying a
small hemispherical drum, accompanied by a boy with a
lantern—go through the streets of the quarter to warn
those who sleep that it is time to partake of the *sahor*, the
last meal eaten before sunrise. Stopping before every
house occupied by Moslems, the Hodja chants the following phrases: "He prospereth who saith, 'There is no God
save Allah! Mohammed, the Guide, is the Prophet of
Allah!'" preluded and followed by four rhythmical taps
on the drum; after which he passes on with the greeting,
"The happiest of nights unto thee, O Ali!" or whatever
may be the name of the householder. The meal partaken of, coffee-drinking and smoking fill up the brief
interval until the boom of cannon announces sunrise, when

the mouth is rinsed with water and "sealed" until evening.

Shortly before sunset the last *namas* of the day is performed either in public or private, previously to which the women of the household will have made preparations for the *iftar*, as the evening meal eaten during Ramazan is termed. It is usual to serve first a variety of *hors d'œuvres*, together with goblets of iced fruit sherbet, and each person begins operations with the word *Bismillah*— " In the name of Allah "—uttered as he helps himself to an olive, some special merit attaching to breaking the fast with that edible. After the *messliks*, as these trifles are collectively named, have been sparingly partaken of, the party sit down to the *iftar*, at which long, flat, unleavened cakes, plentifully besprinkled with sesame seed, are substituted for bread, and the usual courses are supplemented by various dainties prepared only at this season. It is also customary to present plates of these Ramazan dainties to Christian neighbours with whom a Turkish family may be on visiting terms, as well as to poor Moslem households. Shortly afterwards the service of devotion known as the *Terraweh* is performed either in private or in the mosque. In the reign of Abdul Aziz it was customary for the Moslems of Stamboul of both sexes to repair in great numbers after this service to the wide esplanade in front of the Suleymanieh mosque, which, at that hour, would be crowded with elegant equipages containing Turkish *hanums*, or high dignitaries of State, and also with throngs of pedestrians of every rank—a gathering

L

which partook somewhat of a carnival character, petty
missiles being thrown and other liberties indulged in at
the expense of the occupants of the carriages which would
not at any other time have been ventured on. The stricter
régime of the present reign, however, long ago put an end
to all such nocturnal assemblies; and it remains to be
seen whether advantage will be taken of the unwonted
liberty conferred by the Constitution to revive them.

On the twenty-seventh day of Ramazan is celebrated
the anniversary of the "Night of Power," or, as it is also
termed, the "Excellent Night," in which the Koran is
said to have been sent down by Allah from the "Upper"
to the "Lower Heaven," whence it was revealed in portions
to the Prophet by the Angel Gabriel. During certain
hours of this night, which is also called the "Night of
Destiny," it is popularly believed that the waters of the
sea become sweet; that the whole animal and vegetable
creations prostrate themselves in humble adoration before
Allah; and that the destinies of men for the coming year
are revealed to the Recording Angels. The conclusion of
Ramazan is celebrated by the three days' festival of
Bairam, also called by names signifying respectively the
"Breaking of the Fast" and the "Feast of Alms," during
which no work of any kind is done. On the first day
of Bairam, every well-to-do person makes a present
to his children, his slaves, and his subordinates, besides
giving liberally to the poor. In the mornings the streets
are thronged with people in holiday costume, who go
from house to house paying complimentary visits to

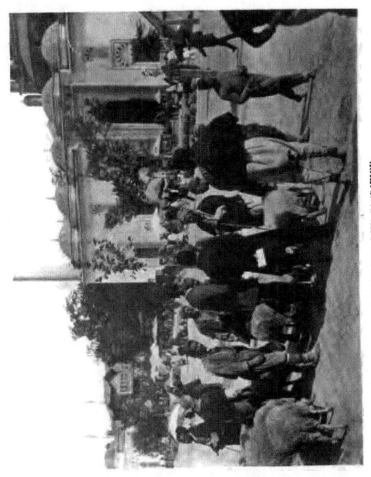

LAMBS FOR THE SACRIFICE

friends and official superiors; and after attending the midday *namas* in the mosques, the whole Moslem population abandons itself to decorous amusement.

A still more important festival than the "Breaking of the Fast" is the *Qurban Bairam*, or "Feast of Sacrifice," which takes place during the season of the pilgrimage to Mekka described in the course of this chapter, its observance forming part of the rites of the pilgrims while at the Holy City. It is commemorative of Abraham's sacrifice, Ishmael being substituted for Isaac in the Mohammedan version of the story. For a week or more prior to this festival the market-place of every town and Turkish village throughout the Empire is occupied by flocks of sheep and lambs, and in the Capital the wide open space in front of the beautiful mosque of Bayazid presents at this season a particularly picturesque and interesting spectacle. For here are gathered countless flocks, chiefly of the broad-tailed Karamanian breed, prospective victims for the traditional sacrifice, tended by a variety of wild-looking nomads in shaggy sheepskin coats—Vlachs from the Balkans, and Kurds, Yuruks, and Turcomans from the hills and plains of Asia Minor. Among them wander Moslem townsmen of all ranks, and each householder who can afford the outlay purchases a lamb for the sacrifice. Until its day of doom the poor victim is made a plaything of by the children, who dye its fleece with henna or cochineal, and cover its budding horns with gold-leaf. When on the morn of the festival the pet is no longer to be found in courtyard or garden, the disconsolate babies are told that it has "been sent to the hills to eat grass, or it would die, poor thing." The flesh is divided into three portions, one of which is given to the poor, the second to widowed or other relations, the remaining third being eaten by the household. The rejoicings connected with this festival last four days. New garments are donned in its honour by both sexes and all classes, and gifts and almsgiving are the order of the day. These mild festivals are also punctuated with the spasmodic firing of volleys of small arms by the youth of the quarter—this being the Oriental equivalent of squibs and crackers—the sound of which seldom fails to create a certain amount of uneasiness among their Christian neighbours, varying in degree according to the political atmosphere of the moment. For in the history of their own times many have had tragical experience of how "great events from little causes spring." Quantities of cheap toys are, during the three days of Bairam, exhibited for sale in the public thoroughfares, and every one calling on friends and neighbours to wish them a "Happy Bairam" will be laden with such offerings for the children, sure to be found with their male relations in the *selamlik* on these occasions.

Traditional custom has made it imperative for the reigning Sultan to "open the Bairam" each year in person. At an early hour accordingly, the Padishah, attended by the highest dignitaries of State, Civil and Military, repairs to the mosque, the roadway being lined with troops who greet his appearance with loyal and enthusiastic cries of "Long live our Padishah!" echoed by the throng of spectators in their rear. A levée is subsequently held by the Sultan, at which a vast throng, consisting of Ministers and high officials, assemble to pay their homage to the "Shadow of Allah;" and the various foreign ambassadors, and other members of the *corps diplomatique*, together with any other foreigners of distinction who may be visiting the Turkish Capital, attend to offer their congratulations on this auspicious occasion. During former reigns this State opening of the Bairam always took place at one of the so-called "Imperial" mosques in Stamboul such as Ayia Sofía, the Suleymanieh, or the Achmedieh, when multitudes of the Faithful would assemble in the streets and squares to greet their Sovereign. And it is hoped that Sultan Abdul Hamid, freed from the baneful misrepresentations of the "Camarilla" who have so long surrounded him, and convinced of the loyalty of his subjects of all creeds, will for the future abandon the semi-private ceremony in the Hamidieh mosque attached to his palace, and resume the time-honoured customs in this respect of his illustrious predecessors.

The *Mevlud*, or Birthday of the Prophet, and the "Feast of the Holy Mantle," are also important Moslem festivals. On the latter occasion it is customary for the Sultan to proceed in state to the "Old Serai" at the eastward point of Stamboul, washed on one side by the waters of the Sea of Marmora and on the other by those of the Golden Horn. For in the private mosque enclosed with

other storied buildings within the encircling walls of this
ancient home of the Dynasty of Osman, is enshrined this
sacred relic, which, at the conclusion of the midday *namas*,
the Padishah, in his capacity of Khalif, or "Successor,"
unfolds with great solemnity from its forty silken wrappers.
The Prophet's mantle, which is displayed to the select
company of high officials who have the honour of accompanying their Sovereign, is said to be merely a small
fragment of cloth of a greenish colour.   The mosques and
public buildings are illuminated on the eve of all these
festivals, the day being reckoned by Moslems, as by
Orientals generally, from sunset to sunset.   Very charming is the effect of the myriads of tiny oil-lamps circling
the tall minarets, outlining the domes and cupolas, and
hanging in fairy-like festoons from point to point.
Occasionally, too, the banks of the Bosphorus present
an endless range of lambent flames, interspersed with
fanals, or cressets, with here and there on prominent
headlands a blazing bonfire ; these myriad points of light,
reflected and multiplied in the broad rushing current,
producing an effect at once mysterious and enchanting.

As mentioned in a previous chapter, pilgrimage to the
Holy Cities of Islam is one of the Five Pillars of Practice
of the Mohammedan religion.   It is indeed considered the
supreme act in the life of a True Believer, its due performance entitling him to a variety of spiritual blessings
in the life to come, and for the rest of his life on earth to
the appellation of *Hadji*, and to accomplish it the pious
shrink from no privation and fear no peril.   Plundered by

brigand bands and slain by Arab tribesmen, tossed on
stormy waters in unseaworthy craft, their bones have for
thirteen centuries past whitened the desert tracks and
their bodies fed the fishes.   The distance lying between
his home and the Holy Cities has never been regarded by
the True Believer as an unsurmountable obstacle to his
visiting them, and attaining his most fervent desire to
behold the Holy Kaaba before he dies ; and should he
chance to perish by the way, he dies resigned to the decree
of *Kismet*, for he has at least the merit of being on the
road to that sacred spot.   Never has danger diminished
pilgrims' zeal, and every year an increasing multitude—
" arriving," to use the Prophet's words, " on foot, and on
every lean camel, by every distant road "—has gathered
to hear the sermon on Mount Arafat and take part in the
time-honoured ceremony of casting stones at the devil in
the Valley of Moona.   Now, however, that the Pilgrims'
Railway reaches Medina, the'Prophet's burial-place, the only
perilous stage of the journey for pilgrims from the West
will be that between this city and Mekka ; and the devout
Turk will, ere long, when the intervening 285 miles of rail
are completed, be able to take the train at Haidar Pasha
on the Eastern shore of the Bosphorus, at Damascus, or at
Haifa on the Syrian coast, and—while still following more
or less the Old Pilgrims' Road—proceed direct to the
birthplace of the Prophet.

   A complete pilgrimage includes, in addition to Mekka,
visits to the Prophet's tomb at Medina, to the shrines of
the Saints at Damascus and Jerusalem ; and also to the

tombs of Mohammed's grandsons, Hassan and Hussein, at
Kerbeleh near Bagdad.   Only dervishes and the most
zealous, however, aim at becoming such complete pilgrims,
the majority being satisfied with having accomplished this
religious duty in the obligatory degree.   The three lunar
months of *Shawal, Dhulkaade,* and *Dhulhajja* are dedicated
to the pilgrimage which culminates in the rites appointed
for the tenth day of the last-named month, after the performance of which a pilgrim is entitled to style himself
Hadji.   Previously to leaving home with this pious object,
a Moslem is required to set his worldly affairs in order,
pay any outstanding debts, and make suitable provision
for the maintenance of his family during his absence.
It has hitherto been customary for pilgrims from Constantinople and the neighbourhood to assemble fourteen
days before the festival of the *Qurban Bairam*—"The
Feast of Sacrifice"—in one of the large open spaces of
Stamboul, where a procession is formed.   This comprises
a number of camels with gorgeously ornamented saddles
bearing the coffers containing the Sultan's gifts to the
holy shrines, together with the alms and presents of his
well-to-do subjects for the religious trustees of their
respective families in the cities of Mekka and Medina.
Other camels carry a kind of palanquin covered with
costly silken stuffs in which lady pilgrims will perform
part of the journey.   A company of picturesquely garbed
Arabs who accompany the Caravan exhibit at every halt-
ing-place, to the accompaniment of kettledrums, feats of
swordsmanship to the crowds of spectators which surround

and follow the procession and its military escort through the streets and across the long bridge spanning the Golden Horn on its way to Yildiz Kiosk, where the pilgrims salute the Sultan before embarking. The best view of this quaint procession is obtained as it mounts the steep road leading to the palace, now lined with troops of the Imperial guard. The rising ground on either side has the appearance of a flower garden, covered as it is with the variously hued cloaks and white headgear of thousands of Turkish women of the lower orders. The Sultan, himself unseen, is believed to be at one of the windows of Yildiz Kiosk to receive the salutation of the departing pilgrims, who, after offering up in unison a prayer for the success of their undertaking, retrace their steps to the quay, whence they embark for the Asiatic shore. Before the construction of the existing railway the pilgrim caravan, after crossing the Bosphorus, made the long journey to Arabia by land ; at Damascus it was joined by thousands of pilgrims from Africa, Asia Minor, and Syria, and thence, under the command of a special official styled the "Steward of the Offerings," and escorted by troops, it began its long journey across the desert to the Holy Cities.

The *ihram*, the "sacred habit" of the pilgrims, is donned just before setting foot on the holy soil surrounding the shrines of Islam, its adoption being preceded by special ablutions and various prescribed formulas of prayers and prostration. It consists of two white wrappers of thin woollen stuff, each woven in one piece without seam or hem ; one envelops the shoulders, leaving the

arms bare; the other is fastened round the waist and falls
to the ankles. On the feet is worn a kind of sandal, a
mere sole of leather secured by a thong passing between
the first and second and the fourth and fifth toes. While
wearing the *ihram* a pilgrim must refrain from shaving,
neither must he trim his beard or nails. It is now incumbent on him to follow with the greatest strictness the
three leading principles of Moslem religious practice,
namely, prayer, fasting, and almsgiving. "Prayer," said
the Prophet, "carries us halfway to God; fasting brings
us to the door of His palace; almsgiving procures our
admittance." The rosary so often seen in the hands of
a Moslem is never absent from that of a pilgrim when
wearing the *ihram*, and it behoves him to be especially
punctilious in the performance of the five daily *namas*
with their preceding ablutions. Additional acts of devotion are also customary during the four days preceding
the Hadj-day, these being generally performed during
the hours of night, and accompanied by prostrations
and other "prayerful exercises." "The odour of the
mouth of him that fasteth is more acceptable to Allah
than the odour of musk." Not only the mouth, however,
but all the other members are required to practise abstinence during these holy days—the ear must refuse to
listen to slander, the tongue refrain from the utterance of
any words save those of a pure and holy character, the
hands from touching that which is another's, the feet from
straying into forbidden places, and the eyes from looking
upon a woman. And the almsgiving incumbent upon a

pilgrim of means includes, besides the legal alms—which range, according to circumstances, from two and a half to twenty per cent. of his possessions—the giving largely to the poor and needy of his camels, kine, and sheep, and of his provisions, coin, and marketable wares.

For pilgrims who have made part of their journey by sea, it is at Jeddah that their worst perils begin to assail them. The natives plunder them to the best of their ability, from the boatmen who convey them from the steamer to the Bedouin camel- and donkey-drivers in whose company they traverse the intervening miles of desert.[1] Caravans consisting of from five hundred to two thousand camels start daily from this port for Mekka during the pilgrimage season until a week before the Great Day of the Hadj, travelling by night for the most part. On arriving at their destination the pilgrims anxiously await the commencement of the Hadj, the date of which is decided by the moon being seen on rising at a certain spot—for, the Moslem year being, as previously observed, lunar, all religious events vary with every succeeding year. The welcome tidings announced, the pilgrims spend the morrow in visiting the mosque and the Kaaba, offering prayers at this and the various other holy places during nearly the whole of the day ;

---

[1] The Constantinople journal *Stamboul* reports (February 16, 1909) that a pilgrim steamer having lately grounded in the Suez Canal, its passengers, who numbered nearly a thousand, were, in consequence of the exactions of the Hedjaz population, found to be in such a destitute condition that the charitable governor of Suez caused money and provisions to be distributed among them.

partaking of the water of the Zemzem and kissing the
Black Stone of the Kaaba also constituting part of this
ceremonial, which is performed fasting. The Kaaba is a
square temple constructed of unhewn stones into one wall
of which is built the famous Black Stone, a meteorite, said
to have originally been white, and to have descended from
heaven. According to Moslem tradition, this temple is
the most ancient House of God, having been built by
Adam and restored by Abraham, as the Zemzem is
probably the most ancient spring of which any record
exists. Its discovery in the desert led to the foundation
of the City of Mekka, and for centuries past it has been
one of the most venerated objects in the Mohammedan
world, the virtues attributed to its waters being doubtless
due to the mineral salts with which they are strongly
impregnated.

At sunset the fast is broken, the ensuing night being
passed chiefly in prayer and devotional exercises. On
the following day a vast procession sets out for Mount
Arafat, on a certain spot on the lower slopes of which
eminence a sheep or goat is sacrificed by each Hadji who
can afford it, the wealthy giving to others of their abundance for this pious purpose. The plain at the foot of
Mount Arafat presents on this day the appearance of a
vast camp, being covered with thousands of tents belonging to pilgrims of the better class gathered here from all
quarters of the world for the fulfilment of one of the most
sacred rites of their common Faith. Their sacrificial
offering made, the pilgrims resume their way to Moona,

where the festival of the *Qurban Bairam* is celebrated. In the valley of Moona is a rough stone structure called the "House of the Devil," at which it is obligatory on all pilgrims to cast stones in order to deter the Father of Evil from approaching this assembly of the Faithful. This festival marks the formal termination of the pilgrimage, the newly made Hadjis being now at liberty to set out on their return journey, though the more devout will not rest satisfied without having also visited the City of Medina and performed their devotions at the tomb of the great founder of the Faith they profess.

This religious duty of pilgrimage, it may here be remarked, is as binding on women as on men. An adult woman must, however, be at least nominally married before setting out, and be accompanied either by her husband or some near male relative who has a right to see her unveiled, while young girls can only go when accompanied by both parents. When their male companions don the "sacred habit," the women are even more hermetically shrouded in their cloaks and veils than ordinarily, it being lawful for the palms of their hands alone to be visible to the other sex.

Should any person desirous of accomplishing this religious duty be prevented by bodily infirmity, or other cause, from accomplishing it in his own person, as may not unfrequently happen, it may be performed by deputy. In order that the full merit of the act may accrue to himself, such a person must, however, defray all the expenses incidental to the pilgrimage, and at the same time satisfy the religious authorities who sanction the transaction that the funds have been honestly and honourably acquired—this being a *sine quâ non* for permission to set out on pilgrimage. Aged or dying persons who have not performed the pilgrimage also repeatedly leave testamentary instructions to the same effect. This practice was curiously illustrated in the case of Khamko, the redoubtable mother of the still more redoubtable Ali Pasha of Ioannina, who, in a codicil to her will, directed that such a deputy should be sent on her part to lay offerings on the tomb of the Prophet and pray for the repose of her soul. It was, however, found on inquiry that the lands directed to be sold for this purpose had been taken by force or fraud from their original owner, a Christian ; and the pilgrimage was consequently disallowed by the religious authorities.

In addition to this obligatory pilgrimage, Moslems, and especially Moslem women, make frequent visitations to the shrines of famous saints, who are for the most part the deceased sheikhs of dervish orders. *Ziarets*, as these lesser pilgrimages are termed, are generally undertaken in fulfilment of a vow, or for relief from sickness or other distress, in obedience to the traditional sayings of the Prophet, "If thou art perplexed in thine affairs, go seek assistance from the inhabitants of the tombs," and "If thine heart be oppressed with sorrow, go seek consolation at the graves of holy men." They are usually made on the *Mevlud*, or annual feast day of the saint—should not the circumstances demand immediate recourse to his good offices—when it is customary for suppliants or visitors to bring with them, in addition to gifts in coin or kind, a lamb or fowl for sacrifice, the flesh of which constitutes the perquisite of the guardian of the *turbeh*, generally a dervish.   Benefits which are believed to have resulted from the intercession of the saint are gratefully acknowledged by wealthy recipients with gifts of rich shawls as coverings for the *sunduk*, or catafalque, which stands over the resting-place of the holy dead.

CHAPTER IX

INTELLECTUAL PROGRESS

FOREIGNERS coming for the first time into contact with Osmanlis belonging to the higher classes of society, are often surprised to find how high a degree of education and culture has been attained by both men and women. In official circles at least the generality of men speak French, and many read, if they do not speak, English ; while in every large town there will probably be found more Turks well acquainted with a foreign language than would be met with in a corresponding class in any Western country. It must not, however, be supposed that a proportionately high level of instruction exists among the Moslem subjects of the Sultan generally. For, as will be evident from even a cursory survey of present methods, the establishment of a less antiquated system of primary national education constitutes one of the most pressing needs of the Turkish people. At the present day in educational, as in other departments in Turkey, two distinct systems exist side by side, the Ancient, instituted at the Conquest and common to all Moslem countries, and the Modern, initiated in the earlier half of the last century, and greatly developed during the last forty years. The educational establishments belonging to the first class comprise the *Mahallah Mektebs*, or parish schools, and the *Medressehs*, or Mosque Colleges, both supported by the funds of the mosques of which they are for the most part dependencies. Though now left so far behind, there is perhaps no country in Europe in which primary education was provided for at so early a date as in Turkey, and so many inducements held out to poor parents to allow their children to participate in its benefits. The *Mektebs* afford primary instruction to children of both sexes over eight years of age, for which a nominal annual fee is sometimes paid, though at some of the better endowed parish schools each pupil is entitled to receive two suits of clothing a year, while at others the benefactions of pious donors provide in addition free meals and pocket-money. The *Hodjas*, or masters of these parish schools, are at the same time functionaries of the mosques to which they are attached, and the instruction given by them is chiefly of a religious character, though elementary lessons in reading and writing have of late years been added to the curriculum. Squatting in rows on the matted floor, the children learn partly from their books, but chiefly by rote, reciting the lesson in unison, while the Hodja, who sits cross-legged at a low desk, expounds to them the doctrines of the Koran which, being invariably used in Arabic, naturally present considerable difficulties to the infant mind. Inattentive pupils receive severe corporal punishment, and are further disgraced by having also the *felakka*, a kind of hobble, attached to one of their ankles.

M

In former centuries the Moslem population of Turkey was divided into two distinct classes, the *Ulema*, or learned, and the unlettered, the former comprising only the graduates of the *Medressehs*, from whose ranks came those who were at the same time the exponents of religious dogma and the administrators of the law of the land, there being at that time no secular system of jurisprudence, as at present. The changes in the legal administration effected during the past century have, however, deprived the Mosque Colleges of their former importance, and their graduates now consist chiefly of those who aspire to become permanent members of the *Ulema*, functionaries of the mosques, professors in their turn in the *Medressehs*, or legal practitioners in what may be termed the Ecclesiastical Courts of which the Sheikh-ul-Islam is the head. These *Medressehs* resemble in some respects the Universities of Continental Europe as they existed in mediæval days, and, as already observed, owe their origin to the munificence of Sultans and grandees of former centuries, whose endowments of the mosques supported also their educational and charitable foundations attached to them, the lectures being very frequently given in the mosque itself. The revenues of the majority of these religious foundations have, however, of late years, owing to changes in their administration, greatly diminished ; and the students who in olden days invariably received, in addition to free quarters, certain daily rations from the college kitchen and oil for their lamps, now enjoy such free commons only on special days, and even the fabric of many of these ancient edifices can hardly be saved from ruin. The residential quarters occupied by the students are usually built in the form of a quadrangle surrounding a courtyard, and the arrangements are quite mediæval in character, several youths often occupying one apartment in which they study, sleep, and do their own frugal cooking. The latest freshman is also required to "fag" for the tutor who supervises the studies of the class to which he belongs. Very poor are many of these youthful students of the Sacred Law; but living is fortunately still cheap in Turkey, and from 12*s.* to 15*s.* per month suffices for their subsistence. In the Capital alone there are said to be no fewer than a hundred of these *Medressehs*, and one or more may be found in every provincial town. At the present day, however, the main subjects of study in the *Medressehs* may be classed under the two heads of "Theology" and "Language," the former including, besides knowledge of the Koran and Moslem Law, the *Hadis*, or Traditions, with the Commentaries thereon, and the latter comprising grammar, rhetoric, poetry, and calligraphy. The number of *Softas* accommodated in the *Medressehs* of the Capital at the present day is estimated at about six thousand, the majority of whom are quite impecunious; and in such great religious centres as Konieh, the ancient Iconium, they are also very numerous. The diminished revenues of the religious foundations no longer affording maintenance to students at the *Medressehs* as heretofore, many undergraduates during the month of Ramazan make tours among the provincial towns and villages, where they preach or do special duty in the mosques, returning equipped with funds derived from fees and alms sufficient to enable them to continue their frugal college life.

The instruction afforded in the Mosque Schools and Colleges at the present day, being of so restricted and conservative character, is, it must be admitted, hardly calculated to advance the cause of general enlightenment in the Ottoman Empire. But limited though their curriculum now is, and antiquated as their methods undoubtedly are, these *Medressehs* constituted in former days important centres of learning, as they then afforded not only theological teaching but also instruction in all the branches of knowledge then available. And seeing that the numerous poets, historians, and philosophers, of whose literary eminence Turkey can rightly boast, were, during many centuries, graduates of the *Medressehs*, it must be admitted that they have in the past done good service and more than justified their existence. Few Europeans are, indeed, aware of the literary wealth to which the Turkish people can lay claim, or have any idea of the high degree of culture that has prevailed during the centuries of the Ottoman dominion. Many of the ablest rulers of Turkey, for instance, were wont to find in poetic composition distraction and solace amid the great enterprises that signalised their respective reigns, and displayed a degree of taste and ability that would have made the literary reputation of private individuals. Out of the thirty-four Sultans of the House of Osman, no fewer than twenty-one have been men of letters, and eleven of these are adjudged by posterity to have been poets of distinction— a record surely unparalleled in the annals of any European Dynasty. Following their example, not only princes of the blood—such as, for instance, the gifted and unfortunate Djem Shah [1]—but also Viziers, Muftis, and more or less the whole lettered class of the nation added to their functions, civil, military, and political, the cult of the poetic muse.

It is, I believe, generally admitted that climate and scenery exert an important influence on character and intellect, as well as on sentiment and belief. And the serene spirit of Islam, combined with the clear blue skies, the soft sun-pervaded atmosphere, the flowery and fruitful plains, and the grand grouping of mountain, stream, and sea in the fair regions occupied by the Turkish people, may be said to have given to their national poetry a character at once mystically religious and languorously romantic. With the establishment in the fifteenth century of the native language as a legitimate medium of literary expression—instead of, as previously, the acquired Persian —verse-writing became general, and never since has the

[1] Djem Shah was a younger brother of Sultan Bayazid II., with whom he claimed to share the sovereignty of Turkey. Defeated in battle, he took refuge with the Knights of Rhodes, who transferred him to one after another of their Commanderies in Europe. On March 13th, 1489, Prince Djem was imprisoned in the Vatican by Pope Alexander VI., and six years later, on being compulsorily handed over to Charles VIII. of France, he died at Naples, it was believed of poison, which had been previously administered to him by this Borgian Pope.

land of the Sultans lacked poets to sing the prowess of
Moslem arms, the beauties and mysteries of Nature, and
the charms of harem *hûris*. The names of quite an
extraordinary number of writers both of verse and prose
are consequently to be found in Ottoman biographical
dictionaries ; but no work exists, I believe, in any language
giving a complete history of the literature of this nation.
Persian had been the Court language of the Seljukian
Sultans who, before coming into Asia Minor, had overrun Persia, the less civilised race adopting the language
and culture of the more civilised people they subjugated,
and Persian became also the literary language of the
Osmanli Turks on their becoming heirs to the Seljukian
kingdom.

One of the chief peculiarities of Ottoman, as of Persian
poems is, it may here be remarked, that they almost
invariably contain concealed beneath their literal meaning
an esoteric and spiritual signification. A certain number
of famous poems may, indeed, be read for the most part for
what they appear on the surface to be—religious or moral
works. But to those who possess the key to their hidden
meaning, many constitute spiritual allegories representing
the yearning of the soul of man for union with the Deity,
or its love of and quest for the highest type of spiritual
beauty and virtue. The *Ghasels*, or Odes, present the
same characteristic as the longer poems. Though on the
surface either mere bacchanalian verses or voluptuous
love-songs, the initiated can recognise in their symbolic
imagery the fervent outpourings of hearts ecstasied, or,

as they express it, "intoxicated" with spiritual love. For every word in these effusions has its accepted mystical signification. The "Fair One" for whom sighs the Lover, Man, is the Deity, the "Beloved" whom he entreats to throw off the veil that conceals her perfect beauty from his sight. The "Ruby Lip" signifies the unspoken, but heard and understood communications of the Divinity; "Nestling in the Fair One's tresses," comprehension of His hidden attributes; the "Embrace" is the revelation to man of the Divine Mysteries; "Separation," or "Absence" from the "Loved One," is the non-attainment of Oneness with the Deity; "Wine" is the Divine Love; the "Cupbearer" is the spiritual instructor, the "giver of the goblet of celestial aspiration"; the "Zephyr" is the breathing of the Spirit; the "Taper" the heavenly light kindling the torch in the heart of the Lover, Man. And so on through every detail. This peculiarity of Ottoman poetry is no doubt largely due to the fact that of the long line of poets who have during the past six centuries contributed to the treasure-house of Ottoman literature not a few of the most famous names have been those of Dervishes. So great, indeed, during several centuries was the influence exercised on literary taste by the Dervish Schools that every poet endeavoured to give a mystical turn to his or her effusions.

From the first half of the fourteenth century onwards Persian began to be abandoned for literary purposes in favour of native Turkish. Both the prose and verse productions in that language, previous to the end of the following century, are, however, adjudged by critics to be for the most part somewhat rude and uncouth, though one of the earliest Turkish writers who flourished in the reign of Orchan was of such eminence that he is to this day styled "The Father of Ottoman Literature." Oriental writers have always affected anonymity, and this author wrote under the *takhullus*, or pen-name of A'ashik—"the Loving"—to which name, according to the custom of those times, was added the title of "Pasha," to denote his high rank among scholars. This honorific title, together with such others as *Sheikh, Emir, Hunkiar, Shah,* and *Sultan,* are often found affixed to the names of Turkish poets and men of letters. Among A'ashik's numerous productions is an "Ode to Culture," from which the following lines, literally translated, have been taken :—

"Empty form is nothing more than body without soul
Structure in the world is of the great world-soul's design.
Culture vivifies the world ; else would there be but soulless form,
Knowledge is the breath of soul, and soul of all the souls.
Wanting knowledge, soul is dead, and like unto the dead.
Knowledge giveth to the Sultans empire over human souls.
Knowledge wanting, life is wanting, this my word is truth indeed."

A'ashik Pasha was, however, chiefly eminent as a mystic, having been a member of the *Mevlevi,* or "Whirling" Order of Dervishes, which has produced so many poets of distinction, its founder Jelalu'd Din, who wrote in Persian his famous *Mesnevi,* being deemed by Orientals a very "prince among poets." A'ashik's principal work is a long mystical poem known as the *A'ashik Pasha Divani.* It consists of rhymed couplets, the following

translated lines from which may give some idea of the
character and sentiment of the Turkish poetry of that
period :—

> " All the Universe, one mighty sign, is shown ;
> God hath myriads of creative acts unknown :
> None hath seen them, of the races *djin* and men,
> None hath news brought from that realm far off from ken.
> Never shall thy mind in reason reach that strand,
> Nor can tongue the King's name utter of that land.
> Since 'tis His each nothingness with life to invest
> Toil nor pain attendeth ever His behest.
> Eighteen thousand worlds from end to end
> Do not with Him one Atom's worth transcend. [1]

Another work of this literary period is the *Mukkam-
mediyya* of Mohammed Yazedji Oglou (Mohammed the
Son of the Scribe), who flourished in the first half of the
fifteenth century. In this work, which consists of 9109
couplets, is comprised the whole doctrine of Islam as well
as the history of the Prophet. The description of the
creation of the celestial Paradise concludes with these
lines—

> ' All these glories, all these honours, all these blessings of delight,
> All these wondrous mercies surely for his sake He did prepare [2]
> Through His love unto Mohammed, He the universe hath framed ;
> Happy, for his sake, the naked and the hungry enter there.
> O Thou perfectness of Potence !   O Thou God of Awful Might !
> O Thou Majesty of Glory !   O Thou King of Perfect Right ! "

---

[1] Translated by Mr. Gibb in his *Ottoman Poems*. I have ventured
to make some verbal alterations in the eighth line, which Mr. Gibb
has rendered—

> " Trouble is there ne'er at His behest."

[2] The love of the Deity for Mohammed forms a frequent theme of
Moslem writers.

Mohammed II., the Conqueror of Constantinople, appears to have been, like so many others of his House, a great patron of men of letters. The poet Sati was given by him a post at the Court as Laureate with the obligation of composing annually three *khasidas*—poems on special subjects—one in honour of the Great Bairam, or Feast of Sacrifice, another for the Lesser Bairam, or Feast of Alms, and a third for the Spring Festival at which the Oriental New Year is also inaugurated.

Notwithstanding the acknowledged ability of a few of these earlier writers in Turkish, the true classical period of Ottoman literature is held to have commenced only with the accession to the throne in 1520 of Suleyman "The Magnificent," and to have terminated two centuries later. Under the rule of this able Sultan "sword and pen," it was customary to say, "were never dry," for no less keenly did he fight the foe abroad than foster the arts at home. A golden age for Turkish scholarship and poetry was indeed inaugurated in this reign. Among poets Baki composed his charming lyrics, Fazli earned undying fame with his famous mystical allegory, "The Rose and the Nightingale," and Khalil surpassed all rivals in elegiac verse; while the prose writers of the period, historians, theologians, legists, and romancists, were as numerous as they were distinguished. To about the middle of this classical period belongs the eminent prose writer Hadji Khalifa, one of the most famous men of letters Turkey has ever produced, who left behind him at his death in 1658 a great variety of works on history, biography, chronology, geography, and other subjects. This important literary period may be said to have closed with Nedim, who flourished at the beginning of the eighteenth century, and is held by critics to stand alone among Ottoman poets, his verse being characterised by a joyousness and sprightliness which clearly distinguish it from the work of any previous singer. His *ghasels* are not only written with extreme elegance and finish, but contain an extraordinary variety of graceful and original ideas, and the words he made use of invariably appear to have been most happily chosen with a view to harmony and cadence. His *khasidas* are also esteemed almost equal to his sonnets, being less artificial and less dependent on fantastic conceits than is usually found in this class of poetic composition.

The Post-classical Period, which may be said to have endured until about the middle of last century, produced a variety of poets of distinction, the productions of each of whom possessed a style as original and peculiar to himself as in the case of the most eminent among their predecessors. Among these may be instanced Ghalib, whose *Magnum Opus*, "Beauty and Love," an allegorically mystical romance, is full of tender sentiment and shows a high degree of imaginative power. And among prose authors of this time may be mentioned such names as Rashid, the Imperial historiographer; Asim the philologist, who translated into Turkish two great lexicons, one from Arabic and the other from Persian; and of writers in a lighter vein, Kani the humorist.

The reign of Mohammed II., "The Reformer," constitutes the great transitional period of Ottoman literature, as it does also of Ottoman history. For during this reign, in which the West entered on the latest stage of its struggle with the East, we find the first indications of the successive changes which have during the past ninety years completely revolutionised Turkey. In the works of writers belonging to the first half of the nineteenth century the old Persian manner still predominates, and only an occasional attempt at composition in the new style is discernible. Pre-eminent among the poets of this time were Fazil Bey, Izzet Mollah, Pertev Pasha, and Wasif, the last named having broken new ground in a not entirely unsuccessful attempt to throw off ancient conventions by writing verse in the vernacular of the Capital. The more intimate relations cultivated with Europe from which naturally resulted acquisition of the French language and study of its literature, combined with the steady progress of the reforming tendency initiated under Mohammed II., resulted in the latter half of the century in the birth of a new literary school, whose aim was the substitution of truth and simplicity for the ancient inflated and grandiloquent style of diction. The first clear note of change is to be found in the political writings of Reshid and of Akif Pashas; but the man to whom more than to any other this literary revolution owed its success was Shinasi Effendi, who applied the modern method of composition to poetry as well as to prose. This important innovation—though not, however, established without violent opposition from literary conservatives—is at the present day alone used by writers of repute, anything now written according to the ancient Persian standards of composition being merely as a sort of scholarly *tour de force.* The whole tone, sentiment, and form of Ottoman literature has consequently changed; poetical forms hitherto unknown have been adopted from European prosodies, and a form of literature altogether new to the East—the drama—has arisen. Thousands of new words have during this period been adopted, or adapted, from other languages to express the wants of modern civilisation; and the language has been thereby so much enriched, simplified, and modernised, that many of the numerous novels, scientific books, and periodicals which are now published in Turkish may be said to be quite on a par with similar contemporary productions in Western Europe.

Nor are the names of women absent from this long and brilliant list of Turkish writers. During the centuries when European culture was a sealed book to them, the fair denizens of the harem not infrequently found its calm undisturbed life conducive to poetic composition; and from the fifteenth century onwards a daughter of the Osmanlis has from time to time delighted her contemporaries with her pen, and given evidence of a degree of talent entitling her to rank with the literary celebrities of her day. And how generously recognised and acknowledged by their countrymen were the poetic attainments of these ladies may be gathered from the following

extracts from Turkish biographers. Kimali Zadé, writing
in the sixteenth century, thus extols in figuratively
Oriental language the gifted Zeyneb, the earliest Turkish
poetess of whom any record exists. "The learning and
poetic talent of this Bride are not covered and concealed
by the curtain of secrecy and the veil of bashfulness; but
the rosiness of her beauty, and the down and mole of her
comeliness are beheld and admired by the world, and
are the object of the gaze of every man and woman."
The same writer applies to her an Arabic couplet which
may be thus rendered—

> "Her woman's sex dims not the sun's effulgent ray ;
> Though masculine the Moon, he lighteth not the day."[1]

And Latifi, the poet biographer and critic, speaks of
her as "an exceptional woman." "May Allah," he continues, "veil her shortcomings. She was a noble
daughter, a chaste and virtuous maiden, endowed with
many agreeable mental qualities. Learned men marvelled
at her understanding. Her father, when he saw sparkle
the rare jewels of her talent, supplied her with masters in
the arts and sciences, and placed in her hands the Persian
and Arabic poets." In his *Teskera*, Latifi appends to a
ghasel by this lady the following appreciative reply :—

> "*Húri*, again our feast as shining Paradise array !
> With thy sweet lip the beaker fill brim high with Kevser's spray[2]
> O Súfi, if thy cell be dark and gloomy be thy heart,
> Come then, and with the winecup's lamp light it with radiance gay ;

---

[1] In the Arabic as in the German language the Moon is masculine
and the Sun feminine. [2] See p. 15.

Heap up like aloes-wood the flames of love within thy breast ;
From thine own breath to all earth's senses odours sweet convey.
O Zephyr ! shouldst thou pass the home of her we love so well,
Full many blessings bear to her from us who her obey." [1]

Equally appreciative are the notices found in literary biographies of other Osmanli poetesses of the classic period who concealed their identity under the pen-names of *Mihri* ("Follower of Love"), *Sidqi* ("Sincerity"), and *Fitnet* ("Restlessness") respectively, as also of Hibetulla Sultana, sister of Mohammed II., and Leyla Hanum, who belonged to the first half of the last century, such facts surely contributing to prove the willingness in every age of men—even when "Unspeakable Turks"—not only to recognise and appreciate the possession of talent by women, but also to concede to them every facility for higher education whenever a sincere desire for it has been manifested.

Thus far as to indigenous Turkish education and culture. Let us now give a glance at what has of later years been borrowed from European methods and organised on modern lines. In addition to the parish *mektebs* above mentioned, there are now to be found in all the cities and larger towns of Turkey, State-supported primary schools called *Rushdiyeh*, to which boys are admitted gratuitously and taught, besides reading and writing, such usual elementary subjects as arithmetic, Turkish history, and geography. In the *Idadiyeh*, or secondary schools,

---

[1] Gibb, *Ottoman Poems.*

which are also State-supported, but as yet very inadequate
in number, older boys receive more specialised instruction
while qualifying for admission to one of the modern
Superior Schools and Colleges modelled on the system of
the educational institutions of France and Germany, in
which all the subjects necessitated by modern requirements are taught. Among the latter are Military Schools
and Colleges, a Naval College, Medical Colleges civil
and military, besides various institutions specially devoted
to the training of civil servants, lawyers, civil engineers,
etc., and a Lyceum organised in imitation of such establishments as they exist in France. In the last, founded
in 1869 by the joint efforts of Ali and Fuad Pashas, the
great reforming statesmen, it was proposed to afford a
liberal education to all subjects of the Sultan throughout
the Empire, irrespective of race and creed. Notwithstanding the difficulties which naturally arose in connexion
with organising a system of instruction which should take
account of the prejudices of members of three different
religious systems, the *Lycée* was opened with some 350
students belonging to seven different sects, and in two
years' time the attendance was doubled. Instruction was
imparted in French by French professors, and every
facility was afforded for the acquisition of both classical
and modern languages. Though the proposed provincial
branches were never established, the original institution
has continued to prosper, some of the most eminent
contemporary Osmalis having received part of their
education in its class-rooms.

STUDENTS AT THE TURKISH AGRICULTURAL SCHOOL, SALONICA

In no department of education is the progress made of late years more apparent than in the Military Colleges, their present state of efficiency being due in great measure to the personal interest and supervision of the Sultan. Elementary military education is afforded in the thirty-six State-provided schools known as *Mekteb-i-Rushdiyeh* to boys between the ages of ten and fourteen, who, on passing into the *Idadiyeh*, or Secondary schools, have already attained a fair degree of proficiency in the French language, and in certain military subjects. The system of education pursued in the seven *Idadiyeh* military schools is especially adapted for youths intending to make the army their profession; and after three years or so of further study, if they can satisfy the examiners, the pupils may enter one of the six superior Military Colleges, those possessing any special aptitude for mathematics entering the Artillery Academy on the banks of the Golden Horn. In these higher colleges the course of study pursued is purely professional and lasts for three or four years, the graduates being then gazetted lieutenants iu the army corps to which their college is attached. Ten per cent. of the cadets of each year are, however, retained for a further three years' course of study, at the end of which those who have successfully passed the examiners are gazetted to the Staff of the Army as captains. The drawback to this system is that the Staff officers are entirely ignorant of regimental work, and consequently unable to cope with the many difficulties which confront the regimental officer as well in peace as during a campaign.

N

Considerable progress has also been made in the department of Medical Science during the present reign. As mentioned in a previous chapter, there is a Naval and Military Medical College in the Capital devoted solely to the training of medical officers for the united services, and the Civil Medical College at Stamboul affords instruction to 1200 students preparing for a medical career, open to all Ottoman subjects without distinction of race or creed. Its teaching staff include a number of fully qualified German professors. The training obtainable here being much appreciated, the College is usually filled to over-crowding with eager students. The course of study lasts six years, at the end of which period the most promising graduates are sent to France or Germany for further instruction, or to attend post-graduate courses in special departments of medical science.

Save, however, in these two branches of medical and military science, intellectual progress had, under the late Palace System, become completely paralysed. Prominent literary men were forced into exile, numerous printing and publishing offices closed, and newspapers and periodicals suppressed, the few that continued to be issued being strictly prohibited from publishing any news of a political or national character, or indeed any information whatever of national interest. The people generally were in consequence entirely without precise information of what was taking place either at home or abroad, and the wildest rumours were often current in the cafés and bazars of the Capital. This dearth of news was, however, evidently equalled by the desire for it. For, on the morrow of the Proclamation of the Constitution, not only was every suppressed newspaper resuscitated, but a number of new journals appeared in the Capital and elsewhere. So great indeed was the immediate demand that the supply fell far short of it, and the fortunate possessor of a copy of the *Serbesti* or the *Sabah* might have been seen on these eventful days surrounded by an excited group eager to share in the unwonted privilege of a free Press. Another notable and highly satisfactory result of the new *régime* has been a wide demand for books of an educational and scientific character, a corresponding feature being an immensely increased demand on the part of the Turkish youth for admittance into the various educational establishments, many of which are already overcrowded. Every College has also now its Club established for the purposes of study, debate, and mutual help, one of the best being a sort of "Old Boys'" Club founded by former pupils of the Mulkieh Superior School, which has a membership of 1600, and possesses commodious premises near the Sublime Porte.

In the department of female education a great advance may be looked for in the near future. An Imperial Lyceum for girls is now in process of establishment under the immediate patronage of his Majesty the Sultan, who has not only placed a palace at Candilli at the disposal of the Committee of Administration, composed of ministers, deputies, and eminent educationalists, but has also generously offered to defray all the expenses

of its furnishing and equipment. The Consulting Committee will be composed of Turkish ladies, and his
Majesty has expressed the wish that his daughter, the
Princess Naïlé Sultana, should be nominated as its President.
Harem restraints have hitherto naturally prevented girls
over twelve continuing to attend school, as on attaining
that age custom forbids them to go abroad save under
the wing of their mother or a female attendant of mature
years.   In this particular, however, as also in others
affecting the welfare and intellectual progress of women,
and with it that of the nation generally, many modifications and ameliorations will doubtless by degrees be found
possible, and brought into operation.   A considerable
number of Turkish girls of the better class have during
the last half-century been educated at home by foreign
governesses, and have become proficient in European languages, accomplishments, and general culture ; day-schools
for girls of the middle classes exist in all the cities and
larger towns, and are well attended; and where statistics
are available, it appears that as many girls as boys receive
instruction in the elementary parish *mektebs*.

Printing, I may mention in conclusion, was not introduced into Turkey until the year 1728, the first printed
book published having been a Turkish translation of an
Arabic dictionary.   To this day, however, the Turks prefer a beautiful manuscript to a printed book.   They have,
indeed, always cultivated and esteemed calligraphy more
than Europeans, and even more than any other Orientals
except, perhaps, the Persians.   Copying books, as a trade,

has not even yet completely died out, as with us; for books of a religious character have only of recent years been allowed to be printed; and the Koran is still always used in manuscript. Letter writing has, however, remained an art not understood of the vulgar. Even among those who can read few are able to write, and for their convenience the professional scribe still sits at the street corners, ready to set down in literary Turkish the simple messages of his customers to friends at a distance, who in their turn will probably have recourse to the erudition of the village *Imām* for the deciphering of the missive. The trade of the seal-engraver, who, like the scribe, is invariably a Moslem, also continues as flourishing as when the art of writing was less common, Orientals generally considering a seal preferable to a written signature, their argument being that any one may imitate a man's handwriting, but no one but himself can be in possession of his seal. The Turks, however, in common with Orientals generally, are not afflicted with the *cacoethes scribendi*, neither social, intellectual, nor commercial activity being so great as to call for a frequent exchange of written communications; and it is still customary, not only among the Turks, but also among the better classes of Christians, to send both business and social messages by word of mouth.

Native Turkish music, it must be admitted, is still very primitive in character. The airs are generally either wild and plaintive, or sentimental and melancholy, presenting little variety and—in common with the folk-music of Southern

Europe generally—they are invariably pitched in a minor key. The popular idea of singing in the country among all races I once heard not inaptly characterised by a Roumanian as "pirouetting around a single note." The repetition of the Turkish words "*Aman Aman !*"—which may be translated as "Oh dear!" or "Have pity!"— appear sufficient to express the sentimental feelings of the lower classes of the population ; and the muleteer on the road, the fisherman in his boat, or the town 'prentice taking his *kaif* at a coffee-house by the seashore, will, for hours together, make nasal excursions up and down the scale from the keynote on which he enunciates his *Aman, Aman !* The wild native marches, as played by military bands, are, however, not unpleasing; but both military bands and barrel-organs now produce for the most part airs from French and Italian light opera, and "La fille de Madame Angot" in particular appeared at one time to have a greater vogue in Turkey than even in her native land. This year has, however, seen the inauguration at Stamboul of a National Conservatoire of Music which, supported as it is fortunate enough to be by the patronage of Prince Ziaeddin Effendi, has, it may be hoped, a prosperous future before it.

The musical instruments in ordinary use among the populace are the *rebeck*, or lute, the *kanoun*, a kind of zither, the reed flute, and the small hemispherical drum. But the favourite instrument of the Oriental rustic generally is the bagpipe—not the complicated instrument, be it understood, of the Scottish Highlanders, but a much more primitive one made from the skin of a sheep fitted with a mouthpiece and a single reed pipe by means of which the notes are produced. The inflated skin is held against the chest of the player, who moves his fingers over the holes, producing sounds discordant enough to Western ears, but pleasing in the extreme to the unsophisticated Turk, as also to the Arab, Bulgarian, or Armenian, especially when accompanied, as is generally the case, by the equally primitive *doubana*, or native drum.

CHAPTER X

MYSTICISM AND FREETHOUGHT

THE Mystics of Islam are to be found in the conventual establishments of the Dervish Orders who constitute the monks and saints of the Moslem world. Monasticism is, however, not only contrary to the spirit of Islam, but was explicitly forbidden by its founder. But so attractive to the Oriental mind has always been a life passed in retirement from the world for the purpose of contemplative devotion, that this natural tendency proved stronger than the injunctions of the Prophet; and very early in the history of this religion societies were formed—and by no less eminent persons than Mohammed's nephew Ali and his friend and father-in-law Abu Bekr—for the purposes of mystic meditation and beneficence. Mysticism, being in principle rather a mode of practising religion than a religion in itself, adapts itself to all dogmas; and the earlier members of these fraternities invariably took a vow of fidelity to the doctrines of the Prophet and continued to perform their duties as citizens. It was not long, however, before many of the followers of these first Khalifs abandoned the rules of the original fraternities.

And the great religious movement of the ninth century, which shook Islam to its foundations and resulted in the formation of a multitude of new sects within that creed, gave birth also to the system of religious philosophy known as *Sufiism*, which enters so largely into the mystical doctrines professed by the Dervishes generally. In the thirteenth century twelve Orders were recognised, but the number of these mystics rapidly increased during the next two centuries in all the Asiatic countries which had come under the influence of Islam.

The founders, at least, of these early Dervish Societies were evidently men of great learning and wide culture, as well as of saintly life. Under Orchan, the first Turkish Emir—the title of Sultan was not assumed until much later—they spread themselves over Asia Minor; and after the conquest of Broussa, this prince, who attributed his extraordinary successes to the presence in his armies of these holy men, founded and endowed for them convents and colleges throughout his dominions, at the head of which he placed the most distinguished of their Sheikhs or Priors, conferring upon them the honourable title of Pasha, joined to such names as *A'ashik* ("The Loving") or *Müchlis* ("The Sincere"). The slopes of the Bithynian Olympus, which had long been the resort of Christian hermits and cenobites, were now also taken possession of by these Moslem recluses who there established themselves among the flocks of the Turcoman nomads; and the coolness and quiet of the retreats which had favoured the holy idleness of Christian monks now charmed the reveries of Moslem poets and the meditations of Sufi philosophers. The honoured tombs of the more famous among them may still be seen at the foot of the mountain on which their peaceful days were passed, or in the vicinity of the schools in which they studied and taught. And in the nineteenth century, as in the days of Orchan, their influence has been made use of by Sultans and generals to excite the zeal and courage of their troops in battle. Whenever a military campaign has been organised, a number of Sheikhs and others from nearly all the Orders have hastened to join the army. Commanding officers gladly engage their services and treat them with every respect and consideration, as their presence in the camp—where they spend whole days and nights fasting in their tents while offering supplications and making vows for the success of the arms of the True Believers— maintains a most desirable religious enthusiasm among the troops. On the eve of an action, the Dervishes roam excitedly through the camp, rehearsing the benefits promised by the Prophet to all who fight for the Faith of Islam, or who die in arms, and seek by their own religious enthusiasm to rouse the zeal and animate the courage of the soldiery. During a battle their voices may be heard above the din of war, shouting, "O Victors!" (*Ya Ghasi*) "O Martyrs!" (*Ya Shahid*) "Ya Allah!" or "Ya Hoo!" ("O Him"). If they fancy the Holy Standard, the Mantle of the Prophet, to be in danger, they crowd round the sacred relic to strengthen the lines of the officers stationed as its guard, and not only sustain their efforts, but themselves perform prodigies of valour. A Dervish of high renown in his day, Ak Shemsi 'd-Din by name, is said to have foretold to Mohammed "The Conqueror" the day and hour of the fall of Constantinople. Together with seventy-seven other "distinguished and holy men beloved of Allah," he accompanied the Sultan to that memorable siege. The deeds of valour achieved by these enthusiasts, and the miracles performed in answer to their prayers are recorded—and, it need hardly be added, exaggerated—by Moslem chroniclers; and the tombs of many are to this day places of pilgrimage for the True Believers.

Nor were the Dervish Orders held in less honour by succeeding Sultans. After the capture of the Byzantine Capital and the consolidation of the Empire, their poets and writers remained in high favour at Court, and there were few Padishahs who were not enrolled as members of one or more of the Orders. The long reign of Bayazid II. (1481–1512) also bears traces of the influence of mystic philosophy on the Court. The most renowned Dervish of that time, the Sheikh Jasi, had, when about to start on a pilgrimage to Mekka, foretold to Bayazid, then governor of Amasia, that on his return from the Holy City he would find that prince on the throne: and it fell out even as he had predicted. This eminent man received the titles of "Sheikh of Sultans" and "Sultan of Sheikhs," and his cell was the meeting-place of all the dignitaries of the Empire. The Turkish writers Seadeddin and Ali narrate the biographies of thirty eminent Sheikhs who flourished in the reign of this Sultan, called by many Ottoman historians "Bayazid the Sufi." The influence of the Dervish society by which this Sultan surrounded himself may also be seen in his poetry, which breathes a spirit of mysticism markedly absent from the writings of his talented but unhappy brother, Prince Djem, and his son, Selim I.

Although the Dervish Orders of Turkey have always outwardly professed adherence to the orthodox *Sunni* sect, many points in their doctrines would seem to lend colour to the accusation of being heterodox *Shias*, so frequently brought against them by their secular opponents the Ulema. The *Shias*, as is well known, trace the Khalifate, or succession to the authority of the Prophet, through Ali, his nephew and son-in-law, while the *Sunnis* maintain its descent through the Ommiade Khalifs to the successive representatives of the Ottoman Dynasty. But notwithstanding the persistent hostility of the Orthodox, it does not appear that, previous to the sixteenth century, the Orders were ever subjected to active persecution. For so long as the substance of the doctrines held by the higher grades of these mystics was kept secret, the denunciations by the legists of their ascetic practices, their vows, the dancing and other peculiar exercises performed in their *Tekkehs*, their pretensions to miraculous gifts, and claims to direct communion with the Deity, had but little effect. But as the influence and prestige of the Dervishes increased, many of the Orders relaxed by degrees the prudence and severity of their original rules, and allowed

much of their doctrine to become publicly known. Their
enemies were now enabled to make definite and serious
charges against them. They were accused of attempting
to make innovations in the dogmas of Islam ; of following
practices forbidden by the Koran; of denying the very
existence of a personal God ; of teaching disrespect for all
established institutions ; and of setting at nought all laws,
both human and Divine. Their religious exercises were
denounced as profane acts ; and it was asserted that all
kinds of abominable practices were indulged in by them
in the seclusion of their monasteries. The general
tendency of the Dervish institutions appeared to the
Ulema to threaten also the introduction into Islam of
something analogous to the "Holy Priesthood" and
"Apostolic Succession" of the Romish Church—ideas
utterly at variance with the spirit of the Koran. An
alleged discovery that gave a still greater shock to the
Orthodox mind was that the Dervishes concluded some
of their prayers by anathematising the Ommiade Khalifs,
and glorifying the Khalif Ali ; and, consequently, that,
though nominally *Sunnis*, they virtually belonged to the
heterodox sect of the *Shias*.

There seems, however, little reason to doubt that
whenever overt hostility has been manifested against the
Dervish Orders by the Sultan and his ministers, it has
invariably been prompted by political, rather than religious
motives. For notwithstanding the odium cast upon these
Mystics by the Legists, no active measures, as above
remarked, appear to have been taken against them by the

Government until the beginning of the sixteenth century, when political events caused them to be looked upon as a possible source of danger to the State. A new dynasty had been founded in Persia at this period on the basis of religion. The Sufi Philosophy had always been popular in that country; and Persia was at the same time the stronghold of the *Shia* heresy and of the Dervish fraternities. A Dervish Sheikh, named Eidar, who traced his descent from the Khalif Ali, having gained a great reputation for sanctity, and a numerous following of disciples and adherents, assumed the title of Sufi *par excellence*, and declared himself to have been commissioned by Allah to work a religious reformation. Sheikh Eidar perished in the attempt; but his young son Ismaïl was protected by his faithful disciples, who took refuge with him in Ghilän, and carefully trained him in his father's principles. In 1501, at the head of a numerous body of partisans, Ismaïl revived the claims of Sheikh Eidar, and gradually overcoming all opposition, he at length became the Founder of the Sufi Dynasty, and the ruler of an extensive Empire. His doctrines gained also many adherents in the Asiatic provinces of the Ottoman Empire, where Selim I. took early and vigorous measures to suppress this new heretical sect. For, as Church and State are, in Islam, identical, a blow aimed at the one menaces equally the other; and the great schism of the *Sunnis* and *Shias* is not a mere diversity of opinion purely religious and theoretic, but also a practical political dispute concerning the succession to the Khalifate, the headship of the Moslem

Church. Sultan Selim, whose inquisitorial talents are celebrated by Ottoman historians, organised a system of secret police, by means of which he caused to be made out a list of all his subjects belonging to this sect. Their number amounted to 70,000, 40,000 of whom were massacred, the rest being imprisoned or exiled. In Damascus a few hours sufficed for the extermination of the whole community of schismatic Mohammedans. The Persian monarch shortly afterwards declared war against the destroyer of his co-religionists, and a sanguinary campaign ensued. The Ottoman Dervishes in European Turkey, whose *Shia* tendencies were more than suspected, were, very naturally, also looked upon with disfavour during the course of these events, the Ulema making the best of this favourable opportunity by exciting the minds as well of the populace as of the authorities against their rivals.

A new Order, created about the beginning of the sixteenth century by a certain Sheikh Hamza, and called after him the *Hamzavi*, appears to have been from its very foundation held in bad repute, and Sheikh Hamza was arrested and subsequently executed under a *fetva* of the Grand Mufti, the ostensible charge against him being that he omitted to repeat at his devotions the full number of the *Isma-i-Sherif*, or "praises of the Prophet." He was naturally regarded by the rest of the Dervishes as a martyr, and his reputation for piety and extraordinary powers still survives in the Capital. Another Sheikh of the same Order was put to death shortly afterwards on an

accusation of heterodoxy, together with forty of his
disciples, who, it is said, voluntarily gave themselves up to
the authorities. And so great was the effervescence of the
Orthodox under several succeeding reigns, and particularly
in that of Mohammed IV., that the Ulema and other
rigid Mohammedans even ventured to propose the extermination of all the Orders, the confiscation of their
revenues, and the destruction of their monasteries. An
attempt was, indeed, made by the Grand Vizier of that
Sultan, Achmet Kiupruli, to suppress the *Mevlevi*, *Khal-
vetti*, *Djelvetti*, and *Shemshi* Orders. Like all former
and subsequent attempts, however, it succeeded but
partially, as the Government was overawed by the Janis-
series, whose intimate connexion with the *Bektashi* Order
made them the allies of the Dervishes generally ; and the
Porte feared to do anything that might arouse the resent-
ment of this formidable military force. The action of the
Sultan, too, seems to have been but half-hearted. For it
is recorded that even Selim I.—whom Mouradjà D'Ohsson
describes as "poet, parricide, and fratricide, mystic, tyrant
and conqueror"[1]—made pilgrimages to the tombs of
deceased, and to the cells of living Sheikhs of repute ; and
that he raised at Damascus a mosque over the grave of
the eminent saint, Muhajjin-el-Aràbi. Suleyman I. also
built at Konieh, in honour of Jelalu-'d-Din, the founder of
the *Mevlevi* Order, a mosque, a *tekkeh*, and public alms-
kitchen. At Sidi Ghazi he erected a great establishment
with a *tekkeh* and college for the *Bektashis;* and he also

---

[1] *Histoire de l'Empire Ottomane*, Part I. p. 377.

repaired the *tekkeh* covering the tomb of Abdul Kadr Ghilani, the sainted founder of the *Kadiri* Order, thus drawing upon himself the benedictions of three influential fraternities.

After this stormy period the Orders appear to have enjoyed a long interval of freedom from persecution. For the Turkish author, Evliya Effendi, writing towards the end of the seventeenth century, makes no mention of the existence of any ill-feeling towards the Dervishes, with whom he was closely connected during his long and adventurous life. The massacre of the Janissaries by Sultan Mahmoud, "The Reformer," in the beginning of last century, was, however, followed by the persecution of the *Bektashi* Dervishes, who were accused of having been concerned in the revolts that followed the suppression of this military branch of the Order, and consequently of high treason against the State; and the Grand Mufti and the chief Legists agreed with the Sultan that a severe sentence should be passed upon this Brotherhood. Its three principal Sheikhs were consequently publicly executed; the Order was declared abolished; many of its *tekkehs* were destroyed; and its members generally were banished from the capital, those who remained being compelled to abandon their distinctive dress.[1]

This determined action on the part of the Government spread consternation among the Dervish Orders throughout the Empire. Their members feared for the moment that they, like the *Bektashis*, were all doomed to destruction

[1] Ubicini, *Lettres sur la Turquie*, vol. i. p. 107.

o

or dispersion; and, to quote a contemporary chronicler, "They remained motionless, expecting their last day, devoured by anguish, and with their backs resting against the wall of stupefaction." But here Sultan Mahmoud paused in his work of destruction. "Though" —as recorded by the historian of the massacre of the Janissaries—"he had not feared to open with the sword a road for public happiness by cutting down the thorny bushes that obstructed his progress and tore his Imperial mantle," he hesitated to decree the entire destruction of institutions which had enjoyed the respect and devotion of his predecessors and of Moslems generally for upwards of a thousand years. This "hesitation," is, however, not so surprising when we learn the fact, of which Ubicini appears to have been ignorant, that Sultan Mahmoud was himself an affiliated member of the *Mevlevi* fraternity of Péra, and frequently visited it; and that he also honoured with his presence the meetings of a *Nakshi-bendi* fraternity established in the suburb of Foundoukli.

The Dervishes, however, on finding that the blow dealt at the *Bektashis* was not followed by the suppression or even persecution of the other Orders, soon recovered from their consternation; and the more fanatical among them set on foot a secret agitation with the object of inciting the populace against a Sultan who had dared to raise his hand against the "chosen of Allah." In 1837 Mahmoud narrowly escaped falling a victim to the frenzied zeal of one of these ascetics. As he was crossing the Bridge of Galata, surrounded by his escort, a long-haired cenobite, commonly known in the Capital as "The Hairy Sheikh" (*Sheikh Satchlü*), darted from among the by-standers, and seizing the bridle of the Sultan's horse, exclaimed, "*Giaour Padishah* (Infidel Sultan)! Art thou not yet satiated with abominations? Thou shalt answer to Allah for thy impieties. Thou destroyest the institutions of thy Brethren; thou ruinest Islam; and drawest down the wrath of Allah on thyself and on the Nation!" The Sultan, fearing that popular feeling might be roused against himself by the ascetic's denunciations, commanded his guards to remove the madman from his path. "Madman!" echoed the infuriated Dervish. "Sayest thou that I am mad? The spirit of Allah, which inspires me, and which I must obey, has commanded me to declare His truth, and promised me the reward of the Faithful!" The fanatic was, however, seized and put to death without delay. His body was given up to his brethren, who buried it with the honours due to a martyr; and on the following day a report was circulated that the watchers had seen a *Nûr*, or supernatural light, hovering over the grave of the Sheikh—a convincing proof of the favour with which Allah had regarded his action. It needed, however, a bold reformer to put a noisy fanatic to death, and the majority of Sultans and statesmen have contented themselves with exiling to some remote part of the Empire a Dervish whose influence on the populace they had cause to fear.

Whenever, on the other hand, public hostility has been excited against the Dervish Orders it has had its

foundation in the horror with which the orthodox *Sunni*
Mohammedans regard the *Shia* heresy, and this hostility
seems never to have been very general, nor of long continuance. Those whose religious principles and devotion
to the purity of the creed of Islam has incited them to
combat the growing power of the Dervishes have invariably been, in their turn, combated by other principles
drawn from the same source. For the majority of the
Turkish nation has always regarded the Dervishes, their
Sheikhs, and, above all, the Founders of the Orders, as
the beloved Sons of Heaven, and in intimate relations
with spiritual powers. These opinions have for basis the
tradition that the different Orders originated, as above
mentioned, in the two congregations of Abù Bekr and
Ali, and that the grace which these had received from
the Prophet, both as his relatives and Vicars, has been
miraculously transmitted through the series of Sheikhs
who, from age to age, have governed the monastic
societies. It is also popularly believed that the legion
of saints constituting the Mohammedan spiritual hierarchy, alluded to in a previous chapter as perpetually
existing among mankind, is to be found among the
members of the Dervish fraternities. Consequently, to
condemn, persecute, and destroy them, as was the unanimous cry of the Legists, would have been to call down
upon the whole nation the wrath of all the holy saints
who have ever lived.

Even the less enthusiastic did not dare openly to
declare themselves hostile to the Dervishes. Moslems

generally respect what is beyond their comprehension;
and they hold this mixture of religious practices and
profane exercises to be a mystery which True Believers
should treat with silent unquestioning reverence.   The
superstitious ideas which these ascetics have the talent
of perpetuating in their nation have always served as their
shield.   So persistent, too, is this influence of, and veneration for, the spiritual character of the more eminent among
the Sheikhs, that even those Osmanlis whose education
and intercourse with Europeans might be supposed to
have freed them from national superstitions are often
found to be still under the influence of the ideas inculcated
in early youth.

From the earliest times to the present, the most general
and, at the same time, most harmless weapon used against
the Dervishes has been that of ridicule.   Turkish and
Persian literature teems with satires in proverb and story
on their peculiarities of dress and practice.   Even the
mystic Sadi does not spare them in his epigrams, though
his satires are chiefly directed against those who are
Dervishes in outward appearance only, and not in heart.
For instance, he writes—

> " Of what avail is frock, or rosary,
> Or clouted garment ?   Keep thyself but free
> From evil deeds, it will not need for thee
> To wear the cap of felt, a Dervish be
> In heart, and wear the cap of Tartary."

A humorous story is current in the Capital of a Dervish
who, when on his pilgrimage to the holy cities, had the
misfortune to lose by death his ass, a gift from his Sheikh,

the guardian of a shrine. He buried the animal by the roadside, and giving out that a deceased companion was the occupant of the recently made grave, soon obtained from the charitable passers-by sufficient funds to erect a *turbeh* over it, of which he constituted himself the guardian. Years passed. The *turbeh* became a famous place of pilgrimage; miracles were performed at it, and the fame of the rival shrine reached the ears of the old Sheikh, who had heard no news of his disciple since his departure, and lamented him as dead. One day, accordingly, he locked up his *turbeh* in order to pay a visit to his brother Sheikh. He was hospitably received, and recognised the rival *turbedji* as his former disciple. When evening came, and the last of the pilgrims visiting the shrine had departed, the old Sheikh asked with much curiosity who was the saint buried below, as he knew of none formerly residing in that part of the country. After some hesitation, Sheikh Ali confessed that his dead ass was the only occupant of the tomb. As his Superior did not seem much disturbed by the announcement, the younger Dervish ventured to inquire who the saint might have been who was buried under his master's *turbeh;* and learnt at length that it was no other than the parent of his own sainted donkey.

The most wildly fanatical of these ascetics are found among the wandering Dervishes, who, by their prophecies and adjurations, often excite the Moslem population against their Christian neighbours. Shortly before the outbreak of the troubles in Bulgaria in 1876, one of these zealots completely terrorised the Christian inhabitants of

Adrianople. He knocked at one door after another in the Christian quarter, forced his way in when they were opened, and declared to the startled inmates that Allah had revealed to him His desire that the infidels of the town should be destroyed within three days after Easter. He finally reached the house of the Bishop, to whom he repeated his menacing prophecy. The reverend gentleman, apprehensive of the possible consequences to his flock of these "revelations," went at once to inform the Governor-General of the incident. The Dervish was sent for, asked if he had said what was reported of him, and what he meant by it. The wily ascetic merely shrugged his shoulders innocently, and replied that, as he was in his *hal*, or state of ecstasy, when he made the declaration, he was not responsible for anything he might have uttered. The Governor-General deemed it prudent to send him out of the town under escort, with orders for his conveyance to Broussa. The Dervish, however, managed to elude the vigilance of his guards—perhaps with their connivance—and continued his fanatical mission in other parts of the province.

The monastic establishments of the Dervish Orders, called by the various names of *tekkehs*, *khanakahs*, and *zanriyehs*, but more commonly by the first, and the *turbehs*, or shrines of their Saints, are at the present day as numerous in European as in Asiatic Turkey. In Constantinople and its environs, many of the Orders possess several establishments; and every town contains the monastery and shrine of one or more of their communities.

The *tekkehs* occupy, for the most part, picturesque and commanding situations, sometimes in the middle of towns or cities, but more frequently in their suburbs. The buildings are grouped round the *sem'a khaneh*—the hall in which the brethren meet for their collective devotions and religious exercises—a square building of whitewashed masonry, with a tiled and domed roof. The interior arrangements vary according to the Order, but are always marked by extreme simplicity. In the halls of the *Mevlevi* and *Rufāi*—the so-called "Whirling" and "Howling" Dervishes—a circular space in the centre is railed off from the rest of the floor, which is covered with matting for the accommodation of the spectators; and when there is no gallery for the women, part of this space is partitioned off for their use. The only attempts at mural decoration are tablets inscribed with texts from the Koran, verses from the poets, the sacred names of Allah, of the Prophet, the Khalif Ali, etc. As in the regular mosques, the direction of Mekka is indicated by a niche in the wall, surmounted by the name of the *Pir*, or founder of the Order, by the Moslem profession of faith previously mentioned, or the word *Bismillah*—"In the name of God." In a corner is usually a catafalque covering the tomb of a departed Sheikh, covered with costly carpets and rich draperies, the pious offerings of those who have there sought and found healing benefit or other boon.

The courtyard surrounding the sanctuary gives access to the cells of the brethren and the apartments of their Sheikh, the convent kitchen and offices. The cells vary in number

according to the Order, and form a quadrangle of low buildings, with a roof sloping to the front, and covering a broad verandah, into which all the doors and windows open. Beyond are flower and fruit gardens, shaded by cypress, mulberry, and plane trees, the haunts of storks and pigeons ; and, enclosed by the arched gateway and tile-topped walls, are cisterns and fountains of sparkling water furnished with iron ladles for the use of the thirsty. Sometimes, as within the precincts of the convent outside the Vardar gate of Salonica, there are also cool, shady cloisters, and raised terraces and kiosks, commanding magnificent views of mountain, plain, and sea. And here, when the evening shadows are lengthening, the mystics, in their picturesque and symbolic attire, may be seen pacing tranquilly to and fro ; or, seated on the broad wooden benches, meditatively passing through their fingers the brown beads of their long *tesbehs*, or rosaries, on their faces that expression of perfect repose which indifference to the world and its doings alone can give.

Though all the Dervish Orders, in accordance with their principle of poverty, are considered mendicant, few are so in reality, for most monasteries possess *vakouf*, or landed property bequeathed to them by pious persons. The revenues from these endowments are applied chiefly to the support of the monastic Dervishes, though the wants of a needy lay brother may occasionally be relieved from them. The monasteries vary greatly in point of wealth, and the more prosperous are expected to assist others less largely endowed. The *Mevlevi* Order is the most popular

—one might even say the most fashionable—of all, and has, ever since its foundation, included among its members men of high rank.   The late Sultan Abdul Aziz was, for instance, a lay brother, and occasionally, it is said, took part in the religious exercises at one of the *Mevlevi* convents in Constantinople.   This Order is, consequently, very prosperous, and its monasteries and shrines surpass those of all other Orders.   The Monastery of its General, at Konieh (Iconium), in Asia Minor, possesses considerable lands bequeathed as *vakouf* by the old Seljukian Sultans, these bequests being ratified by subsequent princes.   Murad IV., too, when marching against Persia in 1634, bestowed many favours and distinctions upon the "Sheikh of Sheikhs," as their Grand Master is termed, and endowed his community as a perpetual *vakouf*, with the proceeds of the *kharateh*—the poll-tax imposed on the non-Moslem inhabitants of the city in lieu of military service.

Notwithstanding, however, these substantial endowments, the Dervishes have never, like the Monastic Orders of Christendom, departed from the original principles of their Founders.   Their manner of living is still as frugal as was that of the original Twelve Orders, and the architecture of their convents is marked by extreme simplicity, both of form and material, any ornamental articles they may contain being the gifts of the pious.

The brethren resident in the well-endowed *tekkehs* are supplied with food and lodging only, their frugal repasts being usually served to them in their cells and eaten in solitude, though on certain occasions the brethren dine together in the common-room. Each Dervish is accordingly required to provide himself with clothing and other necessaries, and to follow some trade or profession. Those who are calligraphists occupy themselves in making copies of the Koran—which is always used by Moslems in manuscript form, and of other books of a religious character. Should any of these recluses be entirely without private resources, an allowance from his Sheikh, or a pension from some wealthy individual, will supply his modest needs. Many Moslems also reserve their alms exclusively for the Dervishes, and make it their duty to seek out those of high reputation for sanctity, visit them frequently, and supply their wants. Others, again, in the hope of drawing upon themselves, their families, and their fortunes, the blessing of heaven, lodge and board in their houses such among these holy men as may lack the necessaries of life. Should a convent possess surplus revenue, it is, after relieving the wants of other less well-endowed communities, given directly to the poor in the shape of alms, or employed in the foundation of almshouses, schools, or public baths, such charitable institutions often constituting the dependencies of *tekkehs* as of mosques. In accordance with their principle of poverty, the Dervish Orders are all, nominally at least, mendicant, and dependent for their daily sustenance on "what Allah may send them." Yet the *solicitation* of alms is equally forbidden by their rule. For though some members of the *Bektashi* Order certainly frequent the public thoroughfares, and the doors of the charitable, soliciting alms with the words, "Something for the love of Allah," the better sort deprecate mendicancy, and support themselves by handicraft trades, and also by fashioning, in imitation of their learned founder, *Hadji Bektash*, small articles of wood and horn. They also carve in greenstone, jade, and other substances, the fastenings used by Dervishes generally for the belts and collars of their garments, besides a variety of symbolic objects used or worn on the person by members of their own Order.

The holy mendicants—wild-eyed, shaggy-haired, and ragged, so frequently met with in the streets of Eastern cities—are for the most part *Kalenderi*—the "Kalenders" of the *Arabian Nights* — and other wandering fakirs belonging to none of the established Orders. The rule of this Brotherhood—for, not being descended from either of the two original congregations, they are not, strictly speaking, an Order—requires its members to subsist entirely upon alms, to wander perpetually, and for the most part barefoot, and to practise the severest asceticism. For thus alone, according to Sheikh Yussuf, its Founder, is to be attained "that state of ecstasy, of light, and of perfect sanctity, which is the portion of every true *Kalender*, and which alone can render him worthy of that high designation." This same title of *Kalender*, it may be remarked, is also given to Dervishes of all Orders who are distinguished among their brethren for superior spirituality. It is this class of "enlightened" beings which has produced so many dangerous fanatics in every age of Mohammedanism. From it have come the assassins of Sultans, Viziers, and grandees of the Empire, and all the "inspired" impostors who, under the title of *Mahdi*, have misled thousands, and desolated whole countries by their supposed prophecies and divine revelations.

A celibate Sheikh resides permanently in the convent, but one who is married visits it only periodically, his authority during his absence being vested in a deputy called the *Naib*. Twelve being the sacred number of the Bektashi Order, Twelve Initiates constitute a *Bektashi* Congregation of Elders, under whose guidance the novices pass through the preliminary stages. Certain rules were, in the early history of Moslem mysticism, drawn up for the admission of new members into a Brotherhood ; and though subsequently elaborated by some of the Orders, these original rules still form the basis of the ceremony of initiation generally. A neophyte of the *Mevlevi*, as also of the *Bektashi* Order, is required to perform a noviatiate of 1001 consecutive days, during which, whatever his worldly rank, he performs the menial offices of the *tekkeh*, and holds himself the subordinate of every other member of the community. During this period he also attends the services in the *sem'a khaneh*, and receives instruction from one of the Elders. The formalities observed in the reception of new members by the *Bektashi* Order are perhaps the most peculiar and elaborate. On the expiration of the probationary period, a candidate is recommended to the Sheikh by two initiates of the Community,

who are called his "Interpreters;" and on the evening
appointed for the ceremony of initiation—for the services
of the *Bektashi* Order are always held by night—the
neophyte takes with him to the convent a sheep and a
small sum of money. The sheep is sacrificed on the
threshold of the *tekkeh*, part of its wool is twisted into
a rope, the rest being preserved to be made later on into
a girdle for his use. If the candidate desires to take the
vow of celibacy, he is stripped naked; but if he proposes,
as in the generality of cases, to take merely the ordinary,
or secular vow, his breast only is bared. With the rope
round his neck, he is led by his "interpreters," one of
whom carries a curiously shaped symbol termed the *tebber*,
into the hall of the *tekkeh*. The Sheikh and the twelve
Elders are already seated around the hall on their sheepskin mats, and before each of them stands a lighted
candle. In the posture of abject humility called by the
special term of *buyun kesmek*—his arms folded across his
breast, his hands on his shoulders, his great toes crossed,
and his body inclined towards the Sheikh—he takes his
place on a dodecagonal stone called the *maidan tash*, while
one of the "interpreters" announces to the Sheikh that
he has brought to him a slave, and begs that he may be
accepted. Various collects and litanies are recited by the
Sheikh and the postulant in turn, at the conclusion of
which the following exhortation is addressed to the latter:—

"Eat nothing forbidden; speak no falsehood; quarrel
with none; be kind to your inferiors; overlook the faults
of others, and conceal them. If you cannot do this with

your hand, do it with your skirts, your tongue, and your
heart."

The novice then kisses the hand of the Sheikh, who
continues—

"If thou now accept me as thy father, I accept thee
as my son. Be hereafter the pledge of Allah breathed in
thy right ear." He then repeats after his Sheikh the
words, "Mohammed is my leader, and Ali is my guide."
The Sheikh asks, "Dost thou accept me as thy guide
(meaning as the representative of Ali)?" to which he
responds, "I accept thee as my guide;" and the Sheikh
adds, "Then I accept thee as my son." The postulant
now approaches the Sheikh, before whom he first bows
low and then prostrates himself, touching the floor with
his forehead. Kneeling opposite to him so closely that
their knees touch, the Sheikh takes the postulant's right
hand in his, and the thumbs of both are raised to repre-
sent the Arabic letter *Alif.* The latter places his ear to
the mouth of the Sheikh, who imparts to him in a whisper
the *Ikranamek*, or secret vows of the Order.

The disciple does not, however, even after this formal
reception into it, become at once a full member of the
Order. This grade is only reached after, it may be, years
of further probation, and its attainment depends upon the
proofs he is able to give of his progress in spirituality.
His final admission to full brotherhood is usually determined by a revelation from the *Pir*, or from Ali, received
simultaneously by himself and his Sheikh. While passing
through these intermediate stages, the aspirant is under

the guidance of the Sheikh, or of an initiate who has
himself reached the highest degree.   During the first
stage, which is termed *Sheriat*, or "The Law," the disciple
observes all the usual rites of Moslem worship, obeys all
the commands and precepts of the Koran like any other
True Believer, and is treated by the Brethren of the Community as an uninitiated outsider.   He is taught at the
same time to concentrate his thoughts so completely on
his "guide," as to become eventually absorbed in him as
a spiritual link with the supreme object of all devotion.
This "guide" must be the neophyte's shield against all
worldly thoughts and desires; his spirit must aid him
in all his efforts, accompany him wherever he may be,
and be ever present to his mental vision.   Such a frame
of mind is termed "annihilation into the *Murshid*," and
the guide discovers, by means of his own visions, the
degree of spirituality to which his disciple has attained,
and to what extent his soul has become absorbed into
his own.

The *Murid* now enters upon what, in Dervish phrase-
ology, is called "The Path."   During this period, which
forms in reality the transition from outward to hidden
things, the disciple is familiarised with the philosophical
and poetical writings of the great Sufi doctors, which
form the chief subject of the lectures and studies of the
Order.   He is taught to substitute spiritual for ritual
worship, and led by degrees to abandon the dogmas and
formulas of Islam as necessary only for the unenlightened
masses.   This method is, however, pursued with great

tact and caution; for a disciple is not released from the usual observances of religion until he has given proofs of sincere piety, virtue, and exceptional spirituality. This period is consequently one of extreme asceticism; and a Dervish at this stage of his training passes most of his time in solitary contemplation, endeavouring to detach his mind from all visible objects in order to attain the desired union with the Deity, his guide meanwhile imparting to him his own mystical philosophy as he finds him capable of receiving it. If the disciple's religious feelings appear to be shocked by any maxim to which he has given utterance, a jesuitical expedient known as the *ketman* supplies him with a double sense which enables him at once to convince his disciple of the groundlessness of his objections. If, on the contrary, a "guide" finds his disciple's theological digestion robust, his advance on "The Path" will be correspondingly rapid. He is now supposed to come under the spiritual influence of the *Pir*, or Founder of the Order, in whom he in turn becomes spiritually absorbed to such a degree as to be virtually one with him, acquiring his attributes and power of performing supernatural acts. Not every Dervish, however, attains even this degree of spirituality; and the highest, in which the mystic believes himself to have become absorbed in the Deity, is reached only by the favoured few. It is during the forty days' fast performed in the solitude of his cell at this period of his training that the disciple has the visions which, interpreted by his guide, announce the distance he has travelled on "The Path." The Pilgrimage

P

is forthwith undertaken, in which it is incumbent on him
to visit not only the Holy Cities of Islam, but also, at
Bagdad and Damascus, the Shrines of the most renowned
Dervish Saints.

The attainment of a high degree of sanctity being thus
the aim of every true Dervish, he seeks, in order to attain
this, to lead a life of sinless retirement from the world,
and spends his days and nights in prayer and meditation.
Fully impressed with the possibility of ultimately attaining intimate divine communion, the ardent aspirant looks
upon every mundane interest as unworthy of consideration; his mind becomes more and more completely
absorbed in mystic contemplation; and as the result of
his constant invocation of the name of the Deity, he hears,
even when in the midst of a noisy crowd, no other sound
but *Allah! Allah!* unless, indeed, it be some divine
command addressed to him in return. The more destitute a Dervish is of worldly goods, the fewer are his ties
to earth; the more emaciated his body with privation and
fasting, the greater his advance in spirituality; the ills of
existence affect him not, and death has for him no terrors.
His solitude is cheered by the presence of angelic visitors,
who impart to him wondrous things hidden from the ken
of ordinary mortals; or they are the bearers of direct
messages from the Deity, who thus makes known to His
servants His holy will concerning men. And when commanded to do so, the Dervish fearlessly denounces, in the
Name of Allah, the great ones of the earth who, by their
misdeeds, have incurred the divine displeasure.

PART III

DOMESTIC LIFE

CHAPTER XI

THE HAREM SYSTEM

THE Social, rather than Religious, Law which lies at the root of the Harem system enjoins that no free woman or girl over twelve years of age must appear unveiled before a man outside the prohibited degrees of relationship. As among the Osmanlis first cousins may marry, the circle of male relatives possessing the privilege of access to a harem is thus strictly limited to fathers and grandfathers, brothers and uncles of its female inmates. Inseparable, therefore, from the harem system is the institution of domestic slavery, for to slave women, who are the absolute property of their owners, the above restrictions do not apply. The demand for slaves for the service of Turkish households is practically perennial, seeing that, instead of forming a permanent class or caste in the country, the vast majority of those who have entered it as bondmen and women obtain, in a few years, their freedom. Slavery, however, as now practised in Turkey, is in direct contravention of the law of Islam, which only recognises as legitimate property non-Moslems who have fallen as spoils of war into the power of the True Believers. For the vast majority of the slaves brought to Turkey at the present day are drawn from the Circassian race, who profess the creed of Islam, and their purchase and sale are, consequently, illegal acts which the Sheikh-ul-Islam himself would have some difficulty in justifying. Purchasers, however, get over this difficulty by asking no questions as to the provenance of the girls and children offered for sale by the dealers, and absolve their conscience with the convenient formula, "Theirs be the sin." The slave-market in Constantinople has, in deference to European opinion, long ago been closed; but the demand for slave women being undiminished, the only consequence of the enactment against slavery has been enormously to increase the horrors of the traffic in its initial stage. For the Circassian women and girls—who, purchased from their kindred, are not generally unwilling emigrants—instead of travelling to their destination as formerly with but little discomfort, are now usually conveyed across the stormy Black Sea in the depth of winter when the Russian cruisers are withdrawn, and many of the wretched little vessels in which they are embarked are never heard of again. The result of Europe's humanitarian endeavours to "suppress the slave-trade" is consequently not only to increase to a horrible degree the sufferings of those it is desired to benefit, but also to subject a still greater number to such sufferings, as, in order to allow for losses by the way, the number originally recruited is largely in excess of the demands of the market.

Once safely landed, the slaves are dispersed to the houses of the various dealers to whom they have been consigned ; and when recovered from the effects of the journey, they are disposed of either to the Imperial Palace or to private persons. As the Sultan's household is said to contain even in its present reduced state, over a thousand persons, all of slave origin, a certain proportion of these immigrants are destined to keep up the number of these Palace inmates. Negresses and others who excel rather in strength of muscle than in beauty of form and feature are purchased for the menial labour of a household, those more highly gifted by nature being reserved for higher duties. Since the abolition of the slave-market, private trade in slaves has become much more general and widespread than formerly, this traffic being often carried on by ladies of high rank, some of whom are themselves emancipated slaves. On being informed of the arrival in the capital of a fresh batch of girls, these ladies either drive to the slave-dealer's establishment, or have the human chattels brought to their *konaks* for inspection. Children of from six to ten years of age are most sought after by these amateurs, who pay considerable sums for them in the expectation of realising a large profit when the girls are grown up. The selection made, and the bargaining concluded, the girl is taken to her new home and placed under the care of a *kalfa*, or head servant, who carefully trains her for the position she will probably be called upon to occupy. Should she be endowed with personal charms, this may be that of odalisk, or even wife, of some grandee, or she may be presented to the Sultan by her mistress, or sold for that purpose to some other person anxious to acquire Palace influence. Many of these amateur slave-dealers are the wives of Ministers and other State or Palace functionaries, who vie with each other in having the most beautiful and expensively dressed girls in their harems. For a lady with slaves to dispose of naturally dresses them well and otherwise makes the most of their personal charms in order to attract customers. When the mistress and her daughters go out walking, driving, or shopping, calling, picnicking, or to the public baths, a number of slaves invariably share the treat. And it is no doubt greatly owing to this custom of including some of the slaves of the household in every pleasure party, or out-door excursion, that misconceptions have arisen in the minds of foreigners as to the general practice of polygamy. A carriage or carriages filled with smartly dressed Turkish *hanums*—or what appear to the inexperienced eye as such —are by the tourist put down as the wives or odalisks of one Pasha, while, as a matter of fact, they are his wife's private property, over whom, consequently, he has no rights whatever. I remember, indeed, in the early days of my residence in Turkey, being myself considerably puzzled as to the status of the half-dozen or so richly dressed young women who arrived with a Pasha's lady to

pay an afternoon call—or rather a three hours' visitation
—and who, on arriving, divested themselves, according to
custom, of their outdoor cloaks and veils.

Domestic slavery, accordingly, as practised in Moslem
Turkey, it need hardly be said, differs widely from the
same institution as it existed until recently in Christian
America. In Islam, slaves are protected by many humane
laws; they are, on the whole, treated quite paternally;
and not being looked down upon as a class apart, are
speedily absorbed into the free and native population.
Food of an inferior quality is not deemed by Moslems
"good enough for servants;" but, according to the command of the Prophet, a slave fares as well as her owners.
Whatever her faults and shortcomings, she may not be
sent adrift into the wide world, her owner being responsible for her maintenance. At the end of seven years'
servitude she can claim her liberty, and generally obtains
with it a trousseau and a husband. Occasionally, of
course, a slave may fall into bad hands, and be resold
before the expiry of the seven years, in order that her
owner may not lose the purchase-money; or may become
the property of persons of violent temper and cruel
character, who take advantage of her helpless position
and ill treat her.

Female slaves have, however, on the whole, little to
complain of. The good fortune of those gifted with personal attractions is assured from the outset, as many
Turks prefer, for various reasons, to marry women who
have been brought up as slaves. For marriage with a

free woman—as will be seen in a subsequent chapter—is
an expensive matter for a young bridegroom and his
parents, owing to the lavish outlay in presents and entertainments obligatory on such occasions. Consequently, if
a father cannot afford to marry his son to a maiden of his
own social standing, he purchases for him a slave girl who
has been brought up in some great lady's harem, and no
expense is incurred beyond the purchase-money. A slave,
having no position of her own, is likely to be submissive
and obedient to, and anxious to please her lord and
master ; she has no troublesome pretensions or caprices,
and no interfering relatives to take her part against him
should any disagreement arise. A free woman, on the
other hand, is by no means always disposed to have,
according to her own expression, "neither mouth nor
tongue," but is fully aware of her rights, and capable of
asserting them ; and the moral support afforded by her
family gives her an assurance which her husband often
finds extremely inconvenient. Should a slave bear a child
to her master, she cannot be resold, but has the right to
bring up under its father's roof her offspring, which is considered legitimate, and may inherit the family property in
equal shares with the children of a free wife, should there
be any. The distinctive provisions of the Moslem Social
and Marriage Laws, indeed, ensure that there shall be no
relations whatever between men and women—whether
free women or slave women—in which the latter, from the
very fact of such relations, shall not have enforceable legal
rights for herself and her children. In all probability her

owner will, in course of time, set her free and marry his child's mother, in which case she assumes the social status, and is invested with all the rights and privileges of a free-born Osmanli matron.

Nor are these rights and privileges inconsiderable, but compare favourably with those enjoyed by women generally in Christian Europe. As a daughter, an Osmanli woman is entitled, on the decease of her father, to inherit his property in common with her brothers in a proportion determined by law according to the number of his children. As a wife, she retains the uncontrolled possession both of the wealth which may have been hers before marriage and of that which may subsequently accrue to her. She can inherit property without the intervention of trustees, and dispose of it as she pleases during her lifetime or by Will. No doctrine of "coverture" exists for her; she can sue or be sued independently of her husband; sue or be sued by him; and plead her own cause personally in the Courts of Justice. But, whether a Turkish wife be or be not an heiress, her husband is equally bound to support her and her slaves according to her rank and his means, and also, to quote from the *Hedaya*,[1] "to provide a separate apartment for his wife's habitation, to be solely and exclusively appropriated by her, because this is essentially necessary to her, and is therefore her due, the same as her maintenance."

As to the much-discussed question of the custody of children, this was settled for Moslems at the outset by

[1] The *Hedaya*, or "Guide," is a Commentary on Moslem Law.

Mohammed, who decreed that a son must remain with his mother so long as her care is necessary to his well-being, and a daughter until she arrives at puberty. And in the case of a child born after the separation of its parents, should the mother nurse it, the father is required to pay her for so doing, and also, if wealthy, "to expend proportionately for the maintenance of the mother and nurse out of his plenty." On the death of a mother the right of custody reverts to her female relatives, the child's maternal grandmother having a prior right, and after her, failing a sister of suitable age, its aunts.

A husband might appear, at first sight, to possess great privileges in the matter of divorce, for he has merely to say to his wife in a moment of anger, "Cover thy face, thy *nekyah* is in thine hand!" and the separation is legally effected. Women are, however, on the other hand, safe-guarded against a too arbitrary exercise of this prerogative by certain wise regulations which to a great extent modify, in practice, such facilities. In the first place, there is the religious restriction—"The curse of Allah," said the Prophet, "rests on him who, without just cause, repudiates his wife;" in the second, the social restriction—for parents would hesitate to give their daughters to a man who had thus acted; and thirdly, a serious obstacle to a hasty divorce is offered by the *nekyah*—the settlement upon the wife of a considerable sum of money, varying naturally according to social position, payable to her in the event of such dismissal from her husband's roof. So essential, indeed, to a Moslem marriage is such a dower considered, that even were mention of it omitted from a marriage contract, the law would presume it by virtue of the contract itself. Being a civil act, consisting of a proposal on one side and an acceptance on the other, and rendered legal by the presence of two witnesses, a Moslem marriage can also be dissolved by the contracting parties by three several methods of procedure. If a couple, for instance, are not on good terms, and all the attempts at reconciliation made by their friends prove fruitless, a divorce *by mutual consent* is pronounced, and the woman returns to her father's house, taking with her, besides the *nekyah*, everything she brought with her, or has become possessed of since her marriage. If a man divorce his wife without her consent, she leaves his house equally well provided. And a *hanum* can, on her side, obtain release from a distasteful union, with payment of the *nekyah*, for various reasons, among which are the husband's desertion, cruelty, or neglect to maintain her in the degree of comfort to which she is by law and custom entitled. If, however, a wife, without such adequate reason, and contrary to the desire of her husband, quit his roof and demand a divorce, she very properly obtains it only by forfeiting the *nekyah*.

Divorce being thus a simple process for a husband with money at his command for payment of the *nekyah*, a conjugal quarrel may easily end in a pronouncement of divorce, when the lady will immediately leave the abode of her irate spouse. Reflection, however, and the intervention of relatives and friends, may lead him to regret his hasty action, and a second marriage will follow the reconciliation of the parties. But this privilege has also its limitations. For after a third divorce, the parties may not again contract marriage, unless the lady has in the mean time entered into a formal legal union with another man. And great is the consternation and gossip in the harems of the neighbourhood, when it is reported that quick-tempered Achmet Bey has pronounced "the threefold divorce," and his pretty but provoking wife has returned for the third time to the paternal roof. This difficulty may be, and usually is, got over by marriage with, and subsequent speedy divorce from, some elderly and impecunious individual, who receives a fee for his good offices in the matter. There is always, however, a certain amount of risk in such a procedure, as the husband *pro tem.* cannot be forced to liberate the lady should he be minded to retain her as his wife. Indeed, I once heard of a case in which, the *hanum* being a woman of independent means, the temporary make-believe husband chose to be a husband in permanence, and no power on earth could release the unhappy woman from her intolerable position. The fact, however, that the words, "May I divorce my wife if——" constitute to Moslems the most solemn and binding of oaths, is sufficient evidence of how repugnant to them is the use, and still more the abuse, of their privileges in this respect.

Notwithstanding the fact that the law of Islam allows a man to marry as many as four wives, and to be the owner of an unlimited number of slave women, an Osmanli household is by no means composed—as is popularly supposed in the West—of a large number of women, all of whom stand in wifely relations to their lord and master. Indeed, as a matter of fact, at the present day among Turks of the industrial classes one wife is the rule, and among those of the upper classes more than one wife is the exception. And thus it has, apparently, always more or less been among Moslems generally. For the Khalif Ali, the nephew and son-in-law of the Prophet, married a second wife only after the death of his beloved Fatima; and if we search the biographies of the eminent philosophers, theologians, historians, and poets, who flourished in the palmy days of the Ottoman Empire, we shall find that very few of them took advantage of their privileges in this respect. For in addition to the numerous other considerations which render a plurality of wives undesirable, there is the very serious obstacle of expense. A second wife means an extra apartment, or suite of apartments, an extra slave, or train of slaves, according to her rank in life—for each *hanum* must have her own special attendants—and an extra allowance of pin money, as a Turkish bride rarely brings a dowry to her husband. There is, besides, no great superabundance of women in the country, notwithstanding the continual influx of slaves, and every mother of a marriageable girl naturally prefers to see her daughter become a *Bash Kadin*, or chief wife, as she thus would take rank before successive wives. Lack of progeny by the first spouse is most frequently the reason of a Turk's incurring this extra expense, and also the risk of having his domestic peace disturbed by taking a second. He may, of course, if so disposed, divorce the first; but, as above remarked, divorce for such a reason alone would not only entail social odium, but he would in that case be obliged to pay to the discarded wife the sum stipulated in the marriage contract.

Two wives, indeed, seem to be the extreme limit nowadays; and only once during my long residence in different parts of the Ottoman Empire had I the opportunity of visiting a harem containing even this number. It was during a brief visit made from Smyrna to the ancient and picturesque town of Magnesia—Magnesia under Sipylus—in Asia Minor, and the harem in question was that of the Sheikh, or Prior, of the "Dancing" Dervishes, whose office is, when possible, hereditary. The first wife, to whom he had been married a dozen years or so, was childless, and the *Ikindji Kadin* was a bride of a few weeks only. After having been courteously received in the *selamlik* of the *tekkeh* by Sheikh Ali, we were conducted to the courtyard gate of the *haremlik*. This was opened to us by an old woman, who, while we entered, kept her face concealed with what seemed to us unnecessary care from the gaze of any chance male passers-by, and then conducted us up an outside staircase to a broad covered balcony on which all the principal rooms opened. Over the doors hung the carpet *portières* so common in Turkish houses; and raising one of these, she held it back while we entered the *divan khané*, or sitting-room. A pretty and pleasant young woman with blue eyes and brown hair hanging below her waist in two thick plaits, uncurled herself from the divan and salaamed low in acknowledgment of the greeting of the *doyenne* of our party; but, divining with ready tact that we other Europeans were unaccustomed to the performance of this graceful Oriental salute, she offered her hand to each in turn, and begged us to be seated. This lady was the Sheikh's second wife; but in a few minutes the *Bash Kadin* entered—a tall, dark, imperious looking dame, just beginning to lose the freshness of youth, with heavy black eyebrows artificially extended until they met over her aquiline nose. Both ladies were dressed in trailing *intaries*, or house-dresses of cashmere-patterned stuff worn under short cloth jackets lined with fur, the season being winter; a kerchief of coloured muslin being so adjusted as to form a sort of little cap surmounting their simple coiffure. Half an hour is the minimum time in which a Turkish visit can be paid. But as soon as etiquette permitted—which was not, of course, until sweets and coffee had been served and partaken of—we rose to take our leave.

Slaves, however, whether male or female, are by no means always compelled to wait seven years before receiving their freedom and its attendant advantages. For it being considered by Moslems a pious and meritorious act to free a slave, Osmanli men and women frequently, either in their Wills or on their death-beds, bequeath their liberty to the slaves of the household. A male slave thus set free becomes, so far as civil rights are concerned, the equal of his former owner, and may aspire to the highest offices of State; while his wife, whatever her origin, can claim the status of a *hanum*. In former centuries, indeed, many an officer in high rank and Minister of State has been of slave origin. It is also a very common practice for childless couples and widows to enfranchise and adopt as their heirs slave children to whom they have taken a fancy. I was some years ago in the habit of meeting a lady, a Circassian by birth, who, brought to Constantinople as a mere infant, had herself been purchased and adopted by a lady of high rank; and when left in middle age a childless widow, she in her turn enfranchised and adopted two little girls of her own race, whom she brought up and found husbands for.

In former centuries the slaves, both male and female, brought into the Turkish slave-market were drawn from a great variety of races and nationalities, European and Asiatic; but at the present day the white slaves are brought chiefly from Circassia, the rest being Yezidis from Kurdistan, or Georgians—though, since the occupation by Russia of that former happy hunting-ground of the slave-dealer, this traffic has only been carried on clandestinely. The traffic in white male slaves has of late years become comparatively insignificant, free men, both Moslem and Christian, being now employed in the service of the *selamlik* in the capacities of cook, pipe-bearer, coffee-maker, and body-servant, as well as in the stables as coachmen and grooms.

A considerable number of negroes, as also of Abyssinians and other Africans of both sexes, are, however, still annually smuggled into the country.

Circassian women who have passed through the slavery stage are said to evince a certain racial sympathy for each other, and also to be very charitable to those who have been less fortunate than themselves. The discovery that an acquaintance is also of slave origin forms immediately a bond of union between two women. This race feeling is not, however, perpetuated in their offspring, who are, of course, Osmanlis. It is only the negresses who always remain a class apart, and fall not infrequently into penury and want. As a rule, however, they are themselves chiefly to blame for their misfortunes. For, after they have been freed and married, it not infrequently happens that their ungoverned tempers cause them to quarrel with, and separate from, their husbands, when they are obliged to support themselves as best they can by hawking parched peas and such trifles about the streets. The quarter inhabited by the negro population is squalid and miserable in the extreme, being a mere collection of wretched tumble-down hovels. The thousands upon thousands of negroes and negresses who have, since the Turkish Conquest, been brought into the country, might lead us to expect to find a considerable admixture of black blood in the lower classes especially of the population. That is, however, not the case. Though negresses and Abyssinians marry both whites and men of their own race, the climate does not seem favourable to the

Q

propagation of the coloured races, and the few negro or mulatto children who come into the world seldom survive infancy.

Low, however, in the social scale as are the negresses of Turkey, there exists among them an *esprit de corps* which has led to the formation in the Capital of a society for mutual aid and protection, not only against the tyranny of masters and mistresses, but in sickness and other accidents of life. This association constitutes also a centre of reunion for the observation of those superstitious heathen rites which its members have brought with them from their native land, and still cherish, notwithstanding their profession of the Faith of Islam. The society possesses a number of local lodges, each under the direction of a president, called the *Kolbaski*, who, while acting as the priestess of their strange cult, manages also the property of the community which has been amassed little by little from the contributions regularly made by its members. From this fund she is expected to purchase the freedom of negress slaves who are on bad terms with their owners, as also to receive in her house freed women who are sick or without employment. Men of negro race are also entitled to receive assistance from this association, but they take no part in the rites and ceremonies of which the lodges are periodically the scene.

CHAPTER XII

FAMILY CEREMONIES—(1) BIRTH AND CIRCUMCISION CEREMONIES

IT is a noteworthy fact that the more secluded the domestic life of a people, the greater the publicity given to such family events as births, marriages, and deaths. The Turks form no exception to this rule, the celebration of all these family happenings being made the occasion of much display and large accompanying hospitality.

The anticipated arrival of a "little stranger" is announced to the neighbourhood by the arrival of the *Ebé Kadin*—the Turkish Wise Woman—preceded by a *hamal* bearing on his porter's saddle the emblems of her calling. As soon as a baby is born its mother is placed on a state bedstead, used only on such special occasions, which is spread with elaborately embroidered and fringed sheets of native gauze and covered with quilts of satin encrusted with needlework in gold and silver thread. At the head are piled half a dozen long narrow silken pillows enclosed in "slips" matching the sheets. Round the lady's head is bound a crimson kerchief to which is attached a bunch of charms, a gauze veil of the same hue being thrown loosely over them—the whole *coiffure* being designed to keep the *Peris* at a distance. For although these imaginary beings are not, like the Nereids of Modern Greek mythology, credited with the power of carrying off bodily new-born infants, their baleful influence is none the less to be carefully guarded against, and the mother and babe should never be left alone for a minute until after the bath ceremony has taken place. If, as among the poor, this is sometimes unavoidable, a broom to which a head of garlic has been tied is placed by the bedside to keep away uncanny visitors.

In the mean time the baby has been dressed. But no dainty *layette*, like that which awaits the arrival of a "little stranger" in the West, has been prepared for the little Osmanli, however wealthy his parents may be. His small body is at once tightly swathed in cotton bandages under a *libardé*, or gown of quilted cotton stuff; and various quilted wrappers bound one over another convert the poor mite into a shapeless bundle, its head being covered with a little cap of red silk from which hangs a tassel of seed pearls and a bunch of amulets—coral horns, turquoises, or pieces of blue glass, etc.—to ward off, besides the *Peris*, the "Evil Eye," as much dreaded in Turkey as in Southern Italy. Its toilette completed, the baby is laid on a handsome quilt in the walnut-wood cradle, and over it is spread a large square of crimson gauze.

When all these arrangements are complete, the happy father enters to congratulate his wife, and confer upon the baby the name by which it is henceforth to be distinguished.

Carrying the infant outside the door of the natal chamber, its sire repeats a prayer, invoking the blessing of Allah on his offspring, and then pronounces three times in its ear the name chosen for it. Should he be unacquainted with the formula, the parish priest is called in to assist him in the performance of this duty. The Moslem equivalent for the rite of baptism is of course circumcision, but this may be, and often is, deferred for many years.

Among the many restrictions to which the mother is subjected by custom and the *Ebé*—as the Turkish Mrs. Gamp is termed—is that of refraining from pure water either for drinking or ablutionary purposes. If thirsty, she may partake of "sherbet" made from sugar-candy and spices, or a *tisane* of lime-flowers or maiden-hair fern. Little rest is allowed her, for, as soon as the event is made known, her chamber is crowded with friends and neighbours who hasten to offer their felicitations, and sit for hours discussing the sweets, coffee, and other refreshments which it is customary to offer on these occasions. On the third day a *djemiet*, or formal reception, is held by the mother, for which invitations have been issued on the preceding day, conveyed verbally by an old woman whose profession is that of *musdadji*, or "bringer of tidings," and accompanied by bottles of the above-described "sherbet." "Open house" is also kept on this day, and all visitors, whether invited or not, are hospitably received, but with this difference—the bidden guests sit down to luncheon, while the unbidden are regaled only with light refreshments. Hired musicians receive at the door of the

haremlik and escort upstairs the more distinguished
guests, who arrive in parties preceded by servants carrying
baskets of sweets prettily decorated with flowers, enveloped in gauze, and tied with ribbons. If the father holds
an official post, it is customary for his fellow officials and
subordinates to send with the baskets of sweets more or
less valuable presents. Among the poorer classes, however, gifts of coffee, sugar, cakes, etc., are, on these
occasions, brought by the visitors in order to lessen for
the family the expense of the customary hospitality.
After divesting themselves of their out-of-door veils and
cloaks in an anteroom, according to Turkish custom when
paying calls, the visitors are ushered with ceremonious
formality into the state bed-chamber. "*Mashallah*—in
the name of Allah—long-lived and happy may it be!"
exclaim the matrons in turn to the happy mother, who
kisses their hands in acknowledgment of their good
wishes. Little or no notice is, however, taken of the
infant personally, as its near relatives are best pleased
when its presence is altogether ignored, and so spared the
risk of the "Evil Eye" being cast upon it. Should, however, feminine curiosity and interest in babies prove too
strong to allow of the "little stranger's" being entirely
neglected, the *hanums*, after feigning to spit on it to avert
the "Evil Eye," conceal their private approval under such
disparaging remarks as "Nasty ugly little thing," to show
their good will. For, in the East, it is most unadvisable
openly to express admiration for either persons or things,
as any future accident or misfortune is certain to be

WHERE THE SWEETS ARE MADE AND SOLD

attributed to the malice or ill-will underlying the honeyed words of commendation.

But amulets, spittings, and abusive epithets notwithstanding, it is considered expedient to make doubly sure that no ill effects of the dreaded " Evil Eye " have been left behind. So no sooner has the last guest departed than the Ebé Kadin, assisted by the women of the household, proceeds to ascertain this by the following process. A handful of cloves are procured and thrown singly on the hot embers of the *mangal*, or charcoal brazier, one for each visitor. If the clove explodes with a report, it is held to be proof positive that the person named with it has cast the *nasar* on mother or child—or, it may be, on both. As an immediate exorcism, snips of their hair are placed on the charcoal embers, and the supposed sufferers are fumigated with the smoke arising therefrom. This is followed by spittings, blowings, prayers, and divers mysterious incantations which are persisted in until a fit of yawning announces that the spell has been removed. An old woman is, however, next despatched on some pretext or other to the dwelling of the person suspected, with the object of surreptitiously obtaining possession of some scrap of her clothing with which to make a further fumigation ; and this successfully accomplished, the minds of the . mother and her friends are, for the time being at least, set at rest.

Among the poorer classes, the bath ceremony usually takes place on the fourth day after the birth of a child, but with the wealthy it is often deferred until the eighth day. On the occasion of the birth of a first-born, great formality is *de rigueur*. If the ceremony takes place in the private *hammam* usually attached to the *haremlik* division of a mansion, a number of friends are invited to join in the ablutions, and partake of luncheon and other refreshments ; if at the public baths, the invited *hanums*, accompanied by their attendants bearing the bath requisites in *boktchas*, or bundle-wraps, assemble at the house, and, preceded by the Wise Woman carrying the baby, walk in procession to the baths. After being formally divested of her garments in the *saouklik*, or "cool room," the mother is enveloped in a silken bath-wrap, and, shod with a pair of high pattens of walnut-wood inlaid with silver, is led to the hot chamber, supported on one side by the *Hammamdji Hanum*, or Head Bathwoman, and on the other side by a relative, and followed by the rest of the company. The baby is first taken in hand, and after it has been well rubbed and scrubbed, the Wise Woman turns her attention to the mother. Before commencing operations, however, she throws a bunch of keys into the marble basin, mutters a spell of a religious character, and then blows three times into the water. These preliminary precautions taken against the Peris who especially haunt the waters, the usual ablutionary routine is proceeded with by the company generally. At its conclusion the mother is placed in a reclining position on the raised marble slab in the centre of the apartment, and her body thickly plastered over with a sort of ointment composed of honey and various aromatic condiments, held to possess strengthening and recuperating properties. This is left on for about an hour, the tedium of the process being enlivened by the ladies of the company with songs and conversation, and every now and again they transfer with their forefingers some of the spicy compound to their mouths, it being considered lucky to get a taste of it. When what remains of the unguent after the *hanums* have thus regaled themselves has been washed off, the mother is wrapped in her *havlu*, or robe of Turkey towelling, the fringed borders of which are worked in gold thread, and conducted back to the spacious "cool room." The *Hanums* seat themselves cross-legged on the raised and cushioned platform surrounding this apartment; but before taking her own place the hostess proceeds to kiss in turn the hands of all the elderly ladies present, the salute being acknowledged with the good wish, "May it be to your health." Refreshments are offered at intervals during these ceremonies, which occupy the greater part of the day.

The circumcision of a boy is made the occasion of another important family ceremony called the *Sunnet dughun*, the festivities with which it is celebrated extending over a whole week. Hospitable on all occasions, the Turks are pre-eminently so on this, when it is held to be a religious duty to show special attention and regard to the poor and needy. Consequently, people of the labouring class who cannot themselves afford the expense of a *Sunnet dughun* for their boys, defer the rite until they hear that the son of some grandee in their neighbourhood is about to be circumcised, when they send in the names of their boys with the request that they may be allowed to participate. The rich man, if a good Moslem, will grant such permission to as many of the sons of his poor neighbours as his means allow of, such acts of piety being held well pleasing unto Allah. When a circumcision ceremony takes place in the Imperial Palace, custom requires that the Padishah should place no limit on the number of participants. As the head of the house in which a *Sunnet dughun* is celebrated is in duty bound to furnish each candidate for initiation with a complete outfit, and defray all other attendant expenses, it is often an exceedingly expensive affair for a man of rank; and even among the middle classes, who limit the festivities to one day, the obligatory minimum expenditure is seldom under £10.

The formalities begin on a Monday, when the boys are sent to the Public Baths, their heads being then shaven for the first time, with the exception of a tuft of hair left on the crown, which is plaited with tinsel thread. The grandee's son is richly dressed, his coat and fez being studded with pearls, the number of ornaments considered necessary for this important occasion being so great that they have in part to be borrowed from relatives and friends, even the humblest urchin being bedecked with gold and gems. Their ablutions performed and gala clothes donned, the boys leave the baths escorted by a number of old ladies to make a round of calls at the houses of their friends, whom they formally invite to the *dughun* festivities. In the afternoon, and also on the morrow, a series of entertainments is given in the *selamlik* of the mansion, Wednesday and Thursday being reserved for the subsequent festivities in the *haremlik*, which are enlivened by music and a variety of amusements. On Thursday morning the women of the household busy themselves in preparing couches for the boys, who meantime, mounted on gaily caparisoned horses led by grooms, and accompanied by the Hodja, or family tutor, the barber, and a crowd of male relatives, make a progress through the streets of the quarter.

On returning to the house of festivity, the children are received at the door of the *selamlik* by their respective fathers. As the horse of the young bey is brought to the mounting-block, and his father is about to help him to dismount, his hand is stayed by the Hodja with the words, "With what gift has my lord endowed his son?" The father mentions the destined present, which may be landed property or some object of value, according to his means, and then lifts him down from his horse. For the other boys is also claimed and received a gift from their next-of-kin, or, failing these, from their entertainer, who is held to occupy for the occasion a father's place.

The rite of circumcision is performed in the *selamlik* on the morning of Friday, and this accomplished, the boys are again consigned to the care of the women, who place them on the couches previously prepared, and make every effort to amuse and distract them. They are also visited during the day by their female relatives, who bring money and other gifts, not only to the children, but also to the barber and the *musdadji* who has announced to the mother of each boy the completion of the sacred rite. On the following morning the children are removed to their respective homes, but the entertainments are prolonged for another couple of days, during which liberal hospitality is offered to the poor.

CHAPTER XIII

FAMILY CEREMONIES—(2) MARRIAGE CEREMONIES

IN common with all Moslems, the Turks hold the estate of marriage in great esteem. For it is related in the *Hadith*, or "Traditions," that Mohammed said, "When the servant of Allah marries he perfects half of his religion."[1] Early marriages are, consequently, for this as well as for other reasons, the rule among the Osmanlis, the patriarchal customs alluded to in a previous chapter making it unnecessary for a youth to wait until he has a home of his own before taking a wife. Formerly, youths of eighteen were married to girls of from twelve to fifteen; but nowadays such very youthful couples are seldom met with, though at a friend's house I once saw a bride of twelve who was the wife of a Turkish orderly in the service of the Pasha, my friend's husband.

When, accordingly, it has been decided by the family council that the time has arrived for a youth to marry, his mother, if she has not already chosen a bride for him,

[1] It is also related that the Prophet, being informed that a certain man was unmarried, asked him, "Art thou sound and healthy?" "I am," replied the bachelor. "Then," said the Friend of Allah, "thou art one of the brothers of the devil" (*Mishkat*, bk. xiii. ch. 1).

makes inquiries among her friends and of the old women brokers—who act also as *koulavous* or "go-betweens" in matters matrimonial—as to families having pretty and marriageable daughters. This ascertained, she drives to each harem in turn, accompanied by one or more near relatives and the *koulavous*. Introductions are unnecessary, but the object of the visit is mentioned to the slave who, on their entering, comes forward to remove, according to custom, the outdoor veils and cloaks of the visitors. The lady of the house, informed of this, hastens to receive her guests with all honour, and should there be more than one daughter, the eldest proceeds to dress and adorn herself for inspection—for among the Turks, as with their Greek neighbours, daughters are married according to seniority. The two mothers meanwhile exchange conventional compliments until the *portière* is raised and the maiden enters, and after saluting the strangers by kissing their hands, she offers to each in turn a cup of coffee from the tray which has been brought in at the same time by a slave. While this is being partaken of, she stands in modest attitude, and after receiving the empty cups salaams and vanishes.

"*Mashallah !* What a beauty! Your daughter, *Hanum Effendi*, is like a full moon!" So the visitors, whatever their private opinion, are required by etiquette to exclaim. Other compliments follow, and then the chief *Guerudji*, or "Viewer," proceeds to expatiate on the good qualities of the would-be bridegroom, mentions the amount of the *nekyah*, or settlements, he or his family are prepared to offer, makes inquiries as to the girl's age and fortune, if any, and finally departs with the conventional remark that, should *Kismet* have decreed it, they will become better acquainted. It is considered no slight if nothing further comes of the visit of inspection, which is allowed to be, in legal phrase, "without prejudice." After some half-dozen harems have been thus visited, the lady returns home to describe the damsels to her husband and son ; and, the selection made, intermediaries are despatched to the family of the fortunate maiden to settle the preliminaries.

Meanwhile, though the youth may not, of course, see the maiden unveiled, she, on her side, is naturally anxious to see her future husband, and an opportunity for this is usually arranged by the respective mothers in the course of a drive abroad, when he will be found at some spot previously agreed upon. Boy and girl friendships, how- ever, not infrequently survive the intervening years of separation, and, developing into a warmer feeling, end in happy marriages. For in the young, romance is stronger than social and religious conventionalities, and love can surmount even the barriers of harem restraint. When the parties to the contract are mutually satisfied, the customary betrothal gifts—a silver jewel-box, hand-mirror, and other toilet requisites—are sent to the bride, who in her turn presents the bridegroom with a jewelled snuff-box, cash- mere shawl, etc. His mother then visits the bride, taking with her some yards of red silk and a basket of bonbons. The former is spread on the floor in front of the divan, and on it the bride stands when she approaches to kiss the hand of her future mother-in-law, who presents her with the sweets and her blessing. Half a bonbon bitten in two by the girl's pearly teeth is conveyed back to the bridegroom, presumably as a first love-token. A few days later the *aghirlik*, a sum of money which is practically the bridegroom's contribution to the expenses of the wedding festivities, is sent to the maiden's father; and eight days after this betrothal is followed by the legal marriage.

According to the law of Islam, marriage is not a religious, but a civil contract, the validity of which consists in its being attested by at least two witnesses. The ceremony takes place in the house of the bride's father, in the *selamlik* of which the amount of the *nekyah*—the before-mentioned sum to be paid to the bride in the event of divorce—is finally discussed and formally agreed to. The contract drawn up and attested, the bridegroom stands up and thrice proclaims his desire to wed the daughter of Selim Effendi, or Ali Bey, as the case may be. Thereupon the *Imâm*, who is present in his legal capacity, proceeds with the maiden's father to the door of communication with the women's apartments, behind which the bride and her friends are assembled, and after declaring the amount of the *nekyah* offered, asks the maiden if she is willing to wed So-and-so. When the question has been thrice asked and thrice affirmatively answered, the *Imâm* returns to the *selamlik*, the contract is formally signed and witnessed, and the parties are legally man and wife. But before the young couple may see or hold any communication with each other, this Legal Sanction must be supplemented

by the Social Sanction, which is manifested by public par-
ticipation in the various ceremonies and festivities which
precede the transfer of a bride from her father's roof to
her new home, such festivities being termed collectively
the *dughun*. Some months may, however, pass before the
dughun can take place, as elaborate preparations must be
made for its due celebration, according to the social position
and wealth of the contracting families. The wedding-dress,
together with sundry accessories which it is customary for
the bridegroom to furnish, are sent with great ceremony
to the home of the bride a week before the date fixed
for the commencement of the *dughun*. The rest of her
trousseau is provided by her parents, as also is the
"plenishing" of household linen and bedding. To these
are added a supply of kitchen utensils, all of copper;
furniture for two rooms covered with costly material; a
handsome brass *mangal*, or brazier and stand; various
articles of walnut-wood inlaid with mother-of-pearl, ivory
or silver, such as dinner-trays and stands, dustpans, bath-
pattens, etc.

The wedding festivities extend over a week, and however ill a father can afford the expenses inseparable from
their due celebration, custom compels him to incur them.
Such festivities are, in fact, the delight of the general run
of Osmanli women, and it is a point of honour with a
mother to celebrate her daughter's *dughun* with as great
éclat as possible. Like the *Sunnet dughun* above described,
it begins on a Monday, when a number of relatives and
friends assemble at the bride's home to escort the *trousseau*

R

and plenishing to the bridegroom's abode. The luggage is carried on the backs of porters under the supervision of the ancient go-between, who is responsible for its safe delivery, the former receiving at the hands of the bridegroom's mother, in addition to their fee, a *chevrek*, or embroidered napkin. The ladies follow on foot or in carriages, according to the distance, and after partaking of coffee and sweets, proceed to decorate the apartments destined for the bride's special occupation. Some fasten strings along the walls, on which they display the various articles of the *trousseau*, together with the cashmere shawls and Persian prayer-carpets, the embroidered sheets and pillow-slips, towels and bundle-wraps, all disposed with a view to artistic effect. In one corner of the room a canopy is constructed of gauzes, embroideries, and crape flowers, beneath which the jewels and other objects of value are arranged on a table under glass shades, while garlands of similar flowers are suspended along the four walls. This satisfactorily completed, the party turn their attention to the second apartment, where they set out the furniture and bedding, the stools of inlaid wood, the *hoshaf* tray, with its service of crystal bowl and ivory spoons, the candelabra, and the household requisites before mentioned.

On Tuesday the bride is taken with great ceremony to the public bath, the fees for the whole party being, on this occasion, paid by the bridegroom. When ready to leave the inner hot chamber, the maiden, wearing of course only her bath robe, is led by her mother three times round the central platform, on which the guests are seated, and kisses the hand of each *hanum* in acknowledgment of the customary formula of congratulation and good wishes. The clothes she dons after this ablution, and wears until arrayed in her bridal finery, should not, according to traditional custom, belong to her, but be borrowed for the occasion.

Early in the afternoon of Wednesday the bridegroom's lady relatives proceed in a body to the home of the bride, preceded by the go-between, who announces with great formality their arrival. The bride's mother and all her assembled friends hasten to the foot of the staircase, and forming a double row in the entrance hall, the first couple place each a hand under the arms of the bridegroom's mother, supporting her as she ascends the stairs, the rest following suit with the other guests.[1] The new arrivals, after having been divested of their outdoor garb, are conducted to a room set apart for their reception—it being contrary to etiquette on this day for the two sets of guests to mingle—around which they seat themselves on the divan and are served with unsweetened coffee and cigarettes. An hour later sweetened coffee is handed round ; and as soon as the cups have been removed the bride enters, still wearing her borrowed garments ; and supported on either side by a matron who has been only once married, she makes the tour of the room, kissing the hands of all present, beginning with her *Kaïn Validé*, or mother-in-law, and not omitting the youngest girl

---

[1] A survival of the ancient Oriental practice of carrying upstairs distinguished guests or persons of high rank.

present. A chair is then placed for her close to this lady, on which she remains seated for a few minutes during which this lady transfers some sugar-stick from her mouth to that of her daughter-in-law, a custom which, together with the half sugar-plum sent to the bridegroom at the betrothal, would seem to be a survival of the ancient and widespread marriage-rite of food-sharing. After having been entertained for some time by the performances of musicians and dancing girls, the bridegroom's mother and her party take their leave, receiving at the same time an invitation to return in the evening for the *Khena* ceremony. The bride then again comes forward and conducts the guests to the foot of the staircase, where they throw over her a shower of small coins, which are forthwith scrambled for by the beggars, children, and hangers-on always to be found in great numbers at the door of a *haremlik* during the progress of a *dughun*.

When the company are again assembled in the evening, a taper is handed to each of the younger members of the party, who, led by the bride and escorted by the musicians and dancing girls, descend to the garden. Winding in a long and wavy line, now between the fragrant flower-beds, and now in the shadow of the trees and shrubs, their rich dresses, bright jewels, fair faces, and floating hair fitfully lighted by the flickering tapers, their feet moving to the rhythm of the tinkling castanets and wild strains of the dusky-hued Gypsy girls, one might imagine them a troop of Peris engaged in their nocturnal revels. Returning to the house, the bride, divested of her gay attire, enters the reception-room, holding her left arm across her brow, and seats. herself on a stool in the centre of the apartment. The fingers of her right hand are then covered thickly with henna paste, on which the bridegroom's mother sticks a gold coin, the other guests following suit. This hand, covered with a silken bag, is now held across her face, while the left hand is similarly plastered and decorated by the bride's mother and friends. When the maiden's toes have also been similarly treated, the ceremony is terminated with a wild pantomimic dance by the Gypsy performers, at the conclusion of which these women fall into exaggerated postures before the principal ladies in order to receive their guerdon, which is looked for as much from the guests as from the hostess. The bride is then left to repose until the henna is considered to have stained her fingers to the requisite amber hue, when it is washed off. If left on too long the skin assumes a blackish hue, which would be considered a bad augury for her wedded life.

The bride is usually conducted to her new home on the morning of Thursday, accompanied by an immense concourse, the women in carriages and the men on horseback, and preceded by music. But before leaving the paternal roof a touching little ceremony takes place in private : the bride's father, in the presence only of her mother and sisters, girding his daughter with the "wedding girdle." While performing this traditional farewell observance, the paterfamilias is, as a rule, deeply affected, and weeps in company with his wife and children. The

departing bride falls at his feet and kisses them and his
hands. He raises and presses her to his breast, and after
winding the girdle about her waist, gives her his paternal
blessing. Arrived at her new home, the bride is received
at the *haremlik* entrance by the bridegroom, who conducts
her upstairs through the crowd of guests there assembled
—the ladies on this occasion dispensing with their veils
on the pretext that the only man present is too pre-
occupied to look at *them!*—to the seat of honour in the
bridal chamber, and then rejoins his male guests in the
selamlik. The bride's veil is now raised, and she and
her *trousseau* remain for some hours on view, not only to
the invited guests, but to all the women of the neighbourhood who flock in to gaze on the poor girl, the festivities
being continued in both divisions of the house until
evening.

After the customary evening prayers have been performed in the *selamlik*, the parish *Imâm*, who forms one
of the company on such occasions, invokes a benediction
on the young couple; and at its conclusion the bridegroom hurries towards the door leading to the *haremlik*,
followed by his friends, who administer smart blows on
his back and also throw at him with no gentle hand the
shoes of which a supply will always be found in the
entrance hall.[1] The door at last shut between the happy
man and his pursuers, he is led upstairs to the bridal

---

[1] This attack on the bridegroom would seem to be a survival of
the custom of Bride-capture still simulated, if not actually practised,
at the present day in Asia Minor by the Tartar, Circassian, and other
tribesmen.

chamber by the old *koulavous*, who, on this occasion, acts as mistress of the ceremonies to the young couple. The bride rises from her seat as he enters, steps forward and kisses his hand. Her bridal veil of crimson silk is spread on the floor, and on it the husband kneels as he offers a brief prayer, the wife standing meanwhile on its edge. Bride and bridegroom are then seated side by side on the divan, and the *koulavous* shows them in a mirror the reflection of their united faces, expressing at the same time a pious wish for the continuance of their present harmonious union. After serving the couple with coffee, she withdraws to make preparations for their supper. The hour of this meal will, however, depend on the humour of the bride, whose shyness, or obstinacy, must be over-come to the extent at least of inducing her to speak to the bridegroom—an indispensable preliminary to his assuming any authority over her. Oriental brides are recommended by experienced matrons not to respond too readily to the advances of their husbands, who are occasionally compelled to have recourse to stratagem in order to obtain their supper. Once a word has been vouchsafed, the husband makes a signal, and the meal is served.

On the following morning, the couple enter, hand in hand, the principal reception-room of the house, where all the bridegroom's family await them, anxious to ascertain "whether their stars have met," which the women at least have no difficulty in discovering from the expression of their respective countenances. Both salute the heads of

the family by kissing their hands, and receive from them
in return the customary presents. At noon a repast—
termed the "feast of sheep's trotters," from the dish
specially offered to the bride and bridegroom on this
occasion—is served to numerous guests both in the
haremlik and *selamlik;* and the two subsequent days are
also devoted to harem festivities, during which the bride,
in her wedding array, sits in state to receive the con-
gratulatory visits of all the matrons included in the
visiting lists of both families.

In the case, however, of a widow, or woman who has
been divorced, these elaborate formalities are dispensed
with ; and, as previously mentioned, no *dughun* is considered necessary at the wedding of a woman of slave
origin.

CHAPTER XIV

FAMILY CEREMONIES—(3) FUNERAL CEREMONIES

THE divine calm of the Moslem spirit—the spirit of profound and complete resignation to the Will of Allah—is on no occasion more strongly manifested by the Osmanlis than in the presence of death. The pious Mohammedan may, indeed, be said to have ever present to his mind the termination of earthly existence and the life beyond; he considers himself but camped in this world, as his nation has been said to be but camped in Europe; and he regards the joys and allurements of earthly existence as but illusions and shadows in comparison with the everlasting delights which await him in Paradise. *Kismet*, which determines the events of a person's life, and *Edjel*, his "appointed time," are decreed by Allah, who has inscribed them in invisible characters on the brow of every human being.[1] The ill-fated Sultan Abdul Aziz, in the brief interval between his deposition and death in 1876, is reported to have traced with his finger on a dust-covered table in his

[1] Compare the Koran, *Sura*, lvii. v. 19.

prison-house some Turkish lines which may be thus translated—

> " Man's destiny is Allah's will,
> And power is given by Him alone ;
> My fate is written on my brow,
> I humbly bend before His throne."

This unquestioning submission to the decrees of Fate renders death terrible to Moslems only in the abstract, and when viewed from a distance. In polite society it is never alluded to save under some poetical name, such as the " Cupbearer of the Sphere," and prefaced by the words " Far be it from you " ; and the common people before uttering the word invariably spit—an action which has much the same signification.

Such a fatalistic view of life and death causes the Osmanli populace to regard the medical art with scant respect. If a person believes himself to have heard the call " *Return*,"[1] he will die, doctors and " charmers " notwithstanding ; and if the " appointed time " has not yet arrived, he will recover—so why trouble him with drugs ? When the " Cupbearer of the Sphere " is believed to be at hand, the relations of the moribund gather round the

[1] An allusion to the verse of the Koran, which says, " O thou comforted soul ! Return unto thy Lord, well pleased, and well pleased with " (*Sura*, lxxxix. 28). In an elegy by the eighteenth-century poetess Leyla Hanum on the untimely death of her friend the foster-sister of Sultan Mahmoud II. the following lines occur, referring also to this verse :—

" Though her Kind Friend (*i.e.* Allah) never parted from her eyes, sweet gentle beam,
Still did she to God her soul yield and the call *Return* obey."

(Gibb, *Ottoman Poems.*)

couch, weeping silently, or reciting prayers to keep away the evil spirits believed to be ever on the alert to harass and torment a departing soul. If the dying person be conscious, and able to speak, *helal*, or free forgiveness of all injuries, is requested and granted on both sides. Pious bequests, too, are often made on death-beds and slaves set free, charity of this kind having been specially commended by the Prophet.

The wailing of the women commences as soon as the last breath has been drawn. Those most affected by the sad event beat their breasts and tear their hair in a passionate outburst of genuine grief. As soon, however, as this first expression of sorrow has exhausted itself, preparations are commenced for performing the last rites to the dead, and invitations are at once issued for the funeral, which takes place either on the same or on the following day. When the eyes of the dead have been closed and the chin has been bandaged, the body is placed, covered only with a sheet, on the *rahat latak*, or "Couch of Ease," a kind of stretcher on which, in the case of a man, it is borne to the courtyard of the house to be washed by the *Imâm* and his subordinates; but for a woman these last ablutions are performed in private by "washers" of her own sex. As a peculiarly sacred character is attached to this ablutionary rite, great reverence is invariably observed in carrying out every detail of the ceremony. The body is kept covered as much as possible, and handled with great gentleness and care, as any rough or disrespectful usage may, it is believed, draw upon the offending washer the "wrath of the dead."[1] For the traditions of Mohammed, as well as the works of Moslem doctors, teach that a dead body is conscious of pain, and great care is consequently taken to avoid undue pressure while washing a corpse. Seven balls of cotton wool enveloped in calico, over which warm water is poured, are successively used for this purpose; and the dead Moslem has thus performed for him for the last time the *abtest*—the ablution which ensures his being buried in a state of "legal purity." These formalities accomplished, seven hundred drachms of cotton are weighed out, small portions of which are placed under the armpits and between the fingers and toes, and with the remainder the body—over which a sleeveless gown called the *kaftet* has been drawn—is enveloped; pepper and other spices being then placed in its folds and rose-water sprinkled. When the shroud has been bound over all the corpse is reverently lifted, by means of slings passed under it, into the temporary coffin.

These observances concluded, and the hour fixed for the funeral arrived, the door of the chamber of death is thrown open, and the guests enter, preceded by the *Imâm*. The latter, addressing those present, says, "O congregation, what do you consider this man's (or woman's) life to have been?" "Good," is invariably the response. "Then give *helal* to him." The *helal* given, the coffin—draped

[1] A story related by the Turkish author, Evliya Effendi, in his *Narrative of Travel*, curiously illustrates this popular belief. A subordinate washer, having somewhat roughly manipulated the body of a holy Sheikh, received a vigorous kick from the insulted corpse, and shortly afterwards sickened and died.

with rich shawls and stuffs, and bearing, for a man, his turban or fez on a projection at the head, and, for a woman, her *chimber*, or coif—is raised on the shoulders of four or more men, and borne to the cemetery, followed by a long procession of male mourners, clad in their ordinary attire. It being considered a meritorious act to carry a dead body even for a short distance, forty paces only absolving the performer from a mortal sin, the bearers at a Moslem funeral are consequently relieved at short intervals by others desirous of obtaining the benefits conferred by the performance of this religious duty. No lugubrious chants, no noisy demonstrations of woe, such as often attend the obsequies of Eastern Christians and Jews, mark the progress of the Moslem to his last resting-place. In reverent silence the procession takes its way to the mosque, where the first part of the burial service—which is very beautiful and impressive—is read.

"Earth to earth" burial is customary with the Turks, whose graves are orientated, like the holy places of their mosques, in the direction of the Kaaba at Mekka. On arriving at the cemetery, the coffin is accordingly placed by the side of the grave, the lid removed, and the body, gently lifted out by six persons by means of the bands before mentioned, is laid in the grave. When the remainder of the prayers and passages from the Koran constituting the burial service have been recited, two or three boards are fixed in the earth above the corpse, the grave is filled in, and the mourners return home. The *Imâm*, however, remains for a time beside the grave, in order, it is said, to prompt the deceased in his replies to the "Questioners"—the two angels Mounkir and Nekir, who, according to Moslem belief, enter the grave with the dead to interrogate him concerning his faith.[1] If the dead has been a devout Moslem, his reply will be, "My God is Allah; my Prophet, Mohammed; my religion, Islam; and my *Kibla*, the Ka'aba." If, however, he has been but an indifferent follower of the Prophet, he will not be able to remember the formula of his creed. In the former case the angels give the dead a foretaste of the delights of Paradise; while in the latter they afflict him with divers torments.

The aspect of the great cemeteries on the outskirts of the Capital and the larger cities is indeed calculated to inspire supernatural terrors. Groves of tall, gloomy cypresses of incalculable age overshadow the vast areas

---

[1] According to a belief common to many Oriental races, the soul retains after death some mysterious connexion with the body, which cannot be buried without it. This belief may be illustrated by the following little Dervish story. As the corpse of Kera Kadin, the saintly wife of the illustrious founder of the *Mevlevi* Order of Dervishes, was being carried to the grave followed by an immense concourse of the Brotherhood, the bearers suddenly found themselves unable for a time to proceed—an occurrence which greatly exercised the minds of the "Brethren of Love." A holy man of the Order, however, received the explanation that same night in a dream. At the spot at which the procession had been brought to a standstill, a man and a woman had, on the preceding day, been stoned to death for adultery, and the lady's soul had left her body in order to intercede for them with the All Merciful. Their forgiveness obtained, her spirit had returned to earth and the bearers were enabled to proceed with her body.—From the "Acts of the Adepts," in the *Mesnevi* (Redhouse's Translation).

occupied by the bodies of the Faithful—for no two bodies are buried in one grave—casting deep shadows even at noonday ; and as far as the eye can reach in any direction is an interminable array of grey headstones, standing erect, slanting or lying prone. If gloomy in the brilliant Eastern noonday, it is in the twilight weirdly uncanny, and by night a place of fearsome horror, peopled with ghouls and vampires ; and a Moslem would rather face death by knife, pistol, or poison than put himself in the way of encountering these gruesome denizens of the cities of the dead.

The tombstones placed at the head of a grave are usually four or five feet in height, either cylindrical or flat, and tapering towards the base, which causes them after a time to lean in all directions, giving to a cemetery a somewhat fantastic appearance. Round the cylinder or on the flat surface is finely engraved a long inscription, often touched up with gold, consisting of an invocation to Allah or a passage from the Koran, followed by a summary account of the life of the deceased, prominence being given to the spiritual side. The more ancient headstones of men's graves are surmounted by carved representations of turbans ; but since the use of the simpler fez has become general, this has been substituted, painted crimson, and with a dark blue tassel. The headstones of women and girls are often finished at the top with some conventional design of which the sunflower forms a favourite example, and the inscriptions which follow the invocation to the "Abiding One"[1] are, with few exceptions, in verse.

[1] One of the thousand and one " Beautiful Names " of the Deity.

On the occasion of the death of a person in good circumstances, gifts are made to the poor from among his or her personal effects, and money is also distributed as alms to the needy of the neighbourhood. Three days afterwards, a large batch of *loukmá*—a kind of dough-nut or *beignet*—is made, plates of which are sent round to the houses of friends, the poor also receiving their share of these funeral cates, in return for which their prayers are requested for the soul of the departed. This ceremony is repeated on the seventh and fortieth days after the funeral, and on the latter occasion a dole of loaves is added. Prayer for the dead is, indeed, considered by Moslems a religious duty of the highest importance. On the tomb-stones in Turkish cemeteries may often be found engraved appeals to the passers-by to offer on behalf of the occupant of the grave a *Fatiha*, or recitation of the opening Chapter of the Koran—a passage which may be deemed the Moslem equivalent for the Christian *Paternoster*—a customary act with all True Believers on visiting the tombs of departed friends or the shrines of the saintly dead.

No external signs of mourning are used, or periods of seclusion observed by Osmanlis after the death of a relative. Female friends pay visits of condolence to the harem ; and the ladies, after acknowledging the customary expressions of sympathy and good wishes for their future exemption from bereavement, speak calmly and resignedly of the departed. Excessive sorrow for children is con-sidered by Moslems to be not only sinful, but detrimental to the repose of their souls and their happiness in Paradise.

It is, however, on the other hand, esteemed an act of filial duty to mourn constantly for lost parents, and to pray unceasingly for their forgiveness and acceptance with Allah. As mentioned elsewhere, prayers and almsgiving are considered by Moslems most beneficial to the souls of the departed.   It is also customary to read or recite daily passages from the Koran on their behalf.   At the conclusion of the *Khotba*, the sermon or address delivered in every Cathedral Mosque on Fridays after the congregational service, a collect is recited praying for the bestowal of the Divine mercy and grace on Fatima, the daughter of the Prophet and Ancestress of all his descendants; on Khadija and A'isha and the remainder of his wives; and on "all resigned and believing women, living or dead." It is also customary for Moslems to conclude their *namaz*, or daily devotions, with a prayer for the forgiveness of the sins of the suppliant and his or her "two parents."

CHAPTER XV

TURKISH HOMES AND HOME LIFE

AS observed in a previous chapter, almost every Turkish dwelling, even the poorest, has its enclosed courtyard, and often a garden with overshadowing mulberry, acacia, cypress, and plane tree. Each house, too, is completely detached, so that a considerable space of ground may be occupied, even within city walls, by a somewhat sparse population. The houses of rich and poor alike are chiefly wooden or half-timbered constructions, and to this fact are mainly due the disastrous conflagrations that have from time to time devastated the cities of the Ægean. Latticed blinds of unpainted wood invariably cover the lower half of the streetward windows of the *haremlik*, thus distinguishing Moslem abodes from those of their Christian neighbours. A middle-class Turkish dwelling is generally surrounded on three sides by garden and courtyard, the fourth abutting on the street over which the upper story projects a couple of feet or so. The plastered walls are coloured a deep ochre or terracotta, which contrasts warmly and pleasantly with the unpainted woodwork of the window-sashes and lattices. Within the high, tile-topped walls of the courtyard, vines

A TURKISH STREET IN AIDIN, ASIA MINOR

ind creepers clothe the supports of the outside staircase
and landing leading to the living-rooms above, and in the
garden beyond bloom in a luxuriant confusion little
troubled by the unmethodic mind of an Oriental gardener,
the rose and jasmine, tuberose and carnation, orange and
pomegranate, side by side with the leek, bringal, tomato,
and egg-plant, melon, cabbage, and parsley. Two rooms
on the ground floor, having a separate entrance from the
street, constitute the *selamlik*.

Turkish *konaks*, as the mansions of families of position
are termed, vary, however, considerably according to the
taste, wealth, and rank of their owners; according to
whether situated in, or near the Capital, or in the provinces; and also to the date of their construction. All
are, however, roofed with red tiles, and stand either amid
gardens, or on the banks of the rushing Bosphorus. Those
of the latter which are at all of ancient date are, in common
with the humbler abodes above described, built entirely of
wood, with the exception of the marble pillars of the
façade, which have probably been appropriated from the
ruins of some ancient edifice. These old *konaks*, with
their projecting upper stories and irregular outlines, their
elegant kiosks and terraces, bright colouring and verdant
setting, are most picturesque in appearance. The lattices
of unpainted wood screening the windows of the *haremliks*
are constructed with circular openings through which
the *hanums*, themselves unseen, may gaze from their
cushioned divans on the ever-changing scene below—*kaïks*,
steamers, and sailing craft of all nations, borne on the

rapid current flowing between the Euxine and the Sea of Marmora. A towing-path only a few yards wide separates the houses from this wonderful waterway, and is here and there raised, bridgewise, to form a watergate through which the *kaïks* reach a staircase in the basement of the house.

Generally speaking, however, a Turkish *konak* is, whether situated in the Capital or the provinces, an irregularly built, rambling edifice of two stories, divided internally into two establishments—the *haremlik* and the *selamlik*. The former and larger division contains the private apartments of the family, and in the latter are the rooms used by its male members for the transaction of business, for formal receptions, and general hospitality. An apartment termed the *mabeyn*—an Arabic word signifying "a space between two objects"—serves to connect the two divisions of the mansion, the keys of the communicating doors being naturally kept by the master; but a kind of buttery-hatch in the form of a revolving cupboard, called the *dulap*, serves for all verbal communication between the two departments, and also for the transmission of provisions into, and of dishes from, the *haremlik* kitchen when a meal has to be served in the *selamlik*, and no second cook is kept for this department. The *haremlik* has its entrance from a separate courtyard, or garden, the front door opening into a large hall which gives access to rooms on each side, and occupies the whole depth of the building. One of these rooms is the *kahveh odjak*, or "coffee hearth," where an old woman may always be found presiding over a wide, low charcoal brazier, ready to prepare at a moment's notice the fragrant

beverage so beloved of Orientals ; the others are used as
storerooms and sleeping apartments for the inferior slaves.
The kitchen, which is very spacious, is usually an out-
building. One side of it is occupied by the great arched
cooking stove, with its rows of little grates, on which the
contents of the brightly burnished copper pans simmer
over charcoal embers, fanned with a turkey's wing by the
fat negress cook.

A wide, uncarpeted, but well-scrubbed staircase leads
from the entrance hall to the upper floor, the centre of
which is generally occupied by a spacious ante-room, on
which all the other rooms open. In some of the older
houses the *divan khané*, or state reception-room, contains
at one end a recess, the floor of which is raised, daïs-wise,
a foot or more above the level of the rest of the apartment.
A low divan furnishes its three sides, and in the most
comfortable corner, which is the habitual seat of the house-
mistress, is a pile of flat rectangular cushions, and here
may also be found her circular silver hand-mirror and inlaid
jewel-box. If the *divan khané* has not such a recess, one
end and half the two adjoining sides are usually occupied
by a continuous sofa, the fourth wall being furnished with
a marble-topped "console" table surmounted by a mirror
and candelabra, and flanked on either side by shelves in
niches containing porcelain rose-water sprinklers, crystal
sherbet goblets, and other objects both useful and ornamental. A few common chairs stand stiffly against the
wall in every space left vacant, one or two inlaid walnut-
wood tray-stools being placed here and there near the

divan to hold cigarette boxes, ash-trays, and other trifles. The walls are usually whitewashed, those of the principal rooms having, perhaps, a frieze painted in distemper, with designs of foliage and animals, representations of the human form being forbidden by the Koran. The ceilings, which are uniformly of wood, are often ornamented with arabesque work in intricate and delicate patterns.

Bedsteads are not used by the Turks, the bedding being stowed away by day in large cupboards, and the couches spread at night on the divans or on the carpeted floor of each room. Such bedroom furniture as washstands, dressing-tables, and wardrobes are dispensed with in old-fashioned dwellings. Turks prefer to wash in running water, and there is a small washing-room with a hole in the marble floor to carry off the waste. Should the *hanum* desire to wash her hands and face only, a slave brings to her the brass jug and basin, and pours the water from the former over her hands ; and for ablutions on a larger scale she will resort either to the public baths or to her private *hammam*, a Turkish bath on a small scale being an indispensable adjunct of a Moslem house of any importance. Bathing accommodation of some kind may, indeed, be found in the most modest dwelling, even if but a tiny cabinet furnished with a drain for carrying off the water after use. The ladies of the family "do their hair," or have it done for them by their slave-maids, as they sit cross-legged on the divan ; and as to their "frocks and frills," the old carved and inlaid walnut-wood chests and coffers in the treasure-room suffice to store their gauzes and brocades, silks and embroideries. Here, also, may often be found priceless treasures in metal, porcelain, glass, and gems, which, were they displayed in the reception-rooms, would greatly add to their cheerfulness. Such, however, save in dwellings into which European ideas and customs have penetrated, is not the practice of the Osmanlis.

The warming apparatus most commonly used is the *mangal*, a wide, shallow brass or copper pan containing charcoal embedded in wood ashes. This is placed on a stand of wrought metal or polished wood, from two to three feet square, and a few inches high, which occupies the centre of the room. The old-fashioned *tandür*, also, though fallen into disuse in the European provinces, may still often be met with in Asia Minor, even in the houses of foreigners. It consists of a four-legged, square deal table, having a shelf covered with tin a few inches from the floor, in the centre of which is placed a pan of charcoal enclosed in a metal screen. Over all is thrown a large, thickly wadded quilt, which the ladies—for this is an eminently feminine luxury—seated on two sides of the *tandür* in an angle of the divan, draw over their knees. The use of American stoves is, however, increasing year by year, and the picturesqueness of many old *konaks*—as also of humbler dwellings—is often destroyed by unsightly black stove-pipes, which emerge from the windows or walls and climb up to the eaves. The partiality of the Osmanlis for light and fresh air leads them to construct their houses with a superfluity of windows, the space between the lights and the upper story seldom exceeding a few inches; and as

they are often ill-constructed, and warped by sun and
storm, the wind and wet enter in all directions. Within,
their unpainted ugliness is only partially disguised by
scrimpy curtains, most commonly of cheap and gaudy
cretonne with the edges "pinked"!

Such a mansion as I have above described is a fair
specimen of the average dwelling of a Turkish family of
good position, as well in the Capital and suburbs as in the
provinces, unless exceptionally wealthy, or infected with
the *à la Franka* mania for imitating European manners
and customs. There are, however, in Constantinople and
its suburbs a considerable number of new houses, hand-
somely and solidly built, and in outward appearance dis-
tinguishable from the dwellings of foreigners only by the
lattice-protected windows of their *haremliks*. The disposal
of the rooms is naturally that best suited to Osmanli
customs, and the furniture a compromise between Eastern
and Western styles. Native costume and native furniture,
no less than native architecture and art, however rich and
varied in colour and material, never offend a cultured eye
when used in accordance with time-honoured custom, as
evidenced by our appreciation of Oriental embroideries,
carpets, and textile fabrics generally. But the Oriental
mind seems, as a rule, to become confused when it endeavours to assimilate its own notions of luxury and magnificence to those suggested by the civilisation of the West.
The highest developments of art are brought into close
contact with objects of the most tasteless construction,
and magnificence is thrown into strong and unpleasing

relief by juxtaposition with tawdriness; and this chaotic
state of mind not infrequently finds expression in combi-
nations of material and colour calculated to harrow the
soul of the least æsthetic Western.   Crimson is trimmed
with scarlet, and pink with violet; shabby chintz hangs
side by side with rich brocade and velvet; and a cheap
rug "made in Germany," and representing a dog or lion,
is spread side by side with a silken carpet of almost
priceless value.

From the description above given of Osmanli homes it
will, however, I trust, be sufficiently evident that a harem,
or rather *haremlik*, far from meriting the epithets of
"detestable prison"[1] and "place of degradation," often

[1] For instance, in *Forty Days in the East*, the author (E. H.
Mitchell) says, "A visit to a harem was said to be a desirable conclusion to our sojourn in the East, but I, for one, declined to enter
such a place of degradation. Were it possible by such a visit to help
our poor sisters out of their slavery, I should only have been too thank-
ful to make it; but to go and see them penned up in their detestable
prison," etc.   The late M. Servan de Sugny, too, who, as an Oriental
scholar, might have been expected to know better, would appear to
have imagined that the Osmanlis are in the habit of loading their
women with chains and keeping them in dungeons, when he wrote,
"Le croirait-on? Les femmes mêmes, dans ce pays où le sexe est
reduit au plus affreux, au plus dégradant esclavage, des femmes ont osé
saisir d'une main meurtrie de fers la lyre du poëte," etc.—*La Muse
Ottomane*, Préface, p. xv.   It is not, however, surprising that such
popular misconceptions of harem life persist in the West when one
finds even professedly serious publications illustrated by fancy representations which would have been practically out of date a century
ago. See, for instance, the frontispiece to Harmsworth's *History
of the World*, Part 24.   The authors of the chapters illustrated are,
perhaps, however, as little responsible for this, as I myself was for
the frontispiece to my last published book, which represents a so-

applied to such abodes by superficial travellers, is, as a rule, the most cheerful and commodious division of a house. For the term *karem* (in Arabic *haram*) simply means "a sacred enclosure," the same term being applied to the sanctuaries of Islam. The *haremlik* is consequently the *sanctum sanctorum*, the place safe from all intrusion, into which even the husband refrains from entering if one or more pairs of overshoes at the door of the *divan khané* announces that his wife has guests—divested, according to custom, of their outdoor garments. And I will now attempt to give some account of the daily life led by the denizens of these, to many, mysterious abodes.

As with Oriental nations generally, the mother occupies the most honourable position among a man's female relatives. Osmanli women are most indulgent mothers, especially to their sons, who naturally in early youth take advantage of their devotion. Arrived, however, at years of discretion, a young Turk, realising the Prophet's symbolical saying that "Paradise is under the feet of the mother," becomes in his turn her devoted slave. Debarred by custom from intercourse with all women not closely connected with him by ties of blood, a man's mother and grandmother, sisters and aunts, are consequently his only female friends ; and to this fact may, no doubt, be traced the strong affection which exists between mother and son, brother and sister. The harem has, indeed, been termed,

called "Turkish Lady" in an attitude which no decent Osmanli woman would think of assuming in the presence of a photographer, and smoking a *narghileh*—a practice quite at variance with feminine custom.

and perhaps not without truth, "the sanctuary of family happiness." For the wife and daughters, having no outside interests, use their utmost efforts to make home pleasant to their male relatives. The relations between the various members of an Osmanli household, and the deference from younger people towards their seniors required by family etiquette, may appear somewhat curious to Europeans. They are, however, the necessary outcome of the patriarchal system which has obtained among all the nationalities of Turkey, and has only of recent years been to a certain extent abandoned by the Christian element in the seaboard towns of the Ægean. According to the customary laws of this ancient social system, if a man's widowed mother reside permanently under his roof, which is not unusual, his wife's position in the house is but secondary, and she is required to defer to her mother-in-law in all things. Hand-kissing being the usual mode of respectful greeting, the wife kisses the hand of her *Kaïn Validé*, as also that of her husband, on the occasion of any family event, or any anniversary, and also on special Moslem holidays, such as the opening of the Bairam festival. The wife may not seat herself at table before her husband's mother has taken her place, nor be the first to help herself to the dishes, nor may she smoke a cigarette in the presence of "the first lady" until invited by her to do so. It no doubt often happens that a good deal of friction exists between two women occupying these relative positions. But the prescribed etiquette is none the less observed : and the young *hanum* probably consoles herself with the reflection that at some future date their observance will be to her own advantage.

According to Islamic law, the care and maintenance of indigent parents, and especially of mothers and grandmothers, is incumbent on Moslems; and it would be difficult to find in Islamiyeh a parallel to cases of common occurrence in England, in which a progenitor of a family numbering perhaps from fifty to a hundred souls, is dependent for his or her subsistence on public charity. In all matters of etiquette indeed, whether family or social, precedence depends on seniority. If, for example, a married Turk has a sister residing in his harem, the elder of the two would enjoy precedence of the other; and similarly if he has three children, the eldest and the youngest being boys and the second a girl, the girl must defer to her elder brother, while the younger boy, spoilt and indulged though he may be, must give way to her in everything that affects their common interests. Nor do the youthful members of a family presume to sit cross-legged before their elders. In the *selamlik* too, similar etiquette is required of boys; and in the presence of guests they speak only when specially addressed.

As above remarked, the only persons of the male sex besides the master who are permitted to enter the *haremlik* are his sons, his wife's father, and her brothers. In the large cities, however, some members of the "advanced" class of society also admit their own brothers and, possibly, even more distant relations; while a few may introduce to their wives and daughters, in addition to the

above, their more intimate male friends. But in households belonging to the old *régime*, which constitute the
bulk of the population, no male relation of the master is
allowed access to the harem after attaining puberty if outside the prohibited degrees of consanguinity, a restriction
which inexorably and eternally separates first cousins of
different sexes, however close their childish intimacy may
have been—unless, of course, a marriage between them
should subsequently be arranged.

Daily life in the harem is consequently no doubt somewhat monotonous; but it is quite erroneous to suppose that
an Osmanli woman of the better class has no duties or occupations beyond a certain amount of servile attendance on
her Bluebeard of a husband, and that she passes her days
reclining on a divan, "eating sweets and playing with her
jewels." For, having so few interests outside her home,
the *hanum* is very domesticated, and no accomplishments
are so much appreciated in a marriageable maiden as
proficiency in the domestic arts. Needlework especially
is held in great estimation, and for many years before
marriage a girl finds occupation for her leisure hours in
embroidering the sheets, towels, quilts, napkins, and other
articles which will later on figure in her trousseau and deck
the bridal chamber. Like all Orientals, the Osmanli
matron is an early riser, and after partaking of a cup of
coffee and a cigarette, she is ready to wait upon her
husband. She places his slippers by the side of his couch,
and holds his pelisse ready, and as soon as he is comfortably seated on the divan, after making his morning toilet

and performing the first of the *namas* or five daily prayers
previously mentioned, she pours out his coffee from the
little *ibrik* in which it has been brought in by a slave,
places the cup in the silver *zarf*, and hands it to him. The
hanum also fills his *tchibouk*, should he prefer one to the
more fashionable cigarette, hands him the amber mouthpiece, and then proceeds to light the fragrant finely
shredded Latakia by placing on the bowl with a tiny pair
of tongs an ember of glowing charcoal. She remains in
attendance, seated on a cushion at his feet, while the slaves
roll up the bedding and stow it away in the wall-cupboards.
The children then troop in, uncombed and unwashed, in
their quaint night-gear—wide trousers and quilted jackets
of coloured cotton—to kiss the hand of their sire and be
caressed by both parents. No nursery breakfast, however,
awaits them ; and they presently begin to clamour for
pence with which to purchase their morning meal. The
ten and twenty *para*-pieces distributed, the children
scamper down to the courtyard gate near which they are
almost sure to find the *simitdji*, or vendor of ring-shaped
cakes covered with sesame seeds ; or, if he is not in sight,
they make their way to the nearest chandler's shop, where
they have their choice of *halvá*—a sweetstuff made from
sesame seed and honey, cheese, or fruit, as a relish to their
bread. After this irregular meal the boys and girls over
eight years old are tidied up and sent, escorted by a male
servant from the *selamlik*, to the parish *mekteb*, where the
children of rich and poor meet on a common footing. The
babies meanwhile roam freely about the *haremli,* attended

by the *dadi*, a slave who performs, after a fashion, the duties of nursemaid.

The *effendi* finally makes his outdoor toilet and departs to his day's avocations, leaving the womenkind to follow their own devices for the rest of the day.   For the *hanum* is perfect mistress 'of her time, as of her property.   She will probably first inspect with her negress cook the provisions for the day brought in by the *ayvas*—often an Armenian—and passed into the *haremlik* through the *dulap*—the revolving cupboard before mentioned.   For the domestic economy of the natives of Turkey generally is of a somewhat "hand-to-mouth" character, so far as fresh provisions are concerned ; and accounts are settled daily between the mistress and the *ayvas*, either at the *dulap*, or the kitchen door, behind which the lady sits with a muslin kerchief thrown over her head, this transaction appearing usually to necessitate prolonged argument conducted, on one side at least, in language more forcible than polite. If any special culinary treat in the way of pickling, cake-making, or preserving is in the day's domestic programme, the *hanum* will remain in the kitchen to superintend or assist in the operation ; on washing and ironing days, too, she and her daughters will take a more or less active part with the slaves in the day's work.   In the Capital, however, such domestic occupations are being gradually abandoned by the younger and more fashionable *hanums* and their daughters, who, emulating the pursuits of the foreign ladies with whom they now come more into contact, prefer to occupy their time in learning foreign languages and acquiring foreign accomplishments.

Paying and receiving calls, attending *dughuns*, promenading, driving, shopping, and going to the public baths are the chief outdoor amusements of the general run of Osmanli women. Before setting out with any of these objects, a *hanum* must, however, first obtain her husband's permission. If the *effendi* is inclined to be jealous and strict, he may object to his family being much out of doors, and permission may sometimes be refused. But in the majority of households this is merely a polite formality, and leave for an expedition is granted as soon as requested. When a walk or drive is proposed, the children clamour to accompany their mother; and scarcely is this question settled by dint of coaxing and distribution of pence, than another arises among the slaves as to whose turn it is to be of the party—a question seldom settled without tears, entreaties, and even little quarrels and disturbances. At last the mistress herself selects her party, and the important business of the toilet commences. Oriental women are much addicted to the use of cosmetics, and faces are blanched and rouged, eyebrows and lashes touched up with *surméh*, and numerous other little coquetries resorted to, which, toned down by the semi-transparent *yashmak*, are calculated to "put beholders in a tender taking." Then follows a scramble for seats in the carriage, or carriages. The *hanums*, of course, take their places first, and the slaves, regardless of comfort, pack themselves together, and even sit on each others' knees if necessary.

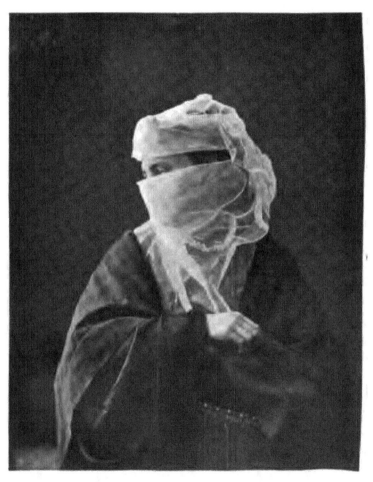

A TURKISH LADY IN *YASHMAK* AND *FERADJEH*

It is indeed curious to see how many can be thus accommodated in one vehicle. Whatever the object of the outing may have been, the party will not remain out of doors after sunset, but will endeavour to be back in time to receive their menkind on their return from the day's occupations. An Osmanli, it may here be remarked, never, under any circumstances, goes abroad in company with his harem, though little girls, before adopting the *yashmak*, may constantly be seen in public with their fathers, and are allowed free access to the *selamlik*. But the veil once donned, a girl enters the ranks of womanhood, and is thenceforward subjected to all the restrictions of the harem. And the reason of this separation of the sexes out of doors is sufficiently obvious. For a father or brother could not frequent the public promenades in company with his female relations without bringing them directly under the notice of his friends and acquaintances, and thus infringing the fundamental principle of the harem.

Going to the bath is made by Osmanli women the occasion of great festivity and ceremony. A complete outfit of garments for each lady is carried by a slave tied up in a square *boktcha*, or bundle-wrapper—the primitive and universal portmanteau—made without of silk, and often richly embroidered ; these garments being donned after the bath, together with their possessor's most handsome jewels, for the admiration—and perhaps envy—of the other ladies they may meet at this favourite rendezvous. Other slaves carry, in addition to fruits and refreshments of all kinds, a variety of rugs, bath-wraps, brass basins, and

T

the multitude of—to the uninitiated—mysterious articles considered necessary for the due performance of this important ablutionary rite. And at the *hammam* the ladies, with their children and attendants, remain for the best part of the day, eating and drinking, singing, frolicking, and gossiping in the intervals of the oft-repeated soapings, rinsings and rubbings, the applications to the hair of crushed laurel berries, and to the nails of henna, and other toilet details impossible to describe.

The Osmanlis indulge in but two meals a day—the *karvaltu*, which is eaten about eleven o'clock, and the *yemek*, partaken of about sunset, and varying accordingly between five o'clock in winter and eight in summer. Men whose vocations take them away from home, rarely return for the early meal, but eat their kebabs and pilaf at one of the numerous cookshops to be found in all business centres ; so it is to the *karvaltu* that ladies generally invite their friends, there being also the additional reason that Moslem women rarely go abroad after nightfall. Sometimes large luncheon parties are given, at which the most rigid etiquette is observed. The hostess leads the way to the dining-room where, in old-fashioned households, the covers are laid on *sofras*—circular tables, or rather stands, raised only some eight inches from the floor, and accommodating at the most half a dozen persons. If the guests are numerous, there will be several *sofras*, at which they are distributed according to their rank. At a genuinely Turkish table the covers consist merely of a spoon and portion of bread. Round the raised leather pad, which occupies the centre, are grouped small saucers containing *hors d'œuvre*—olives, cubes of water-melon or cucumber, radishes, anchovies, etc. As the ladies seat themselves cross-legged on the low cushions disposed around the *sofra*, slaves approach bearing water, soap, and towels. One holds the *leyen*, or basin, made with a little stand in the centre to hold the ball of soap, and a "well" into which the used water disappears through perforations ; another pours water on the hands from an elegantly shaped brass *ibrik ;* while a third tenders the embroidered towel with which to dry them. Other towels with ends embroidered in coloured silks and gold thread—the *chevreh* of which the East has of late years been almost emptied by the demand for them in the West—are distributed as table napkins, and the repast commences. A tureen of soup, very thick, rich, and nourishing, is first placed on the *sofra*. With a wave of her hand, and a polite " *Boyournu Effendi*," the hostess invites the principal guest to dip in her spoon. If, however, all her guests are of inferior rank to herself, she takes precedence, and the first spoonful. When the spoons have returned a few times to the tureen, it is removed and re-placed with a number of other dishes in succession. The *hors d'œuvres*, with various sweets and fruits, fill up the intervals between the courses until the pilaf is placed on the *sofra*. This national dish is composed chiefly of rice and butter, and is, like the others, eaten with the fingers—which may sound a difficult feat. But "practice makes perfect," and it is surprising to see with what neatness and dexterity the loose grains of rice can be picked up by two henna-stained fingers and a thumb, and conveyed to the mouth. The last dish, the *kochaf*, consists of stewed fruits cooled with ice, served in a crystal bowl, and eaten with long spoons of ivory. Water, and occasionally sherbet —the latter, however, not an effervescing drink, but made from fresh fruits—are the only beverages partaken of in the *haremlik*, and these are not placed on the table, but handed by the attendants as required. At the conclusion of the repast the *leyen* and *ibrik* are again carried round, and the party adjourn to the *divan khané*. After a short interval, during which the ladies place themselves on the divan—still, however, observing the rules of precedence— a *kalfa*, or head servant, enters, bearing on a tray draped with a richly embroidered crimson napkin, the coffee-pot, tiny porcelain cups, and *sarfs*, as the cupholders in gold or silver are called. She is followed by a troop of slave-girls, who advance in turn to the tray, pour out a cup of coffee, place it in the *sarf*, and present it to the guests, according to their rank, which it is their duty previously to ascertain, those of equal rank being served simultaneously. Tchibouk-smoking has gone out of fashion among Osmanli ladies, and with it, of course, the ancient ceremonial of pipe distributing and lighting. Cigarettes are now handed on a tray to each lady separately, and when she has adjusted one in her amber mouthpiece, another slave approaches with a glowing charcoal ember on a little brass dish from which to light it. When all the cigarettes are alight, the slaves retire to the lower end of the apartment where, ranged in a line, they stand with arms crossed on their bosoms and eyes modestly cast down until their services are again required to remove the coffee cups. In the interval they are, however, furtively taking mental notes of the dress, conversation, and manners of the guests, who —should the hostess have brought up in her harem girls for sale—on their side submit this galaxy of beauty to a critical inspection, and make their remarks on the girls individually with an outspokenness that would both astonish and amuse more reserved Europeans. Some of the *hanums* have, perhaps, been commissioned by their brothers or sons to select wives or odalisks for them during visits to the harems of friends—for such transactions naturally require the co-operation of the ladies of the family—and may return home with a favourable description of some girl who has taken their fancy. An offer of purchase may in that case be made for the damsel to her owner, who names her price; and this agreed to, the slave is transferred to her new home, probably as a *kitabetli*—that is, one sold with the stipulation that she will in due course be set free and married.

Should, however, the day's programme include none of the above-mentioned distractions, the monotony of harem life may, at any moment, be broken by various incidents—as, for instance, the arrival of a female broker with jewels, articles of dress, or home-made cosmetics and perfumes for sale, and gossip unlimited. These itinerant vendors, who are chiefly old women, are quite an institution in Moslem society, and, under the cloak of their calling, which gives them easy access to harems, they act

as agents not only in affairs matrimonial, but also in
clandestine intrigues of every description. In Turkish
folk-literature, indeed, an "old woman" invariably appears
as the *deus ex machinâ* of a romance or tragedy. And
should the family possess daughters of a marriageable
age, the portress may at any moment announce the visit
of a party of *Guerudjis,* or "Viewers," which, as described
in a previous chapter, is calculated to cause lively and
more or less lasting excitement in the breasts of the fair
denizens of the *haremlik.* For every Turkish girl, whether
handsome or "homely," has a right to look forward to
marriage as her destiny; and an "old maid" is hardly to
be found among the Osmanlis, so rarely does it happen
that a husband cannot be found for a girl of marriageable
age. Good looks naturally add to their owner's value in
the marriage market; but even the most unprepossessing
or deformed spinster, if she belong to a family of position,
need not despair, as she will at the worst be bestowed on
some impecunious but aspiring youth, to the furtherance
of whose ambitious schemes the patronage of her father
is necessary; and many a high official has owed his
success in life to the influential connexions of an uncomely
spouse.

With regard to the dress of Osmanli women, the
incongruities noticeable in the furniture of the majority
of the better class houses prevail to an even greater
extent in the dress of the generality of the ladies who
inhabit them. Out of doors, of course, the *yashmak* and
feradji—the veil and cloak—are still worn as full dress,

and also, on less formal occasions, the *mahrema*, a more
complete disguise, which may perhaps be best described as
a scanty double petticoat—made of a variety of materials
from checked or striped printed cotton to rich brocaded
silk—the upper one drawn hood-wise over the head, and
fastened under the chin, the face being completely hidden
by a kerchief of dark-coloured silk or muslin. But with
regard to indoor dress it would be difficult to say what is
or is not, worn at the present day by Osmanli women of
the upper and wealthier classes, the majority having during
the past thirty years gradually discarded their graceful
and picturesque national costumes in favour of what are
but too often ludicrous and lamentable travesties of
Parisian fashions. The ancient indoor dress of an Osmanli
lady, which may still occasionally be seen in the remoter
provinces, is extremely handsome—a sleeved gown of
white silk gauze, edged with silk point lace, and a *shalvar*,
or full trousers, of red silk worn under a *yelek*, a sort of
long coat tight-fitting above the waist, and buttoned from
the bosom to below the girdle, but open on each side
from the hip downwards, and trailing a few inches on the
floor. For full dress, another *yelek*, wider and looser, is
worn, also open at the sides and trailing, the sleeves of
both garments being rather tight-fitting, but open for
some six inches at the wrists, where they are often shaped
en sabot. This outer robe is usually of some rich material
worked round the borders, or all over, with elaborate
trailing patterns in coloured silks, or in gold and silver
thread, to which pearls are sometimes added. The head-

dress is a little round flat cap, covered with pearls and precious stones or with embroidery and gold braid. The bridal dresses of women of the middle and lower classes are still made on this model, the materials depending on the wealth of the bridegroom.

The everyday dress of women and children of the middle and lower classes generally is of brightly printed cottons, made up in winter into quilted jackets and other garments, which are worn over full trousers of the same material. Before going abroad a Turkish woman tucks up her skirts about her waist as high as possible, and secures them there with one of the large squares of printed muslin that serve her for so many purposes. Having thus made a shapeless bundle of herself, she throws over all her *mahrema*, puts on her yellow *babouches* and black overshoes, and sallies forth. Owing to the disposition of her primitive " dress suspender " and to her heavy footwear, the gait, when in their outdoor gear, of Osmanli women belonging to the middle and lower classes is, as a rule, the reverse of graceful, presenting as it does a peculiar combination of waddle and shuffle.

In concluding this brief survey of the home life and social status of Osmanli women, I may remark that the seclusion of women which accompanies the harem system is by no means, as generally assumed, a proof of their supposed " degraded position," but is, on the contrary, in great part the outcome of the regard entertained for them by the men of their nation. Surrounded as they have always been by people of alien races and religions, in no other way than by restricting them when at home to the inviolable *haremlik*, and by hiding their charms from the public gaze when abroad under disguising veil and cloak, could they be shielded from the impertinent curiosity—to say the least—of the mixed horde, Christian, Moslem, and Jew, who throng the streets of their cities and towns. For the same reason similar customs were formerly, and in some parts of the Empire still are, observed by the women of the Christian population, Armenian and Greek. And, as a matter of fact, the outdoor disguise of a Turkish woman renders her perfectly safe from insult or molestation, whether on foot in the streets, in tram or train, or on the deck of the Bosphorus steamboats, and whatever the provocation she may give.

The keen interest taken by Osmanli women in late events, and especially in the incidents attending the elections of members to, and the ceremony of the opening of the Turkish Parliament, has been the subject of much comment among those foreigners in Constantinople who are unaware of the extent to which the ideas of political liberty and intellectual progress have taken hold of women belonging to the upper classes. Crowds of cloaked and veiled figures gathered in the streets to witness the Sultan's procession to this important function, and it was remarked that many ladies installed at the windows of houses on the line of route had not only ventured to remove the obstructing latticed blinds, but in many cases to appear at their open casements in ordinary European attire.

Few foreigners are, however, aware how important a part was played by Osmanli ladies in the preparations for the bloodless revolution of last July. Taking full advantage of the immunity from molestation or impertinent curiosity which is the privilege of women of their race, and also of the absolute anonymity conferred by their disguising veils and cloaks, the wives, mothers, and sisters of the leaders of the movement in different parts of the Empire were able to act freely as their emissaries and go-betweens, bearing from harem to harem, and from city to city, compromising papers which a man could have carried only at the risk of his life. And, very naturally, Osmanli women of the upper classes are now demanding removal by the new Party of Reform of some at least of the irksome social restrictions by which they are hampered, and many important changes may be anticipated as soon as the political and financial situation may permit the new Government to give its attention to social reforms. As Prince Saba-ed-Din is reported to have remarked when addressing an audience of Turkish ladies at Constantinople in September last, the religion of Islam was not responsible for their lack of social freedom, and that the establishment of a constitutional form of government would have an important effect for them also as women; and he urged them in the mean time to be moderate in their demands, and wait for their fulfilment with calmness and patience. With regard to their legal status, Turkish women, as above pointed out, already possess all the legal, personal, and proprietary rights necessary to give them a social position equal, if not superior to that of European women generally. And the objection to their emancipation from harem restraints being consequently one of custom and prejudice, rather than of religious law—the seclusion and veiling of women being immemorial social usages borrowed from other Oriental races, and not institutions peculiarly Moslem —no religious law would therefore be contravened by a change in these merely social customs.

This question of female emancipation is indeed one which will, in all probability, have to be faced by the Turkish Government in the near future, and some members of the "Young Turkey" Party are frankly in favour of according to the women of their nation all the social and industrial freedom enjoyed by their Christian sisters. Serious difficulties of all kinds stand, however, in the way of this very desirable reform, and one of the most important of these is the fact that the abolition of the harem system must necessarily entail the abolition of that of domestic slavery, its inseparable adjunct. All kinds of restrictions, legal and customary, which now make for morality in the family relations of the Turks would, under the new conditions, be thrown aside, and the result—in the opinion of those competent to judge—would inevitably be, for a generation at least, great social laxity. For if, as is the case, only a very small minority of Turkish women are as yet fitted by education for such new conditions, the same is true of Turkish men. And in a city like Constantinople, the centre of a great military system, suddenly to set free

from authority and make responsible for their own maintenance thousands of ignorant women hitherto protected
and maintained in private households, and for the most
part unaccustomed to any but the most desultory household duties, would be to create a social evil now happily
non-existent. A change so far-reaching in its consequences could, indeed, only take place without great
resulting evil to the nation at large if prepared for by
such organisation for the wage-employment of the emancipated as one can hardly yet expect to see carried out
in Turkey.

Difficult of realisation as such a measure of reform
is of itself, some of its advocates among the " Young
Turkey " enthusiasts, with whom I have discussed the
question, appeared to me to complicate it unnecessarily
by proposing that Osmanli women should be at once
placed, as to employment in factories, shops, etc., on a
level with their self-supporting sisters in the West ; surely
a case of "more haste, less speed !" For the Armenian
and Greek women of Turkey, many of whom are now
at liberty to follow various industries and professions,
enjoyed at the beginning of last century far less personal
liberty than their Moslem sisters, and the gradual change
in their position has been chiefly due to the spread of
education and liberal ideas during the past century among
the men of these Christian nationalities. Economic conditions also differ widely in East and West ; and were
domestic slavery abolished, domestic service would afford
quite sufficient employment for Turkish women of the

lower class; while for those belonging to the educated classes, there would be little necessity for their becoming bread-winners, save, perhaps, as teachers. For, as early marriage is customary for Turks of both sexes, old bachelors being almost as rare as old maids, all native girls would naturally marry under the new *régime* as they have done under the old. In the original Turkish Constitution, as drafted by Midhat Pasha in 1876, the abolition of slavery was advocated, but to this and other clauses the Sultan refused his assent. Were, however, the slave-trade made illegal in Turkey, the abolition of the present system of domestic slavery would naturally and gradually follow. All adults now in a state of bondage would in due course receive their manumission, and all children might be freed within a certain number of years, during which their services would in some measure recoup their owners for the expense of their purchase and maintenance. The harem system thus greatly modified, if not abolished, women of slave origin would no doubt be for a time available as domestic servants, being gradually replaced by the daughters of the working classes, to whom such employment should prove an immense boon, limited as have hitherto been their wage-earning opportunities. And a probable and very desirable result of this economic change would also be the raising of the age of marriage for girls.

CONCLUSION

THE FUTURE OF THE OSMANLI TURKS

IT is impossible, however, that such economic and social changes as I have just hinted at should take place without being both preceded and accompanied by political changes, and changes, indeed, issuing in hardly less than a complete reconstitution of the Ottoman Nationality. It seems desirable, therefore, to say something of the probable character of these political changes. But as I cannot pretend to any degree of authority on such a subject, I shall confine myself to indicating briefly certain large views and assured forecasts which, though published thirty years ago, are so remarkably verified in present conditions that one may have some confidence in their further and complete verification. In 1879, when Mr. Stuart-Glennie published his *Europe and Asia*, the Eastern Question was still regarded as it had long been in England as also in Europe generally—namely, as simply a Turco-Russian Question, dividing men into Philo-Turks and Philo-Russians. The general point of view, however, from which that book was written was " that the Eastern Question could not be adequately treated, save as the question of a readjustment of the relations of Europe and

Asia to each other, and of both to Africa—a readjustment involving that of the States of Europe to each other and that of the States of Asia."[1] But since at least the Russo-Japanese War of 1904, few would probably deny that the Eastern Question is now evidently what it really, though not so evidently, was at the time of the Turco-Servian and Russo-Turkish Wars—such a general question of the readjustment of the relations of Europe and Asia as should raise politicians quite above either merely Turkish or Russian partisanship. And hence, as remarked thirty years ago in *Europe and Asia*, the Future of the Osmanli Turks must be now more generally recognised as inextricably connected with all the great movements of the time, both Asiatic and European.

To gain some definite foothold in taking so wide a view of the Eastern Question, Mr. Stuart-Glennie attempted to discover and demonstrate historically a Law of the Development of Nationalities. As to that great generalisation it is not for me to say anything. But it led its author to a forecast of that renaissance of the Ottoman nationality which has been declared by review writers—ignorant of, or ignoring his work—to have been "wholly unforeseen," though acknowledged to have been the greatest of the political events of 1908.[2] And even more assured appeared to be the rebirth of the European Nationalities as independent, though federated, States. This, however, necessarily involved the withdrawal of Turkish government from

[1] *Europe and Asia*, Preface.
[2] See, for instance, *Fortnightly Review*, September, 1908.

Europe, though Constantinople might remain the Ottoman capital. Yet it will probably now be recognised by all duly acquainted with the strength of the Nationalist aspirations of the various Balkan peoples, that the first point clear in the Future of the Osmanli Turks is—what already, after the last Russo-Turkish War, the more far-seeing of the Commanders in that war did not hesitate privately to admit would sooner or later be found necessary —withdrawal from their European Provinces. And, to illustrate this, I may say that in an interview with the Commander-in-Chief in Macedonia, within the ancient walls of the seaward fortress of Salonica, Mr. Stuart-Glennie, having ventured to state his main conclusions in *Europe and Asia* with respect to the Future of the Osmanlis, was surprised and delighted by His Excellency's response : " I entirely agree with you ! "

The Pasha—with whom I also was acquainted, and whom I greatly esteemed—then further said, "After that War, had I been Sultan, I would have endeavoured to arrange for our gradual withdrawal in the course of a certain number of years from all our European Provinces. The very desirable result for us would have been the setting by the ears of Austria and Russia, and, sooner or later, of probably all the European Powers. In the mean time, instead of wasting the flower of the Osmanlis of Anatolia in the vain attempt to retain provinces which cannot be permanently, or, indeed, much longer retained, without a lavish expenditure of blood and treasure, we should have consolidated ourselves in Asia Minor, and recovered, perhaps, our natural frontier of the Caucasus. Our Nationality thus consolidated, futile would have been the dreams of European Protectorates over our Syrian, Arabian, and African Provinces. And our Khalif's temporal sovereignty would have thus been immensely strengthened, instead of being, as seems but too probable, fatally exhausted."

The time, however, was not yet. And the intimate connexion between the problems of the Near East and the events of the Further East, insisted on thirty years ago in *Europe and Asia*, cannot but be now recognised if one considers how immensely more favourable to a renaissance of the Ottoman Nationality are the political conditions which have followed the Russo-Japanese War and that Russian Revolution which, though suppressed, has been by no means crushed. In a moment of wild enthusiasm members of the diverse nationalities of the Balkan Peninsula may have embraced each other as newly enfranchised "Ottomans." But that can only remind us of similar scenes in the great French Revolution, when the cry was *Fraternité ou la Mort !* and any hope of even a partial union of the Balkan populations as Ottoman subjects can now be hardly even a diplomatic pretence. Conditions, however, are altogether different in Asia Minor. There, the only Christians having National Churches are Greeks and Armenians. But the Greeks are not only chiefly to be found in the cities, and particularly in Smyrna, but belong to what is already a free Nationality ; and they can, therefore, remain Hellenes if they do not care to be

U

naturalised as Ottomans. And though the Armenians are very numerous in the Eastern Highlands of Asia Minor, in no province or *vilayet* do they constitute the majority of the population. They are also, like the Osmanlis, an essentially Asiatic people, and have been not inaptly termed "but baptized Turks." Notwithstanding this, however, the characteristic financial and administrative capacities of the Armenians constitute a felicitous complement to the political and martial virtues predominating in the Osmanlis. The Armenians also have been established in most of their present seats from time immemorial, while the Turks are, in Asia Minor, comparatively but new-comers, dating back, in this their new home, to but the beginning of the thirteenth century. But each is as necessary to the independent existence and free development of the other as are the English of Southern, and the Scots of Northern Britain. And one is glad to see that this is now being more and more fully recognised.[1]

These, then, are the first two points that may now, with more definite evidence than in 1879, be predicted as to the future of the Osmanli Turks—withdrawal from the

[1] For instance, in a " *Lettre d'Erzeroum*," published in the Constantinople journal *Stamboul*, February 18, 1909, and delivered as I write these lines, it is reported that, " Les Comites Arméniens déclarent formellement que si la Turquie leur accordait de sa propre volonté l'autonomie ils ne pourraient pas l'accepter ; car l'Arménie étant entourée d'éléments ennemis, vu sa position géographique, elle ne pourrait nullement se protéger. Tous les Arméniens ont compris parfaitement bien que leur salut est de s'accorder avec les turcs et de protéger ensemble la Turquie, le Vatan [fatherland] de tous."

government of their European Provinces, a withdrawal which those who have any intimate knowledge of the Osmanlis cannot doubt will be at once dignified and honourable; and the territorial consolidation and constitutional development of their Nationality in the immemorial homeland of such constituents of it as the Armenians, Kurds, and Circassians, the homeland also of the Osmanlis themselves for the last seven hundred years. But if thus consolidated, another feature will, as already hinted at, certainly mark the future of the Osmanlis—a renovation of their rule over the great Empire that will still remain to them, an Empire extending from the Caucasus and the Caspian to the Persian Gulf and the Indian Ocean. The renovation of this Empire Abdul Hamid II. has assured by his quiet pushing on, for so many years, of the construction of his splendidly statesmanlike railway from Constantinople to Mekka. Of this and its probable effects much might be said. But here I shall only point out that it, in a manner, forces the friendship of Great Britain. Russia's and Germany's ambitions will be effectively baulked by the consolidation and development of the Ottoman Nationality in Asia Minor, and by the more enlightened government of its Asiatic and African Empire. Not so, however, the just ambition of Great Britain—the ambition to retain her Eastern Empire, and give even fuller freedom to its subjects, of whom a larger number are Moslems than those who acknowledge the temporal as well as the spiritual sovereignty of the Khalif. And the admiration and respect which Britons who have had any real knowledge of the Turks have ever been disposed to feel for them will, granting such a consolidation of their Nationality and renovation of their Empire, be supported by economic and political reasons substantially contributing to an enduring alliance.

That consolidation and that renovation can, however, be worked out only against antagonisms both from within and from without of the most serious character. Immensely can Great Britain aid in smoothing the way of the Constitutional Party amid both classes of obstacles. Thus that friendly alliance with the Turkish People which was only interrupted by the absolutism of Abdul Hamid would be renewed. And it must be admitted that the conduct of the "Young Turks" in the whole of the proceedings connected with and subsequent to the Revolution of July, 1908, certainly justifies all the aid that can possibly be afforded them in the great task they have undertaken. What will be the ultimate fate of Abdul Hamid, and what manner of man the new Sultan proclaimed by the Parliamentary Party will show himself, it is impossible as yet to conjecture. But however great the political changes may be, it will certainly be long before any considerable changes take place in the Social, Religious, and Domestic Life of the Turkish People described in the foregoing pages.

SULTAN ABDUL HAMID II

GLOSSARY OF TURKISH WORDS USED
IN THE TEXT

Agha, a title.
Alaïk, a young slave.

Bakshish, a bribe.
Bektchi, a watchman.
Beshlik, a coin of 5 piastres, value about 1*d.*
Bey, a title of rank.
Bismillah, " In the Name of Allah."
Boktcha, a bundle-wrap.

Daïra, an establishment.
Divan-khané, reception-room.
Djami, a mosque.
Djemiet, period of festivity.
Djereed, a spear.
Djin, a demon.
Dughun, wedding or other festivities.

Effendi, a title of courtesy.
Emir, a prince.
Eskedji, a dealer in cast-off clothing.
Esnaf, a trade guild.
Ezan, the call to prayer.

Fatiha, the Moslem " Lord's Prayer."
Fena guez, the "Evil Eye."
Feradjeh, Turkish lady's cloak.
Fetva, a legal decree.

Ghazel, a sonnet.
Groosh, piastres, a coin worth about 2½*d.*

Hadis, the Moslem traditions.
Hadji, a pilgrim.
Hafiz, one who knows the *Koran* by heart.
Hamal, a porter.
Hammam, a Turkish bath.
Hanum, a Turkish lady.
Haremlik, the women's apartments.
Hodja, a tutor.
Hoshaf, stewed fruit.

Ihram, the sacred habit worn by pilgrims.
Imâm, a priest.
Imaret, an almshouse.
Inshallah, " God willing."
Intarie, a house-dress.

Kadi, a judge.
Kahvedji, a coffee-maker.
Kaif, ease, enjoyment.
Kaïkdji, a boatman.
Kalfa, a head servant.
Khan, a hostelry, a royal title.
Khasida, a verse-form.
Khotba, the Friday sermon.
Kibla or *Kibleh,* the direction of Mekka.
Kiler, a storeroom.
Kismet, fate, destiny.
Konak, a mansion.

Leyen and *ibrik,* basin and jug.

293

Mahalla, a street, a quarter.
Mangal, a warming apparatus.
Medjidieh, a dollar.
Medjliss, a town council.
Medresseh, a theological college.
Mekteb, a parish school.
Mezzlik, *hors d'œuvres*.
Mihrab, alcove in a mosque indicating the direction of Mekka.
Mimber, pulpit in a mosque.
Mollah, a dean.
Musdadji, a "news-bringer."

Namaz, daily prayers.
Narghileh, a water-pipe.

Para, the fortieth part of a piastre.
Pasha, a title of rank.
Peri, a supernal being.
Pir, the founder of a Dervish Order.

Raki, a kind of spirit.
Redif, a Reservist.
Rutbe, social rank.

Saka, a water-carrier.
Saraf, a money-changer.
Sebil, a fountain.

Selamlik, a ceremony, the men's apartments.
Serai, a palace.
Seraili, slave belonging to a palace.
Sheik, a prior.
Sheri or *Sheriat*, the Holy Law of Islam.
Shia, a Mohammedan schismatic.
Sofra, a tray-stand.
Softa, a theological student.
Sunni, an orthodox Moslem.

Tandür, a warming apparatus.
Tcharshi, a bazar or market.
Tchelebi, "gentleman."
Tchibouk, a Turkish pipe.
Tchiboukdji, a pipe-bearer.
Tchiftlik, a country estate.
Turbeh, a mausoleum.

Ulema, Moslem Legists.

Vakouf, Church property.
Vurkulak, a vampire.

Yakli, a villa.
Yashmak, veil of a Turkish lady.

Zaptieh, armed policeman.

INDEX

PRINTED BY WILLIAM CLOWES AND SONS, LIMITED, LONDON AND BECCLES.